To Adám, the monkey; Dinah, the tan and white bitch; the armadillo, a small unrelenting secret; the owl; the hawk; the deer; the mangy little chicken who lived in a cotton nest after its leg was hurt. To the delicious goats, and all the little birds with sunken breasts and rigid claws—my friends who are dead, who loved me for no more than the food I gave them.

INTRODUCTION

During the early months of 1914, New Orleans newspapers carried stories of the sensational 'escapade' of Elsie Dunn, granddaughter of a prominent New Orleans family, and Frederick Creighton Wellman, Dean of the School of Tropical Medicine at Tulane University. She was nearly twenty and he was at least twice her age, married to his second wife, and a father. The furor created by the sudden disappearance and unknown destination of the couple had both immediate and future effects on the runaways and those closely connected with them.

Escapade is the autobiographical memoir of Evelyn Scott's chosen six-year exile with her married lover in primitive and remote regions of Brazil, of her separation from family and friends by distance and circumstance, and the geographic separation from cultural, artistic, and social activity that forced Scott to cope with years of solitude, to struggle against poverty, illness, and social condemnation, and to come to terms with an ordered universe. "It was during the first six early years in the tropics that I came to grips with the bedrock actuality in a primitive sense, and learned, through a geographical remoteness from social stimuli, the full value of self-dependence and an 'inner life'."

The act that produced *Escapade* and the book itself shocked both conservatives who criticized Scott's high-minded, open flaunting of moral codes and social conventions and liberals who criticized society's judgment of Scott's conduct as immoral. The changes in her life that this romantically envisioned but desperate act brought about, and the subsequent publication of *Escapade* and her perceived reception of it, haunted Scott for the rest of her life.

As a literary work, *Escapade* stands alone. While there is no need for knowledge of either of the participants, their backgrounds, or the events leading up to their 'escape,' the intensity of Scott's personality emanating from her interior vision in the writing stimulates one with a desire to know more. When I first read *Escapade* some time in 1977, before I was drawn into the rediscovery of Scott, I knew little about her. Since that time I have learned a great deal about her, but to enforce my statement that the work stands alone, I can say that in my many re-readings of *Escapade*, my acquired knowledge neither adds to nor subtracts from the artistic quality of the impact of the book. So strongly do I believe in the artistic excellence of *Escapade* that were it not for the fact that we are rediscovering an artist's life *and* work, my feeling would be that this Introduction should actually be an Afterword.

But to fan the fires of curiosity and to provoke interest in the author and her career, I believe it is appropriate to reveal some facts relevant to *Escapade* about Scott's life before New Orleans, her meeting with Frederick Wellman, their life together after Brazil, and Scott's obsessive preoccupation with the effects of the Brazil years on her life—particularly her wish to be allowed to take responsibility for her own actions and her change of name.

Elsie Dunn was born January 17, 1893 in Clarksville, Tennessee. Her parents, Maude and Seely Dunn, enjoyed for a time a certain influentially and financially secure aristocratic existence, based on tobacco and railroads. Money and position were lost after the Civil War and the family did not cope well with either loss; Scott's mother's mental condition suffered considerably. Scott says of her in *Escapade* that she "was born with a gold spoon in her mouth and she doesn't understand what has become of it." In *Background in Tennessee*, published in 1937 and reissued by the University of Tennessee Press in 1980, Scott recreates the atmosphere for growing up Southern, and she describes events in the life of a charming child becoming a young woman searching for an identity that eventually led her outside the boundaries of the South in her life and writing. The family's financial condition deteriorated further. When Scott was sixteen, the Dunns were forced to move to New Orleans to be closer to Seely Dunn's parents who could give some monetary relief. Scott was the youngest student ever to enroll in Sophie Newcomb College, but she did not adjust well to the discipline involved in university life. Motivated by simultaneous ambitions to become a writer, a painter, an actress, and a disciple of Pavlova, Tolstoy, Schopenhauer, Nietzsche, Bergson, and Karl Marx, she continued to educate herself by reading. Evelyn's father was involved with another woman; disillusioned with her parents' strained marriage and her mother's worsening mental state, resistant to the notion of being a Southern belle "like everybody else," and homesick for Tennessee, Evelyn was extremely unhappy and, according to Wellman, suicidal.

Frederick Wellman, when he was on a research expedition in Honduras earlier, had met Seely Dunn who was, building a railway line from the port of Telas to the interior of the country, and when he returned to New Orleans, he visited him, and met Evelyn. Wellman, too, was unhappy and felt trapped in a situation, mostly of his own creation. The two were attracted to one another, partly because of their similar interest in philosophy, partly because of their mutual unhappiness and discontent. Wellman later claimed that apart from his attraction to her and the fact that she could discuss philosophy with him, Scott was the only woman who would go to Brazil with him. He made the same claim about his first wife who had accompanied him to Africa.

Elaborate plans were made to conceal their departure and route of escape. Evelyn *did* confide in her mother who begged her not to go and even threatened to shoot herself if she went; but Mrs. Dunn kept silent.

To explain his absence and buy time, Wellman told his wife that he was going on an extended fishing trip. Knowing Evelyn's father could use his knowledge as a railroad man to trace anyone who hadn't "walked or swum" away from the United States, they first took a train North. With only the clothes they wore and very meager baggage, they left the United States for Southhampton, England; they changed their names to Evelyn

Scott and Cyril Kay Scott. Evelyn took two volumes of poetry, Keats and Shelley, and *War and Peace* in three volumes. Cyril took seven hundred dollars. Their planned destination was the Amazon where they would collect beetles.

Behind them they left the woman scorned, who talked loud and long to the newspapers, harrassed Evelyn's parents and threatened to invoke the Mann Act when the couple was found, a major university that wanted to avoid publicity about a missing Dean, and an embarrassed, prominent Dunn family.

Because of Mrs. Wellman's threats and the escalation of World War I in Europe, what Scott envisioned as a romantic fusion became an ordeal that not only lasted six years but forced her to live in isolation and under such wretched conditions that she wished for a "saving insanity" that would blot out her acute awareness of the situation. The physical and psychological deprivation was a reality that Scott, with her sheltered background, could not have begun to imagine. "When we left home with a deliberate intention never to return, we both anticipated hardships. But I had only conceived of some sort of work we could do together. I thought poverty was something which could be more completely shared." Scott's only child, Creighton, was born in Brazil.

Out of this experience Evelyn Scott wrote *Escapade*—an autobiography, but also a deliberately conceptualized work of art. Cyril Kay Scott in 1943 wrote his autobiography, *Life Is Too Short* that contains an account of the experience. We can be sure the accounts tally by comparing the order of events, but beyond this, any similarity—in writing, and *experiencing*—ends. Cyril Scott was critical of Scott's rendering of *Escapade* in two important ways, two ways that point to the fact that the work is not simply a chronological autobiography covering six years spent in Brazil. First he says that the book is so subjective that it might as well have been written in Newark, New Jersey. Secondly, he objected: "My wife was not an observant person, except of her own subjective verities." However, both critical objections that Cyril Scott makes are actually strong evidence of Evelyn Scott's artistic intention and fulfillment. The two books exhibit a perfect comparison between two people writing about the same events. One writer is a chronicler, reciting what 'really' happened, the other, a literary artist conveying personal impressions of the same events. Reading these two books side by side, it would be hard to recognize that these two people shared a common experience. In fact, they did not.

Escapade is purely subjective and Scott sustains the interior design of the work without faltering. The images in the text are conveyed so as to produce a conscious and deliberate literary effect and should not be seen as accessory and subconscious elements in the narrative. Her writing therefore should be seen primarily as emanating from this 'conscious' standpoint. The reader is never exposed to self-pitying, romanticized suffering and anguished spiritual birth scenes, but feeling is conveyed through shifts in focus from naturalistic objectivity to flashes of sensory perception. Scott does not describe to make the reader *see*. She senses the exterior influences—people, poverty, physical discomfort, her bizarre situation—only in direct interrelation with the way they appear to her inner being, what she calls 'inner life'. Everything Scott tells us in this autobiographical account of her life in Brazil is within that context.

So *Escapade* is one of the rarer works of autobiography which consciously uses fictional techniques to achieve certain literary effects. The reader experiences *Escapade* in ways one might experience fiction, such as the type of fiction that begins without explanation of preceding events, who (in terms of character) is there, or why. The deliberate disorientation brought about by the technique comes and goes throughout the book like waves of feeling. The structural sequence is not the usual chronological sequence of most autobiography, but moves backward and forward with the same wave-like effect.

A thematic structure of birth-life-death, a cycle that is repeated and implied even in the end when there is liberation (birth) and return to health (life) but again the darkness (death), is set up in the beginning of the book with the impending birth of Scott's child. Along with the thematic structure, Scott also sets up an isolation motif in the first pages of the book by emphasizing the language barrier she encounters with the native servant girl who converses easily with a man she is with while Evelyn herself is unable to get through to her.

It is fairly certain that Scott did not write *Escapade* while she was in Brazil, but by using the present tense, she lends an immediacy to experiences as though the events were happening at the time of the writing. The permanent impressions created in the mind of the reader by the immediacy are also intensified by the disparity of using lyric, imagist language to describe such dreadful circumstances.

The double fictionalizing of names is a curiosity. Frederick has already been changed to Cyril, but in the book, he is "John"; the son, Creighton, is "Jackie," a derivative of John. Two of the characters, actually her mother and father, not only have different names—"Nannette" and "Alex"—but become Scott's aunt and uncle. The characters in Scott's mind have a particularly strong subjective aura, almost giving them a mystical or ghost-like quality. Never do we have a sense of characters that we could bump into and we never have any feeling of John, Nannette, or Jackie living an ordinary day-by-day existence. We do not experience Scott as a flesh and blood being, but more as a consciousness.

Another unusual aspect of this autobiography is that it has an ending similar to a work of fiction. Just as the most important level on which *Escapade* begins is the esthetic and the literary, so also does the work end on this level. At the end of the memoir detailing and evoking six years in the jungles of Brazil under conditions conducive to madness and near-death, Scott writes: "A heavy iron door opens, rolls back from one world's end to another, and lets me out" symbolizing the author's release from the solitary confinement of exile, or beyond that, her birth through the iron doors of the womb.

This brings us to the final chapter—a beginning, so to speak, *after* the end. The language shifts abruptly, causing the reader's intense participation to move to a satirical, seemingly unassociated epilogue. This chapter epitomizes Scott's individualistic perception of social, moral, and religious conventions. She juxtaposes the world of nature, the hypocritical world of man, and the unrealistic spiritual world. The names, the personified roles of the animals, and the spiritual symbols give the chapter an aura of mixed sources, and the tone, structure, and fable-like base evoke a memory of *Alice in Wonderland*. Only the first line, "Impenetrable darkness. A moment of silence," and the last, "Silence and darkness, as it was in the beginning," that extend Scott's birth-life-death philosophy, relate to Scott's Brazil experience. Without background explanation, one can only read the last twenty-six pages of *Escapade* for what they seem to be—Evelyn Scott's personal satiric commentary on the moral climate of society expressing itself negatively in relation to her past behavior.

The Scotts returned in 1920 to the United States, and after settling Mrs. Dunn once more in Clarksville, they lived in Greenwich Village. Evelyn Scott moved among the most important artists of the time. Both in Greenwich Village and later in Paris. Between 1920 and 1941, she published thirteen major works of fiction, three children's books, two volumes of poetry, an autobiographical history of Tennessee, and one three-act play, performed by the Provincetown Players, short stories, critical essays, and, of course, *Escapade*, all of which were critically acclaimed by many of the foremost authorities.

In each book Scott wanted to create and express an integral part of the completed universal design. She explains this in the following manner: "One book can be only a partial attempt to create or express the universe. There is something in each of my books that makes it an integral part of the architecture of the whole and even if, at my death, a turret should be missing, you will be able to get an idea of the general design . . ." As is clear from the texts, she possessed a rare combination of personal intuitiveness, literary conception and an artistic genius for style and technique. Her books can be read on artistic, philosophical and psychological levels.

When William Faulkner's *The Sound and the Fury* was being considered for publication, Scott was given the manuscript to read for comment. She was asked to expand her comments into an essay that was circulated with advance copies of the relatively unknown novel in manuscript form. Later this essay was published as a pamphlet entitled *On William Faulkner's 'The Sound and the Fury*. It was published specifically to publicize Faulkner's work and was prefaced with this statement by the publisher: "*The Sound and the Fury* should place William Faulkner in company with Evelyn Scott." The irony here of course is that Scott who sustained a high literary image for twenty years, faded while Faulkner, to whose work she brought attention, is our most renowned Southern writer today.

When I wrote *Melancholy Necessity*, an article about *Escapade* for the *New Orleans Review*, in 1979, the only work in print was that piece on Faulkner. I discovered that while she had been forgotten in literary circles, historians still counted *The Wave*, reissued last year by Carroll & Graf Publishers, among the ten great Civil War novels. With the reissue of *Background in Tennessee*, *The Wave*, *The Narrow House* and now *Escapade*, it is clear that Scott's books are as relevant today as they were when she wrote them.

Peggy Bach

There is a little space in the park. Here the grass, yet green, rushes up softly beneath the trees. Bare twigs spray the sky in showers of black glass. The clouds pearl above the blue-white water which is transfixed as by a shiver. The sun is a seared eyeball that melts in sightless intensity. Its pink glows like springtime in the smutted coal-yard. A train rushes past in the distance and chokes the quiet with reverberations. A lather of blue and violet smoke curls slowly upward, and creams along the edges, lifting itself sumptuously, yet delicately, like a great trumpet-shaped flower, unfurling in heaven.

Gray clouds, dissolving, re-form in hard square lines, rigid as an ideal god. I feel pressed between the high buildings. I am like the grape in the wine press. I am a hull, flattened and shapeless. I have a weak sense of being ill-treated. But that is all irrelevant to the majesty of elevated tracks, factories, and church steeples: things too lofty for my interest. The end is resignation, decay: the ungrateful oblivion of a grain of sand, wind-hurled, eon after eon, across a sphinx's face.

The gigantic shadows of my delirium are dim along the bleared horizon. A dwarfed Liberty has ceased to threaten. The fog glistens. The pale air is a stupid resolution. In the deck chairs are rows of sickly quiescent faces. Soon the stony sunshine and the symmetrical palm trees will mark rows of identical graves—the graves of those who masqueraded in differentness.

ESCAPADE

ESCAPADE

THROUGH the only window I saw ragged clothes on a line between outbuildings of unbaked brick that leaned against each other as though about to fall. Because the hill jutted up precipitately behind the Hotel Rio Branco, the outhouses came on a level with my eyes and were very close. In the morning it was delicately bright in the room. John was asleep. The mosquito netting around him made his face dim. There was a knock at the door, and the Portuguese girl entered, very slovenly, her coarse black hair hanging in stiff locks against her full florid cheeks. When she said, "Bom dia," I understood that, but the rest of her speech was a harsh murmur of guttural sound and depressed me with its strangeness.

John's gaze, always so still and kind, opened on me first. Then he talked to the girl. In the interchange of unintelligible noises I felt my exclusion from the life about me, my helplessness. The girl could not grasp the nature of my incapacity. She tried to force me to listen to her. When I remained blank and uncomprehending she began to shout. With difficulty I articulated the few phrases I knew. "Eu não fallo Portuguez. Não entendo o que a senhora está dizendo."

I

ESCAPADE

For a moment she regarded me silently. Her bright-shallow-black eyes were glistening with suppressed amusement, and she finally burst into a loud guffaw, bending forward, clasping her knees with her palms, and rocking her body, delighted by my stupidity. "A senhora não entende nada?" she asked John incredulously. "Nada que eu estou dizendo?"

When John repeated what had been said on the previous morning, that the Portuguese language was a sealed book to me, she was satisfied at last. She placed the tray of coffee and cold sour bread on the stand beside the bed, and turned to go out. As she left the room, she looked back at me, laughed stolidly, as if to herself, and shook her head.

WHEN John had gone to his work I sat there in the room with nothing at all to occupy me—nothing but my thoughts. The hotel faced a narrow street, and the thud and rattle of wheels jolting over cobblestones shook the entire building almost continually.

I took a pencil and some paper from my hand-bag. If I could only write! But I had no thoughts. What possessed me completely was the faint disturbing nausea of my pregnancy. Though I had no appetite when I sat at the table, I was obsessed by the idea of food. Our meals here were all the same—coarse fish reeking with the odor of the olive oil in which it had been fried, bread made without yeast, and tinned butter which suggested underdone cheese. I hated the stupid reiteration of my desire for something else. Perhaps it was not food at all that I wanted.

I had two books, volumes of poetry which I had

2

packed hastily in my suitcase when I went away from home—before we went to London. Besides these I had bought War and Peace in three volumes. I took out my books and tried to read. Keats, I knew by heart, and Shelley irritated me. He was too much concerned with vague ecstasies and mythological figures of speech. War and Peace, which I read and re-read so many times later, did not then interest me in the least.

The sunshine, falling through the one window, intensified. A wedge of light, thrust across the floor, widened, and swept everything with a glare from which there was no escape. The heat seemed every moment more unbearable. I moved my chair again and again. The light always pursued me. There were no blinds on the window and no way to shut out the radiance. I was the more uncomfortable because I had no suitable clothes, and always wore the warm dress in which, in December, I had left the United States. My flesh prickled with heat. I loathed the contact of the woolen material where it touched my naked skin. I sat there. I could not tell the time of day because I had broken my watch.

THE heat of the tropics, as mid-day approaches, seems not so much to descend from the sky as to emanate from the earth in warm clouds of invisible but palpable steam. From the adobe huts, so close to my window that, leaning across to them, I can almost touch the people, comes a reek of hot palm oil with the stench of excrement in a number of unemptied pots set out in a row at the back. Pale naked children run about among the banana plants and scream in play. An old

3

woman, who has been laying out some clothes to bleach, hobbles toward them with a stick. A baby is crawling on all-fours, nearly under her feet. She becomes angry with it also, and slaps it, pushing it aside. I can still see its arrested posture as it gazes at her in astonishment, cries loudly for a moment, and then resumes its investigation of twigs and leaves.

I walk about the room restlessly, lie down on the bed and get up again. My eyes are half-blinded with the whiteness of sunshine. But I can see up the steep side of the hill above which the sun is climbing to the zenith. In the sky of an almost terrible blue, glittering masses of white clouds hang motionless. Now and again one passes between me and the light and makes a shadow across the others—a reddish violet shadow which gives them the appearance of a darkened expanse of snow. The heat is like a ponderous tide which drags me in its depths. The morning has passed with indescribable heaviness.

TRUE love is abnegation of self and in the relation of the sexes it is inappropriate. The sacrifices made to a very young child impose upon it none of the burden of obligation which an adult must feel in similar circumstances. I have seen in my own family too much of what self-sacrifice implies. People who profess to live only for others evade the responsibility for their cowardice and give their self-gratification a subtler form through a trick which allows them moral superiority. I am not disturbed by the thought of having a child.

If I could only believe it! But I am continually in doubt as to what is the matter with me—even though the evidence is so plain.

ESCAPADE

When I take off my clothes and stand sidewise before the cracked mirror I see that my body is no longer hollow and unfilled. It has a swelling line, a trifle grotesque, such as I have observed in the meager figures of old women.

*　　*　　*　　*　　*　　*

I want to be proud of myself, and I am ashamed. When I walk out with John I wear a heavy coat. Conscious of a kind of nudity, I try to ignore the men who stare at me. I allow my coat to swing open in front. I am astonished to hear my pregnancy spoken of as if it were a casual fact.

If I could only *feel* the child! I imagine the moment of its quickening as a sudden awakening of my own being which has never before had life. I want to *live* with the child, and I am as heavy as a stone.

I HEAR echoing steps in the hallway that is so much of the time deserted. I understand their briskness, their decision. John is determined to bring home to me none of the anxieties of the day. He would like to admit nothing of the burden of attempting to keep books for a company that sells sewing machines. Bookkeeping! Something for which John, as a biologist, is totally unfit.

When we left home with a deliberate intention never to return, we both anticipated hardships. But I had only conceived of some sort of work which we could do together. I thought poverty was something which could be more completely shared. We first planned to go to the Amazonas and collect beetles.

5

ESCAPADE

John comes into the room. He makes my eyes cool with his smile. I love him.

THE dining room is the one common room of our hotel. A bar adjoins it, and the front of the place, crowded with small bare tables, is wide open to the street, closed at night with shutters that let down like a portcullis.

The man at the next table has a beautiful face, vivid like an animal's, but without any consciousness of itself. He has rings in his ears, large gold hoops. He wears a red shirt, corduroy trousers, and leggings made of gay colored cloth wound about his legs in strips. A guitar is hung around his neck.

He and his companions begin by ordering drinks. Then they sing an odd song. I cannot understand the words, but John says they are obscene.

Senhor Oswaldo, our landlord, glances at me furtively and uncomfortably. Afraid of losing his respectable patronage, he would like to put the ribald stranger into the street. He sends a meek little yellow-skinned waiter who asks the troubadours to remember that the foreign senhora is present. The answer is another song, more triumphantly shouted.

John thinks that the men are drunk, and that to avoid unpleasantness we had better go out. Nothing but blows stronger than those he can deliver himself will reduce the singer to quiescence. I resent my physical inequality which nothing can overcome. In spite of irritation I am to be treated like a lady. Only extreme anger can override my physical cowardice.

ESCAPADE

WHEN I venture by myself into the low part of the city where we live, something objectionable always occurs. Perhaps it is because I am only twenty years old. Perhaps it is because I am shabbily dressed. I know perfectly well that I am not particularly pretty. Inwardly shrinking and cold with an obscure fear, I make it a point to look very directly at all the men who speak to me. I want to shame them by the straightforwardness of my gaze. Perhaps I am ridiculous. If I could consider sex more factually and with less mystical solemnity I might find amusement in the stupidity of these individuals who can't be so sinister after all.

WHEN John comes home at night he is too exhausted to talk very much—even to plan about our future. He receives twenty dollars a week. Not long ago there was a mistake in his accounts and he was unable to discover it. He brought home the long sheets of paper and we worked together over them. We were certain that the error was beyond us, and that we were going to be confronted with starvation and homelessness again.

I remember growing cold and hard with despair, with resentment—not of John, but of our situation, of people at home who disapprove of what they consider our "immoral" life. I talked of hiring myself out as a servant, but John was hurt when I insisted on it. Servant girls in native homes are very badly treated. The maid who cleans our rooms lives in a kind of dark cupboard under the stairway, a place without any furnishing other than the hammock she sleeps in, and without either air or light. She works often until

7

midnight and has to endure the contemptuous advances of all the men about. I think I was vain of my determination, but I was really glad when John discouraged me.

Sometimes, though, I would be willing to experience something painful that would relieve the monotony of existing as I do. The sun beating in on me gives my mind a dry feeling. I feel like dust.

I ALWAYS detested a needle in my hand. Sewing for an hour at a time has made me vomit with distaste. Now I wish, above everything, to begin my baby dresses at once. For weeks we have been unable to lay aside enough money for such things, but I have fifty milreis—twelve dollars—and I am going to buy the material immediately.

I have felt my child quicken in me. A curious stir, a faint throb like a pulse; and my belly moved in a strange undulation. I undressed to look at myself. I was elated. All at once I had discovered a kind of hard unquestioning satisfaction in my own being. I was strong and important. A new ruthlessness seemed to be born in me, though for what end I could not conceive.

*

*　　　　　*

With my pregnant body it is different. My mind is filled with a kind of stillness of understanding. There is calm in my realization of myself—force that has surpassed motion. I feel integrated like a rock, but warm and breathing. I am afraid of the world—of people—but my fear surrounds me. It doesn't permeate me any longer. I believe in myself, just as I believe in things outside me through the objectivity of touch. I realized a long time ago that a belief which does not spring from a conviction in the emotions is no belief at all. When I am convinced of something, I am convinced with my whole self, as though my flesh had informed me. Now I *know*. Knowledge is the condition of my *being*.

THOUGH I am at loss to understand the unkind assumptions of the newspapers from home that, without a single fact as to what has actually occurred, anathematize John and me in the most vulgar terms, the exposure of injustice gratifies me, and gives an almost mystical assurance to my sense of right. Yes, I want to be an outcast in order to realize fully what human beings are capable of. Now I know that fear and cruelty underlie all of society's protestations in favor of honesty and moral worth.

When I learned something of physical passion and of the violent emotion which might accompany it * * * I was compelled to feel shame for my knowledge, but I gloried in it also. I wanted to * * * construct a universe in which everything was included.

John never conceals anything from me.

WE have moved to the Hotel Globo. On the first day I was terrified by the great number of large mahogany-colored cockroaches that appeared from cracks in the floor, from behind the guarda-roupa, and from a dark square cut high up in the wall, a kind of ventilator in the closet for dirty linen which is next our room. Fully dressed as I was, I hid myself in the bedclothes and stayed there, half smothered under a pillow, until John came home at night.

The building we are in is a ruin. On the second floor is the office, a long bare sala in which there are some bentwood chairs from Vienna and a few ponderous rockers with plush-upholstered seats. A number of elderly men, either very thin or very fat, all of a ghastly yellow complexion, all with untidy mustaches, all dressed in linen clothes that never seem to be fresh, lounge there, smoke and stare, and read the newspapers a little. I seldom go into this sala myself for I don't like to be scrutinized and commented on as if I were inanimate.

The dining-room is very grand. On each of the small tables with their soiled cloths is a blue glass vase filled with some sort of decaying vegetation. On the wall over the desk hangs a huge lithograph portrait of Emperor Pedro the Second. Almoço is at eleven o'clock. We have the same coarse fish fried in oil, the same indescribable meats, and when we request a little lettuce it comes to us half-covered with sand, with oil served in a broken cruet. There is frequently a fly in the stew, and sometimes even a roach. The waiters, small and thin, with Mongolian features, all look alike. I enjoy the theatrical family at the table beside us: some ill-bred children, a young girl who wears spangled dresses in the daytime, and a fat woman in a very gorgeous matinée of soiled lace.

How the people here do love shoddy elegance! There

is something fundamental in the racial attitude toward plumbing. In the indescribable toilets there are signs which request the guests not to throw paper in the bowls, cockroaches rattle through the empty tin provided as a waste-paper receptacle, and from a nail depends a soiled cloth with which to wipe off the wooden seat. There is one tub in the hotel, but I am too frightened of disease to bathe in it.

OUR window is really a French door giving egress on a balcony and nearly level with the street. We have to leave it wide open on account of the heat and the little boys climb up on the railings and stare in at us.

There is a square in front, a church before which bombs are constantly exploding in honor of some saint, and a fowl market. No one in the square ever goes to bed at night. There are cries, calls, curses, the jolting of carts, and the thud of innumerable feet. At two o'clock in the morning the roosters begin to crow, the hens cluck, and the turkeys keep up a sort of bleating. A strong sour smell, like an odor from a hen house, floats into the room with the cold heaviness of the morning air

JOHN has received a promotion. From mere bookkeeper he has become auditor for the score or more of stores the Company has in and around Rio. And we are going to move again. This time to a private boarding house, a pensão in the Praia Flamengo.

On Saturday I bought some more material for baby clothes, we went to a confectioner's on the Avenida and had ice cream, and on the way back John purchased a basket of grapes that cost four milreis.

Our landlady is an Alsatian. From the maid, Maria Theresa, I am learning my first intelligible words of Portuguese address. Our room faces the sea and I have learned the names of boats and waves and of things going by in the street.

At last I have written to Nannette. I have wanted to write to her for a long time, but John's wife, I knew, was in communication with her, and since Louise has been threatening John with arrest I dared not.

After our dreary dinner in a dark dining-room we escape into the street. Sometimes we sit on a bench in the Public Gardens and watch the endless procession of motor cars that, without any regulation of speed, are always sweeping up and down the Avenida. Rio is very brilliantly illuminated, very beautiful at night. The asphalt roadways, stained with the reflections of the lamps, seem composed of black porcelain in which is mirrored all of the color and movement of the street in a kind of apotheosis of agitation. The foliage of the trees has a luster like purplish wax, and the geraniums in the flower beds, shadowed with blue, are a sinister crimson.

Beyond the gardens and the roadway, on the side opposite the houses, the sea wall extends. Ferries traverse the harbor from point to point. Sometimes one of the big ocean liners is visible as it approaches, a low shape, outlined in fire, sweeping with a hundred lights the darkness upon which it floats, into which it now and again appears to sink. Upon the summit of the Pão d'Assucar the electric bulbs look like the circle of a crown, and as the car of the elevator swings upward, suspended by an invisible cable, it resembles a golden insect surmounting, with the hairlike rays of its legs, the blackness of a wall that cuts off an abyss.

Behind us, up the slopes, there are lights and more lights, the darkened spaces between them widening as they approach the stars, until finally, where our gaze rests, it is nearly impossible to distinguish the earth from the sky, except that the shadows of peaks somehow suggest a greater solidity than do the shadows of clouds. Beyond everything, visible and invisible, according to the alterations in the mist, is the lookout on the Corcovado, arrived at from nowhere, a suspended planet in which we realize, nevertheless, there are people moving.

I am crushed by the city which precipitates itself upon us from the looming mountains. I know that I love John, but I remember nothing but weariness. I want to feel, to feel anything—to purge myself of the heavy turgidness of the thoughts that come to me as I sit alone day after day with no definite occupation.

I suppose the truth is that I have not evolved completely from the romantic notion that a great outward expenditure of energy constitutes a kind of super-reality. I imagine that I live only in action. Restraint or passivity of any kind represents to me an inferior condition.

I am ashamed that, loving John as I do, I am not happier. I know that John believes my pregnancy should impose * * * restraint on us. I can not bear his disapproval and I would never admit it to him, but I know in my heart I am longing for * * * some crudity of expression which would be, for me, incontrovertible proof that we are yet alive, that we have not been reduced to a slavery of self-control. I want to remember that we live for something beside the food which sustains us and the place in which we sleep.

I THINK so often of Nannette. When I first told her that I loved John she was less shocked than I had expected. Her moral convictions, like most of the ready-made convictions of the world, meant nothing to her until she reverted to their statement in an instinct of defense. But when she knew that John and I were going to live together she took out an old pistol which belonged to Uncle Alec and threatened to kill herself with it.

IN the Public Gardens the leaves are still. The first lamps diffuse a moist radiance in the clouds of trees. Motor cars, passing quickly, are heavy flashes succeeding one another in the brilliance of the street. The train of pedestrians is endless: English nursemaids in bonnets and long blue capes; stout mothers of the people in what John calls "fatigue," a full silk skirt and a formless jacket of elaborate lace. A wedding cortège has just gone by. The bridal carriage resembled a parliamentary chariot of state. The married couple, behind a wall of glass, were exposed to everyone's gaze. The harness of the horses bore a decoration of flowers. But the funeral procession was even more brilliant. The red and blue hearse, the brightly plumed

horses gave everything the atmosphere of a fête. Even
the coffin, painted with blue and orange and draped with
a carnival wreath of paper blossoms, seemed to celebrate
a victory of the deceased.

The bay, vague as an expanse of silk, undulates
before me. Into the small hollows of little waves, the
pale light floats hesitantly, and rests there in bronzed
pools without ever penetrating that mysterious surface.
I can see the mountains of Petropolis, fifty miles away,
a jagged contour of amethyst.

I think I have given up questioning life, trying to
find a pattern into which I can fit myself. I am satisfied with the vagueness of the evening, the vastness of
the world surrounding me in which there is room for me
and for everything else, in which every suggestion of
conflict disappears. At this moment Rio is more beautiful than anything I have ever seen.

At the little tables across the pavements people sit
and drink coffee or cerveja. There is a river of light
rushing along the Avenida, carrying everything with it
as toward a magnificent destruction. And above and
around this minor torrent is the massive movement of
clouds and sea.

Darker, darker, darker. The night is dark and the
ocean is like a shadow upon another shadow—darkness upon darkness. Around the semicircle of the bay
the lamps, sprung to intense being, reach their little
claws of rays through the vast softness beneath. They
clutch. Reflections like little burning wires sink themselves into the water. But the night remains—the night
in which the light is finally extinguished. Darkness.

15

ESCAPADE

LOUISE has the law on her side—law supposed to be founded on equal rights. Through it she has the power to punish by a terrible separation two people whose only crime has been to prefer each other's society in poverty when they might enjoy the physical security of loveless homes. John is spoken of as a man of vile predilections who has callously ruined a young girl's life. In recalling my adolescence I can remember no true understanding or sympathy from any source; John has given me both. He is the only person I ever knew who was really capable of love, who, without any of the cant and falsity of sacrifice, considers in the most delicate sense the inward happiness of another being.

John and I left the United States with seven hundred dollars. This money came from the sale of some microscopes and other valuable instruments which were John's own property. A fortune has not been left Louise, but at least she has more than we. The ruin of our health and future is to be the indemnity for her chagrin on discovering that something unusual— something indeed not quite nice—has occurred within the most intimate circle to which convention binds her.

Without too much effort of the imagination I can follow Louise's emotion as she awakened to the humiliation of her position—for humiliating it certainly must have been. In a life dedicated to social pretense, how impossible not to be pained by a situation too bald to be glossed over. Louise wants to be seen at the opera on all the most fashionable nights and to know only "the best people." And society is almost as unkind to the innocent participant in its scandals as to the sinful originators of the debacle. We have behaved as

Louise's enemies and she is justified in considering us as such. But I am in rebellion against all those people who make the laws, who edit the newspapers, who, without once inquiring into the personal elements which distinguish every situation, condemn in advance all those who fail in a conformity which has no individual significance.

I am not afraid of men and women as I know them, but of *people*, the world—everything which seems to me huge and formless and blindly motivated. The more we are persecuted the more self-righteous my convictions become. What I resent most deeply is the attempt to deprive *me* of responsibility for my own acts. To have John sent to prison as though *I* had not equally selected the condition to which we have been brought!

JOHN and I sleep together in a bed that is narrow like a prison cot. I lie on the edge of it, almost suspended in space. That is the only way I can show John that I love him—when he doesn't know it. My gratitude to him is like a feeling of sin. I know that he has so much more to give than I have. Of course I never admit that anyone is better than I am. I honestly don't think so. But in the case of John it is almost a pain to realize how much I owe to him.

In the early morning the sea makes a cold heavy sound, massively reiterated against the breakwater across the street. I lie there tensely, trying not to fall off the cot, and I am frightened of John's sleep, as if in it something had already separated us. I could almost pray for the waves to cease, if only for an instant. They go on. I imagine the ocean dragging itself, with an indescribable effort, against the masonry. It falls back.

The street is not wide and the rush of water seems almost in the room. A bellbuoy, anchored a little distance from the shore, clangs monotonously. When I sit up in bed I can just make out the table, the two chairs, the sewing machine I have rented, the silver of the glass. The sky is plain now. Vacant like an empty mirror. The water, too, gives out a gray light. When it strikes the breakwall a frothing cataract pours, with a hushed stir, down into the street. I lean against John and try, without waking him, to comfort myself with the warmth of his body. I want everything warm— warm and bright.

WHEN John said goodbye to Louise he was bound, presumably, on a fishing expedition, and there was no excuse for carrying away the better part of his wardrobe with him. So he has only two suits of old clothes. The elbows of the coats are shiny and the trousers are frayed along the bottom edges. I have mended the suit of blue-striped material with pieces of black.

Pregnancy has so altered my figure that nothing I own really serves to cover me. I have an old coat and I must keep it on both indoors and out. There isn't a simple paper pattern to be bought in Rio, so yesterday I went to an atelier where they design fashionable dresses and asked to have a pattern cut.

The gentleman who was responsible for the models was a small yellow person with moist uncertain eyes and a waxed mustache. While he was measuring me he talked volubly and passed his hand carelessly and caressingly over my hips and breasts. I felt like an animal for sale who was being examined for good points, and I hated myself because I didn't find it possible to say anything. When at last I got out of the shop I wanted to run home. I was conscious of my flesh as of some horrible garment and my cheeks were hot. I am not going back there again no matter how difficult I find it to make a dress.

THE rains are beginning, brief heavy showers that scarcely dissipate the heat. In the mornings processions of porters trot by from market, keeping up the gait of rickshaw runners. The panniers swinging from their shoulders are piled with burry chu-chu the color of pale jade, with parsley like crisp velvet moss, with lettuces that have a faint green blush, and with a deep reddish-orange squash. Sometimes the sun shines a little on all the green things drenched by the rain. In the early stillness the bare feet of the men make a shuffling sound. The street, beneath the lifting fog, is glossed over with amber-colored reflections. The sea is obscure like a dream, and the mountains are invisible.

FOR a time John and I had preserved the fiction of having come to South America to collect natural history specimens for a London firm. Actually we had visited an entomological shop in Great Russell Street and some correspondence had passed between us and the dealer.

Several months ago when we were in Cascadura we went out every morning with our nets: two green gauze ones for butterflies, and two canvas sweeping bags for beetles and the like. The main street of the village was inches deep in a kind of chalky dust. As we walked along the house fronts became suddenly agitated and at every window appeared a face, half concealed by a blind or the fold of a curtain.

I wore an old khaki riding skirt divided in the middle, and John was in overalls with a beach hat too small for him perched high on his head. Before we had traversed a block the little boys began to collect about us, and by the time we reached the last straggling huts the ranks of our followers resembled a circus parade or the advertisers of a negro minstrel show.

The small boys, giggling discreetly, intensely curious, followed us for miles on our walks. We sometimes essayed their collaboration in our hunt, offering them a vintem apiece for their finds. But when they began to bring us by the hatful a large black grasshopper which was peculiarly plentiful at that season we had to desist.

We were at the bachelor establishment of the assist-ant American consul where we were given only our dinner, and our money was so short that we never had more than a few crackers for lunch.

It was a hideous country—red clay hills and dreary vegetation. Occasionally a large mango or a jaca tree offered us a little shade under which to rest. In the center of the village was a cattle market, and to one side of it a large stable with an inn on the floor above. One day we went up the dingy unpainted stairway and looked at a bedroom which an old woman had for rent. Vast and bare—the only furnishings a bed, a chair, a table with a cracked mirror above it, and a stand that held an earthen carafe—its windows overlooked the market directly. It smelled of manure and dust, and the floor, which seemed never to have been swept, was harsh with the stale-looking sunlight cast upon it through the smeary uncurtained glass.

The landlady, drawing a calico dressing-gown about her, talked to us in a staccato whisper, as though she expected the information she was giving us to draw the police. She told us that her husband was dead, her children had left her, and that she had "female complaint," and she wanted us to accept these calamities as a valid excuse for the exorbitant rent she asked.

She introduced her remaining son, a poorly dressed youth whose straggling hair fell greasily over his collar. His back was humped. He clutched his thin coat across his meager chest and coughed continually. He was very close to me and the tubercular spittle fell in a fine spray across my face.

Well, there was one thing to relieve the hideousness of this village in which there was scarcely a tree, a garden, anything green to look at. There were the mountains of Petropolis, closer than I could view them in the city, and in the late afternoon they had a wonderful translucent color. An amethyst dust seemed to have settled about them in the dry still atmosphere and I was almost oppressed by their loveliness.

ON one side of a cajú thicket we came upon a low mud house covered with palm thatch. A thin weak-looking dog ran out and barked fiercely at us while we hesitated, waving our butterfly nets in defense. A thick toothless voice. An old woman squatted on her thin haunches, staring at us enigmatically, a philosopher's pipe between her teeth.

Without altering her posture she watched us as we moved away. When we looked back on the oasis shade of the empty hut, the old woman before it resembled some strange dead old goddess, the smoke of her pipe the fire of offering.

ALL the stores of the Sewing Machine Company resembled each other. A large room facing the street had an array of highly varnished machines which were to be sold, on the installment plan, to poor Brazilians, and for an exorbitant price. At the back of the salesroom behind a dark partition the bookkeeper worked on a high stool, and this was also where John, on his visits as auditor, officiated.

I sometimes went in to talk to the embroidery teacher, pale, with carefully oiled hair and an elaborate homemade dress of sleazy material ornamented with lace. She had an exaggeratedly modest demeanor, a discreet subdued voice, and thin hands covered with pinchbeck rings. Having fallen into the disgraceful extremity of working for her living, the profession of professora de bordado appealed to her as an employment which did not offend the strict conventions of a lady. She was paid almost nothing, but that nothing provided beans and mandioc for herself and an aged relative whom she supported.

John was going to leave these stores of the city. He told me of his new appointment on a Friday. The boat for the North was sailing the next morning and he had already secured our tickets.

ESCAPADE

The professora de bordado, with tears in her dreamy unintelligent eyes, bade me good-by. She commiserated me. In the North she said there was nothing that resembled Rio. The people had no "chic."

THE narrow decks of the Maranhão were crowded with stout dark-skinned women in lace jackets, elaborately dressed children, and oiled and perfumed men in linen suits. When the bell for leave-taking rang, breasts heaved, tears were copiously shed, and men and women embraced each other alike.

At one o'clock we descended for "lunchie," so pronounced by the steward in what he considered the English fashion. We had scarcely quitted the harbor mouth when the ship began to pitch and roll, children cried, and—no receptacles being handy—there was a deluge of vomit in the passageways and on the deck.

I retired to my stateroom. Cockroaches were everywhere, and the close air stank of unemptied slops. The porthole had to be closed.

WHEN the ship went into a trough an undulant expanse of green marbled surface was on a level with my face. The stolid horizon seemed to contract upon us. The colorless sky sagged with the heaviness of the glare it half concealed. A few gulls swooped opposite the glass and their mewing came to me faintly. I had a peculiar sense of drama in regard to myself and my situation. I observed with astonishment my unforeseen actions and the circumstance in which John and I had been caught. Then all at once I became identified with the automaton I was. My anxiety was actual. I was excited—afraid of what might ultimately happen to me.

PART II

PAST Cape Frio the calm was unbroken. The ship slipped through a lake of blue oil which had a metallic tinge. Far away this bronzed liquid congealed in a pale edge that cut across an horizon blanched with light. All at once, out of nothing, a cloud appeared. The blue water was filled suddenly with green reflections. And on this indolent plain a shadow of the tint of crushed grapes floated and sank away from us.

A shower gathered and the big scattering drops hung for an instant like a veil of glass and silver between the ship and the sun. A rushing noise of sudden wind accompanied the rain, but not a fold of our garments was stirred. With a sound like leaves, the drops flattened on the deck.

To our right, faintly, for an instant, appeared a rainbow. Another to our left. So faint these were they were mere insinuations of color. They vanished in the moist heat and the sun once more poured down upon us.

Still, still. Light, so much more intense than sound, has absorbed our senses. Blue deafens us. And above blue a phantasmagoria of radiations in which every hue conceivable is elusively apparent.

JOHN and I have brought our own steamer chair— thank heaven—because none are to be secured on board.

ESCAPADE

We sit in a shaded corner of the deck and are left almost entirely to ourselves. An acrid odor of hot machinery pervades everything. There is a smell of blistering paint, and also, occasionally, of roaches.

As evening approaches the sun dissolves in its own gold emanations, drawing water, as the saying is. The clouds arrange themselves across a ladder of light that suggests a grandiose composition by Doré. The air is moist and sweet. The star that appears in the gray and yellow mist is like a tear—the tear of a giant, a tear that is heroic.

I HAD not yet got over the strangeness of finding my body animate in some way unrelated to my will. The agitation of the journey awakened my child to some dark consciousness which I was unable to share. Instead of finding his wrigglings merely humorous they excited me. I imagined myself carried along in some nameless inevitability.

My breasts were heavy. * * * What I was experiencing could not be articulated. I gave myself to my own flesh and enjoyed the relaxation of an irresponsible state. I wanted to go to the end of myself, to the end of something obscure to my consciousness. Maternity at this period was exclusively an experience of the senses, and, except in rarely reflective moments, almost without any tenderness of the emotions. I longed for physical suffering which, like a light, was to illumine for me my own being.

ESCAPADE

On a headland, on a hill so steep that its summit could be approached only by countless steps hewn in the rocks, a monastery, the peak of the roof ornamented with a gilded cross. The smooth high wall which enclosed the almost barren garden gave the building a medieval appearance.

Almost before we set foot in Victoria it began to drizzle. The unpaved streets, without sidewalks, were already deep in mud. Vultures settled drearily on the roofs of the huts of unbaked bricks. All along the sloppy roadways we heard the muffled flap of huge dank wings ascending as we approached.

After a time the sun came out very weakly. Then the hills by the waterside looked freshly green. The harbor quivered all over its opaque surface with greenish bronze reflections. The monastery, the last light on its windows, resembled the citadel of man's final aspiration to escape the earth.

As night approached the governor's palace was illumined for some festival. A torrent of light rushed into the pale darkness of the sea. But through it one yet had glimpses of sodden streets, dilapidated dwellings, and heard the rising rhythm of heavy wings out of the shadows.

In Cabedello the sun shone very bright. Between the fronds of the palms that kept up a metallic clatter as the wind jerked them about, was spread the same dazzling sky that had hung so amazingly over the ship. The stiff enameled foliage lashed itself against the blueness of a heaven that was angry like a stone. There were some natural avenues among the cocoanut trees and these were designated streets, but the sand was ankle-deep and hissed continually before us in little spiral eddies. The huts were unplastered, built of mud and wattle and covered over with thatch. Their shadows, etched sharply in violet-blue, were like shadows thrown across an expanse of snow. And the shadows of the trees, following the agitations of the leaves, moved forward, shortened themselves, and stretched themselves out again, as if in delicate anguish.

The dwellings, without window glass, presented interiors on a level with the eyes of passersby. We could see the hammocks swung from wall to wall of the bedrooms, the small salas with their proud array of chairs stiffly facing one another, the shrines in the corners where the patron saints, in gowns of red and blue, had wreaths of pink paper flowers draped carefully about their necks.

GOD knows how long it took us to accomplish the short railway journey between Cabedello and Parahyba. There were no stations along the line but the cars moved so slowly that, had walking been possible, we should have preferred the trip on foot. The train was crowded. The sun came through the window on my side of the coach, and, as I was covered by my heavy coat, I began to feel faint with heat and fatigue. John, who irritated me because he never complained of anything, if not for the purpose of definite accomplishment, had to stand up.

The track was laid between salt marshes over which the tide had spread and inundated everything but some islands covered with a harsh gray grass that glittered in the sunlight and seemed coated with rime. On these sterile oases fisher-folk had built huts of mud-daub and wattle with only three walls, across which dry palm branches were sparingly laid to keep out the rain when it should come. One could see that these people had no possessions other than the ragged clothes they wore, an earthen pot or two, and perhaps a net which was laid out to dry on the wall or the roof. Naked yellow children with emaciated arms and legs and huge inflated bellies turned, as the train passed, and stared after it with a long stupid gaze of astonishment.

There was nothing anywhere but this grass, thrust stiffly from brown-bright pools of what—as the tide receded—must have been almost pure mud—rigidly twitching grass and a glaring sky faded with light stretching away and away to the end of a world of misery, past the last poverty-stricken hut.

In the square paved with cobblestones grew a few small jaca trees. Under them ragged barefoot old women squatted on their hams before charcoal braziers and chanted out wares of roast corn and boiled peanuts. Except for these old women and the passengers going by from the train, Parahyba might have been deserted. The sun struck full on the stucco houses we approached, and the blinds across the front of the Hotel were drawn. Contours were dislocated by the gyrations of the heat waves which rushed up from the paving blocks and trembled undulantly before us. The heat was the visible expression of a terrible silence, a silence in which the cracked voices of the old women were as irrelevant as the discordant notes of far-off birds. A stasis of life had created a vortex of intensity, a stillness into which life poured itself with the vividness of death.

THE large room was quiet like the street. Sound was subdued to heavy somnolence. Even though the blinds were drawn the purple mosquito netting suspended over the ‚bed seemed inflated with radiance. The pottery carafe on top of the commode held pink-violet reflections in its terra-cotta surface. On the tin washstand the cracked bowl and pitcher had a dazzling opaque lustre.

Between my room and the next, the partition ascended only a little way toward the ceiling and I could hear a drunken woman sobbing and cursing, her voice broken and thick.

To reach the toilet I had to cross a little garden where men in their shirt sleeves were drinking and playing cards. And the door I had to enter was very conspicuous. Two of the men, seeing a young foreign woman, turned and spoke to me. I did not reply to their greeting but, out of a mixture of fear and irritation, I gazed at them with undeviatingly defiant eyes. On the right hand of one the nail of the fifth finger was elegantly long and twisted at the tip. His eyes were brilliant, black, filled with a hard factual understanding. His expression was admiring and condescending— perhaps there was a little ridicule in it. With an indolent gesture he caressed the few hairs of his mustache.

In the dusk the garden was filled with a greenness

that flowed upward from the earth. The fading light, trembling above the house tops, was like a sea of glass in motion. The shivering foliage of the flame trees resembled black Spanish lace.

I rushed up to my room and, flinging myself on the bed, began to weep with indignation.

AGAIN the sun crept through the blinds and pursued me until there was no corner left in which to escape. I lay down, but if I forgot to pull the mosquito netting across my face, the flies clung limply along my exposed cheek and the back of my neck. There was not even one comfortable chair to sit in, and if I went to the garden the women greeted me with hostile eyes, and the men pursued me with their shallow cloying looks. It was different only for a little while in the evening when John came home from work.

I felt as if I were drowning in ennui. As if the sun had blinded me of any inward seeing. Yes, I was like a blind person. In the long days when John was away I should have to sit there in my white empty prison, a prison in which nothing moved but the irradiation of the glare, in which there was no aim, no interest.

If my brain was dead my hands and arms were dead also, and the baby was dead in me. I did not believe in it. I imagined myself bound in the heat forever. Two white stones were laid upon my burning eyeballs, and I rested woodenly beneath their weight. The heat was cold. It burned me like ice. I wanted to be a writer but I had nothing to write about. The world was a field of light and I was a ghost.

ESCAPADE

OUR trunk was moved. The new room was on the top floor of a four-story house. Passing through the hallway outside our door, we could enter a barn-like apartment, unused, it seemed, for many a day. The walls had a greenish look of mold and the floor was heavy with dust. Spider webs filled the crevices in the broken window panes. From this room a crumbling stone staircase descended outside the house to the garden which was on a hillside and elevated above the street. Along the disintegrating walks, among the banana plants frequented by large coral-striped centipedes, four little naked children, almost of an age, played day after day. In the dark I frequently encountered some of the messes they had made on the most frequented paths. The kitchen of the establishment downstairs was in an ell of the building. When I leaned from my staircase I could see the slatternly servant pounding coffee beans in a mortar. The Dona da Casa was very stout and indolent. She sat by a window and did crochet, every now and then screaming irrelevantly to the children in a shrill choked voice. The eldest daughter played the Grand March from Aïda. The piano, laboriously strummed, had a thin hollow sound as it floated up to me in the empty rooms. I was surrounded by a sterile atmosphere of peace. Time was imperceptible. Occasionally melancholy produced a faint nausea of the emotions.

It is one thing to view such a town and such people from the heights of an independent existence, another to realize that to them and them only one must turn for the vivification of response.

31

ESCAPADE

IN the Public Garden, in the illumined evening, the senhoritas promenade with wizened old women in shawls who chaperone them. There is a surreptitious intercourse of eyes as the young men, lemon-colored, their little mustaches waxed, their clothes a crude exaggeration of the fashions that come from Rio with the weekly boat, pass and repass with affected casualness. I feel gay, stimulated by the shock of alien presences. In the gateways of the park, groups of ragged peanut vendors. The corn on the braziers has a succulent odor. The band in the pergola plays very loud. The men wear a red uniform. The people stamp, clap, and whistle.

IN our bedroom it is too warm to sleep. We take our pillows for cushions and sit out of doors at the top of the long stairway. The smell of salt from the marshes nearby mingles with the pungent fume of the latrina. Some jasmine planted against the wall has an odor that suggests exotic confusion. John points out the Southern Cross and I respond appropriately to this symbol of romantic journeying.

I HAVE had letters from Uncle Alec and from Nannette, forwarded to me from the Consulate at Rio. Nannette, in her large sprawling emotional writing, mingles with her reproaches the endearing terms of her relief in hearing from me. If I had, she says, realized what I was bringing upon her I would have behaved very differently. She has been almost maddened by worry and humiliation, by the scandalous stories of the American newspapers. Why should so much be inflicted upon her

32

when she is innocent. She says that John and I, who have escaped these details, have suffered less. Then she tells me that she looks forward some day to seeing me. That her heart is nearly broken, and that, but for Uncle Alec's fortitude, she would never have recovered herself.

She goes on with an account of Louise who, when the University was trying to overcome the notoriety of the affair, gave everything to the papers. Louise has, as Nannette expresses it, "hounded her" on the telephone with hysterical reproaches—as though she, Nannette, were not undergoing even greater wretchedness.

I am as indignant as Nannette that she has been made to suffer so, but I do not hold John and myself responsible for what she has been through. Society must know that its punishment is heaviest on Nannette who has always adhered to its tenets. If the approbation of the group had been of prime importance to us we should never have gone away.

Perhaps this kind of argument is specious. The simple fact of course is that I love John more than I have ever loved Nannette, and that I am willing to make sacrifices in order to be with him. As yet I don't consider that I have made any. It somehow pleases my vanity to know that I no longer have a respectable reputation.

Uncle Alec is much more coherent than Nannette. His letter indicates an acceptance of the situation which surprises me. He says that when John and I disappeared he was nearly mad with anxiety for some weeks. But after he received our letter, mailed to him from New York, he accepted my decision. He referred to the "stench of public opinion," but he did not recount the scandal to us in so much detail. He says he knows how unhappy I must have been at home, and that he realizes that I had a right to do something with my life.

Nannette has suffered more than he. At one time she showed such symptoms of morbidness that he feared for her sanity. The family finances have not improved. Nannette, who was never educated to the use of her hands, is doing all the housework and even the family washing. I can scarcely imagine it. After we lost our money she was morbidly susceptible to the opinions of others, and her humility as to the social position we had relinquished tortured my pride. But she tried to absorb herself in books and music so that life at home never seemed to me as sordid as Uncle Alec suggests it is now.

Uncle Alec concludes what he has written by assuring me of his forgiveness. This tinges my affection for him with a faint flavor of bitterness. My vanity will not allow anyone the moral prerogative of passing judgment on my acts. Besides John is the only person who understands me sufficiently to be capable of any just comment on what I do.

To-day I had another note from Uncle Alec. It must have been delayed in Rio, for the date showed that it was posted with his letter. He tells us we must beware of Louise, who has refused to divorce John. She is hopeful of trying John under the Mann Act, or at least of beggaring us through alimony. She doesn't attempt to conceal her vengeful frame of mind and everyone thinks she is right.

ESCAPADE

I HAVE asked Nannette to come to see us. I doubt she can, for Uncle Alec is in such straits for cash that the small sum required for her passage and her board here may be more than he can produce. Poor Uncle Alec! He has concocted so many wild schemes of success and they have all ended disastrously. I know his terrible sense of guilt in not providing Nannette with all the luxuries she was formerly accustomed to. Long ago I talked to him of divorce and he was very much shocked. His idea has always been that in giving Nannette and me material happiness he bought some freedom for himself—freedom to live as he liked.

How well I remember the first time I saw Brunhilda in Parahyba. I used to call her that. The clean bare floors and spotless tablecloths did not dissipate the aroma of Valhalla, though it blended with the odor of a German kitchen. Brunhilda showed us the postcard album, the letters from home, and cried when she spoke of little Theodore who died in the yellow fever epidemic. Her husband wasn't good enough for her, though he was an excellent cook. There was the old grandfather, Berthe, Karli and Gretchen—so fat and so pathetic. They were all dependent on her. Karli and Gretchen, escaped from Russia, had traveled with a circus. I didn't know then what that lank old Brazilian with the diamond on his forefinger, the lodger in the best room, was to be to her. If only she had really been the daughter of Wotan!

WHEN we turned out our lights we could see, from the window of our room in the Pensão Allemão, the end-

35

less marshy meadows that lay back of the garden. Thousands of fireflies suspended themselves over the vague grass. The field resembled a lake in which rayless stars were reflected.

THE sea again, a steely sea on which a reddish purple glare trembles. The water lifts from its bed, and across its vast continuity of motion the smaller broken motions of wind make a thousand ebbs and flows of waves, a thousand hissings of froth.

The lift of the ship, its rigid descent is arrowlike. It approaches each declivity through a torrent of sibilance. The ocean rises in leaden hillocks that dissolve finally in veined pools of darkness—darkness threaded with white.

Lines of passengers in steamer chairs resemble rows of convalescent patients in a hospital. As night comes on the glow of lamps along the deck accentuates the stiff attitudes of sick people.

The sea grows colder, heavier—green—gray-blue. The deck quivers with the reverberation of the screws. A newspaper in a man's hand oscillates and its harsh folds glisten with the light. The jerk of the engine is like the beating of a heart. Damp wind. The awnings flap. The ship tilts its stern—tilts, lowers, dips.

At this season there is nothing in the atmosphere to suggest that we are near the equator. We have also had the good fortune this time to go further North on an American boat.

SENHOR EVARISTO has a fat pock-marked face, a squat plump body, and he dresses in soiled linen clothes with a heavy watch chain across his wrinkled vest. He wears glasses with gold rims. When he stares at me I feel his gaze uncomfortably. He is lecherous and timid. He calls one of the hotel waiters to take our bags and show us up to our room.

"I em American, too." He smiles. His teeth are very bad. He breathes heavily while he speaks. "I am seis mezes in de U-ni-ted States." He passes one of his short hands apologetically across his thin hair. He understands American manners and is carefully oblivious to indications of my pregnancy. "De senhora ees well? Natal ees not fine like Rio, but eet ees a nice leetle place."

JOHN was required to report immediately at the Sewing Machine Store. I spent the morning alone in our hotel room. It is over the kitchen and smoke comes up in little puffs through the wide cracks in the half-rotted floor, covering me, the bed linen, everything about with showers of soot. Black snow descended almost imperceptibly upon my hair, my clothes, everything that I touched.

I smelled palm oil and garlic, and listened to the continual dry clatter of plates. The voices that came to me were shrill or gruff but I could not make out any words.

When I took off my outer garments to lie down I discovered that the bed had already been slept in. The sheets were very much soiled and there were other unmistakable indications. So I continued to sit up.

For some reason I was very indignant about the bed. I sat in the stiff chair, facing the glaring window, and simply raged. Of course I should have gone downstairs and, without waiting for John, complained to the proprietor. But I was helpless. The consciousness that I am pregnant makes me feel helpless most of the time. I can not bear to expose myself to the naked gaze of the men I see. It is almost as if they had touched me, and this uninvited contact is more than I can endure. The people around me are full of falseness and shame and they compel me to be ashamed also. And I hate myself because I am contaminated by their suggestions.

I've always been like that. If I listen to someone who is lying to me I understand his guilty sensations and have to endure the most of his embarrassment. And I can feel satisfied in my own body only when I am with people who do not question it.

Ennui is the most awful thing I have ever had to bear. I sit here hour after hour and my brain is clasped with iron. I am dulled to inactivity, but with a stupid ache that will not allow me to sleep.

THE dining room, hung with old mirrors which Senhor Evaristo purchased in Rio at the auction of a fashionable house, is adorned all over the walls with advertisements of a cure for syphilis, and with some large placards on which "Why have worms?" is printed in magnificent red type.

The other women guests of the establishment are prostitutes. As I pride myself on equality with everyone where morals are concerned, I would like to continue my meals in the sala de jantar with the rest. But John is going up the coast to look over some of the smaller stores of the division and he advises me to have everything served in my room, as the male boarders might prove annoying.

We have coffee in a dark hallway under the stair. An old Indian woman prepares it on a brazier. She strains the liquid through a greasy rag on which she afterward wipes her hands. And the rag is never washed. All the same it is a delicious drink.

In the hallway there is a broken-down table spread with oilcloth, some chairs with loose backs—some with the legs off—and a large black cat. The hotel is filled with rats, roaches, enormous spiders, and many small vermin—fleas—the kind that burrow into the flesh and lay their eggs—and bedbugs in abundance.

SINCE John is gone, Senhor Evaristo likes to come to my door and talk to me. He never comes in, no matter how much I insist. I know this is because I am "respectable," and he is afraid of John, and it enrages me. Men show me respect only as they respect the physical belongings of another. They don't really respect me, but John's property. Senhor Evaristo admires me, and on account of John he is ashamed of it. As to the fact that his attentions don't flatter me as an individual—that never occurs to him.

SENHOR EVARISTO has a "girl" in the United States. He showed me her picture and I knew immediately what she was. She despises him also, but it is because he is fat and old and very naïve. Since she is American, pure white, of a superior race, he wants to marry her. "I spen' muito dinheiro on ella. I giv' her a gold ring with a diamon' in it," he says.

ESCAPADE

When I go out into the dingy dirty hall I often meet some of the prostitutes and they talk to me. I like them. I feel they are infinitely superior to most of the men. And Senhor Evaristo warns me not to have anything to do with them. "Dey are not nice wimmin for de senhora. Dey come here. I can't help eet. Eet ees de life. Not like de U-ni-ted States. Sometime I have a nice place for respectable people." He bows grotesquely. His smile is pathetic, but he irritates me. I should like to tell him that his guests are as good as he is—probably as good as I am.

Perhaps I ought to be more humorous on the subject, but I am not cynical enough for that yet.

BETWEEN my room and the next the partition is so low that, if I climb on a chair, I can see over into the next chamber. I wonder, after I have tried it, if the man who lives there is in the habit of doing the same thing.

The dingy electric bulb gives a yellowish glow to the shadows. I have a native bed made of woven cane, without any springs. There is a table in the room, and a washing stand taken out of a ship. Above the tank there is a mirror and under the lavatory a door opens to display vessels for other use.

I go to bed early, but from the dance hall in the building opposite—the "annex" to Senhor Evaristo's hotel—the maxixe reiterates until morning. Even after I am asleep the noisy shuffling of feet is an agitated undercurrent to what I dream.

When I wake in the dawn there is quiet at last, and I lie there in the cool shadow of loneliness. The hushed pearl-colored clouds dissolve their iridescence in the harsh silk water. One large warm star slips through the dawn like a thought of love through the pale torpors of decency.

THE harbor at sundown is cool and still. The chill air has the sweetish smell of salt, the bitter odor of laid dust, and a musty scent that pervades the old buildings along the wharf. The stone stairs of the quay, discolored with age, wet by the encroaching tide, reflect a smoldering and clouded amber. An old schooner at anchor. Her black hull has a charred look, and her spars, fixed against a pellucid afterglow, are like outstretched despairing arms. There is a slight methodical lift of her shadowy bulk as she veers with the outgoing current. Her stern lights, dim red, without any radiance, remind me of eyes sad and unfaltering.

I wonder who I am. Who is this being I am alone with every day, who is already a part of the child she never beheld, the child who knows her more intimately than any other creature can, though it has never seen her with its eyes. My inflated body is heavy about me. I cannot escape from its heaviness. I want John here to give me a name to see myself with. I feel sensual, cold. There is no delicacy or voluptuousness in my flesh. Pain is the consciousness of an incongruity of which one is a part.

CROWDS, crowds, and the babel of voices. Let men, rushing after themselves, trample between my breasts. I will slip away into passive stillness. Because I am utterly abandoned to life I believe I cannot be taken.

ESCAPADE

When there is a kiss upon my mouth there is a colder kiss upon my heart. I feel wide like a field, sown with the seeds of pain. I bloom unseen to myself.

And I wonder if all these emotions are utterly absurd.

SENHOR EVARISTO introduced his little girl to me. She has lank, mouse-colored curls, light brown eyes, negroid features, and a thin anemic little body. She wore a blue dress trimmed with lace, a bright pink sash, and, on one of her meager hands, a gorgeous ring of brass.

Her mother is a prostitute. And her fat old father is the hero, so John discovered, of half the amours and scandals of the town. She is eleven years old.

Senhor Evaristo turned his weak lecherous gaze on her, stroked her hair, and observed her through his tears. Her virginity makes him uncomfortable. He has a religious regard for it. In order to tolerate her innocence, he pretends to himself that children have no sex. He wants to keep her apart in his regard from the sensual motives which govern his life. "Tenha paciencia com seu pae velho," he says to her. Without knowing how to put it into words, he would like to explain to her the inevitability of his being. His helplessness with himself. His sin and his corpulence have something of the same origin and quality.

MR. AMES has come to the hotel. He is tall and has big heavy bones—clumsy hands and feet. His large face is florid and coarse. His hands are freckled and red. His brown eyes are enormous and melancholy.

ESCAPADE

His expression is humorous and patient. His hair is prematurely white.

Senhor Evaristo introduced us, and, because there is no sala de visita in the building, Mr. Ames comes to my room to talk with me. He places his chair at a deferential distance and leaves the door open. This is to disarm scandal.

He has a great respect for me. I am married, he supposes, of his own caste, and of a flawless reputation. When he glances at me I realize that he is trying to ignore what is so extremely obvious—that I am going to have a child. And I resent his obliviousness. I insist on talking about it, on calling attention to myself. He blushes. His eyes keep looking at me, but carefully, without observing any of the details of my appearance. It would not be "nice" for him to do so. He said that Brazil was "no place for a decent woman." Then he turned the conversation to other channels. He is positively wistful in his desire to escape embarrassment.

TODAY Mr. Ames apologized to me for having come to my room so often. He is certain people are talking about us. Indeed Senhor Evaristo has hinted something to that effect. My answer was to invite him here again and to insist, when he came in, that he close the door after him. He thinks that I am too young to be aware of the evil that surrounds me and that John should be here to protect me. He repeated his remark about Brazil. And he has been with one of the prostitutes. I saw them talking together and I am sure of it.

ESCAPADE

When I think that, if the truth about us were known, Mr. Ames's attitude toward me would be entirely altered I can scarcely endure the deception. I should like to tell him just how things are between John and me. Then he could accept our moral standards or get out, as he pleased.

People believe in moral codes because in relation to their immediate acts fear touches their imaginations. But they do not believe in death. They do not believe in life either, or in their own flesh from which their being proceeds.

THERE is something Byronic in my sadness—for I really enjoy it—enjoy it until I convince myself too thoroughly of my own play.

I went into the church today and watched an old woman place a candle before the shrine of the saint. Jesus was wise through weakness. He had discovered the limitations of his own being. There is nothing so impenetrably stupid as the illusion of the strong who believe in their strength. I believe in my weakness, but I shall keep on, with all the determination I have, discovering myself through everything that I am not. My enemies are many, but some day I shall have my revenge. I shall smile, too, you smiling people.

SENHOR EVARISTO presented me with a marmoset. She wears little gold ear rings, and, around her neck, a gold string of beads with a charm at the end. Her small face, wizened and delicate, is framed in a puff of blue-gray fur. She has shallow eyes, cold, full of a melancholy inquisitiveness, and there is always a small nervous frown on her brow. When she leaps from my shoulder to the table she suggests a squirrel. Her tail is an exquisite plume, rising and falling with a wonderful sweep. But somehow she reminds me of a nervous little old woman very much concerned about trifling things.

At night I tie the string that secures her to the back of a chair, and she perches there in a little heap, making the one thin piercing note that is the cry for a mate.

I cannot understand how people who never question the proprieties can endure the presence of pets.

JOHN has come back. I feel now that nothing can harm us. Because the hotel is impossible and we have not yet discovered a house with a cheap rental, we are going to spend a fortnight with the family of the gerente of the local sewing machine shop.

DONA MATILDA has five daughters. The girls are all between fifteen and twenty-one. At home they are very untidy, except as regards their hair which is oiled, combed close to their heads, and fastened neatly with a bandeau of ribbon, or perhaps a rose. Their handsome eyes are brilliant and unquestioning. They are all thin. Their skin is the color of rich cream. They have very white teeth.

As far as I am able to judge they think of nothing but embroidering, marriage and household affairs. This morning I must have examined at least fifty examples of needlework and complimented them all equally.

ESCAPADE

The mother is not more than forty-five or six, but she appears seventy at least. Her manner is timidly cheerful, but her dull eyes are sad and suspicious. She has a weak spine so that, as she sits all day sewing, she has a hump in her back.

These women live in a house filled with their own subjective emanations, and they never go out of it. Even if they walk in the street they carry with them an atmosphere which encloses them like the atmosphere of a dream. And they will die in the same dream, a long dream of little things. After all they are much nearer fundamentals than the people outside. Men come into the House to them. It is in the House that all the matters of birth and death are attended to. I wonder if their "pettiness" is not, after all, a juster sense of proportion than most of us exhibit in careening through space.

THE back yard is called "o jardim," but the bare earth is adorned only by a few banana plants, a large castor-oil tree, and some thin paw-paws cluttered with rotting fruit. When I step out of doors, a goose, elongating its neck, runs forward on its rubbery feet and challenges me with a hiss. The latrina is not particularly private. Over the entrance, instead of a door, hangs nothing but a short, torn piece of matting * * * A tortoise lives there in the dark, and when I must visit him at night he snaps at my feet.

With the macaw in the sala de jantar, the guinea pigs and chickens that run all over the house, Dona Matilda's establishment resembles the ark. There is also a soffré, bright orange and black, with incredibly delicate black legs, a sharp sensitive-looking black beak, and eager expressionless eyes. And a young emu, heavy and gawky, naked about the head, with thick fur-feathered neutral-tinted wings.

THE sala de jantar has only two windows, but a soft shadowed light casts a pinkish reflection from the tiled roof into the farthest corners of the large bare room. The sole furnishings are a cupboard to keep dishes, a very old table, and some battered chairs. Dona Matilda's sewing-machine to one side keeps up a continuous ominous humming like the humming of a gigantic gnat. The macaw, sharpening his beak on the metal of his perch, disturbs an occasional silence. Dona Matilda calls him "o velho." When he flaps his blue and orange wings he squawks, clutches feebly at the bar he stands on, and finally tumbles off. He hangs there, suspended by the chain around his gnarled rose-gray foot, and screeches terrifically. Dona Matilda throws a feather duster at him. He slowly ascends to his former position and, with cold unblinking eyes, regards her sidewise.

I feel as if the life of generations has been arrested here in a moment's scene.

I AM going to dress my baby in a queira such as Brazilian infants wear. She is to have a short shirt of cambric, and I will fold an embroidered cloth around her middle instead of a dress. I am going to have a girl. Girls are unpopular, so I shall love a girl most.

WE have a house at last. I close the door that opens to the street, and I am safe inside myself. I can keep everyone out. To secure our privacy I draw the blinds and a pale lilac glow pours softly through the dim blue slats.

Our house has only one window, the one to the front. The side walls are of adjoining houses. As the doors along our block are unnumbered and some of the windows are the same color, I can recognize our place only by counting five windows from the corner.

The bedroom is set in the middle of the house by a half partition. It has two doors, but as there is no direct opening outside there is very little light. I do the cooking in the courtyard. We have an American kerosene stove, but we haven't paid for it yet.

John works as continuously as ever. He has had no money for clothes, but somehow up here where there are no Anglo-Saxons his shiny elbows and patched trousers humiliate him less. His salary has improved, but everything in that line goes into the guarantee fund which secures him his position. Thank heaven the arrangement is the same as with a bank, and if we ever leave the Company they will return what has been deposited with them, and with a moderate interest.

WE have bought a bed. On Sunday John made me a cabinet for kitchen ware out of some kerosene cases. We have four chairs, and a dressing-table constructed with the base of a sewing machine, some boards nailed across the top. I try not to think how charming the place might be if we had even a little money to spend on it. But I have to confess that the meat safe of bright yellow wood, elaborately varnished, the wire door painted blue, the knobs the color of raw beef and ornanmented with tin, gives me an illness when I look at it. And paint is so expensive we can't buy any yet. I shall never let John know that I cried over it.

IN the sky clouds like wet wool suck up the moisture that has been left to the earth. The vultures, as they flap upward from the roofs, resemble eagles rustling their heavy wings. In the sand old women rock on their haunches, their broad bare feet sunk in the dust. Their eyes, bleared and cunning, stare at me with an expression of reserve. On the ground beside them are malas of cow hide, open to display the wares inside—corn, mandioc, coarse meal, aimpin, and coffee-colored bricks of sugar. On braziers black messes of beans bubble thickly in clay pots. The smoke, brownish in the sunlight, rises and becomes almost instantly obscure; but the heat radiates in transparent ribbons above the white glitter of the street. There are booths festooned with tin ware on which the glare shatters itself in a million pointed rays. Outside the feira cattle are being sold. Steers with long sad faces lift immense twinkling-tipped horns above the leather hats of the vaqueiros.

Because I had reached the limit of my capacity as a seamstress I wore a long loose apron of blue calico over the dress that no longer covered me. And on my bare feet I had wooden-soled tamankos with plush-embroidered tips.

Every time I went to the feira I was fleeced. I did not understand the psychology of bargaining nor what anything should cost. But I felt calm and satisfied with myself. When I reached home the small bare darkness of our house seemed limitless. I did nothing but cook

ESCAPADE

and clean and splash buckets of water upon the brick floors. I had no interest in anything else.

When John returned to me at night I believed in him more than I believed in the law or the cruelty of people in the United States. And because he believed in me, I was actual to myself. I had got over the conviction that I was a ghost.

I AM the weakest person in the world. I cannot withstand the pain of others. To be really good, in a moral sense, one must be occasionally ruthless. But the feeling that someone depends on me is a flattery I cannot resist. I heard from Nannette. She wants to come to us. When I think of her, her despair in our separation responds to a hunger in me—a hunger to be necessary to a great many people. I resent Nannette only when I remember that she wants me to think myself disgraced.

If she comes here and stays with us, something foreign and undigested will be injected into the relation between me and John. I have a sense of sin toward John in having asked Nannette to visit us.

SINCE Nannette lost her money she has always been certain that people slighted her. She imagines those she used to know turn their heads aside when they encounter her in the street.

Nannette's view of life is, from my standpoint, utterly absurd. I am very much ashamed of my need to be kind to her at John's expense. But of course the shame is no extenuation of my conduct since I am not modifying my desire for his sake.

ESCAPADE

THE baby has no crib. We counted over the money we had to live on and I bought her a carriage. It is a German one, decorated with gilt like a circus chariot, with red plush curtains on the leather hood, and red chenille cords to tie them back. I have spent days and days making the baby carriage white.

Strange, I have grown so accustomed to being huge and helpless that I imagine I shall remain like this.

DOCTOR JANUARIO has a small waxed mustache, large cold brown eyes with heavy lids, and he is dressed immaculately in white. He took my clothes off, felt me all over, and said I was very healthy, in very good condition. The baby is in the correct position for presentation and I can have a child without any trouble.

I felt his cold eyes all over me, ignoring me. I wanted to get away from my body that he had touched— to leave it to him. To have one's individuality completely ignored is like being pushed quite out of life. Like being blown out as one blows out a light. I began to believe myself invisible.

However, as long as John can see me I continue to exist.

I had to go into the darkness in the back of the house and find the physician a chair. He is the first person I ever did anything for who made me feel menial.

When he finished examining me, I imagined I had lost something. I couldn't have said what. He takes away something from me.

I detest particularly his emerald watch fob and his immaculate clothing. If he were undressed he would be a great deal more naked to me than I was naked to him. He is a cold little monkey without any true pride to cover him up.

I wish that I could have my baby alone—or at least when no one but John was about. John is glad that I am so well. He tells me not to waste my emotion on Doctor Januario, but to ignore him also—to consider him a mechanism for my convenience.

WHEN the pains began on Thursday I felt that once more there was some meaning to my body. It really belonged to me again. Every time a pain went through me it stiffened my legs so that I could scarcely move. But I was ecstatic about all this sensation. And then the pains occurred only about every hour or so and I had plenty of time to recuperate.

JOHN has brought a servant here. He is afraid to leave me alone. I tried to conceal from him how much I was suffering because I didn't want the servant brought.

But now, on Sunday, the pains are very bad. The paroxysms are so close together that all of my energy is absorbed and my mind, which I wanted to keep clear, goes blank. I have a long, long pain inside my mind— then quiet—nothing. I feel cold inside. Blind.

ON Monday morning I knew that I was caught in a mechanism of some kind that had to go on and on to the end—even if the end were death.

Anything which is entirely beyond my control fascinates me and seems to me to have some awful and particular signficance, so that, while I was frightened, I was pleased also. It is impossible to control creation. I don't mean this only in the sense of giving birth to new physical life. That which really *is* continues with the impetus which propelled its origin. I *am*, and I am going on and on to the end of myself where something else begins.

AT two o'clock in the afternoon Doctor Januario called again. He looked at my body, even touched me intimately to assure himself that everything was going on all right.

But somehow I know that he has never seen me. I hate him more than ever. If nobody recognizes me, then it is a sign that I have ceased to exist. That other impersonal being who lives through pain is all that is.

Somehow my hostility makes me very acute. I know that Doctor Januario, who is accustomed only to treating the native women, is embarrassed in my presence. Because he cannot place me as a type I disconcert him and he dislikes me. We are very poor. He despises poverty. We make him uneasy.

He notices everything about me, and is examining me from the standpoint of his cold sexual curiosity. Even though we are poor he is vain of the opinions of foreigners. All of his gestures toward me are very professional, very pompous and correct. Women exist for him in two categories—those one goes to bed with, and those who are ill. He would like to despise all of them. Woman is an inferior creature. Something quite usual is occurring in regard to me, something about which he has a faint curiosity but which repels him. It also stimulates his sense of power to look on women like this. What he would like most to have explained is my relation to John and the origin of our poverty. He sees at once that John is well educated, has traveled, and has the manner of someone accustomed to authority. Doctor Januario probably thinks that John has made a fool of himself on account of me, on account of sex. And of course that is something which can't be argued. People think that in order to give up financial security one must be intoxicated.

DOCTOR JANUARIO had some business to attend to, so he left me and came back at night. I could not recall how much time had passed for somehow or other pain is timeless, absolute. It has removed itself from space. It always has been and always will be for it exists independent of relations. I feel it as myself, and when it ceases I will cease.

IN suffering intensely one's being cannot be reduced. And the worst of it is that I cannot even establish relations within my individuality. My body fades out and becomes one with the dark turmoil.

Only a faint point of consciousness in me continues to realize itself as separate. It sees Doctor Januario seated by the bedside, yawning, caressing his waxed mustache. Sees his instruments spread elaborately on a chair and glittering dully in the lamplight. Vague reflections are thrown back from the red-black tiling of the unceiled roof, from the blue shadows of the night.

I watch him out of the concave darkness. A breath of wind stirs the flame of the lamp and the clear fire rushes against the glass chimney, reddening it, leaving it bronzed with soot. He comes toward me and lays his hands somewhere about me, out of sight. All that is indefinite.

The absurd thing is that vanity in my own drama persists. I am determined not to make a sound. If I were here alone I would give myself that relief, but not before Doctor Januario. So much of my body has been exposed to him that I shall not reveal anything more.

John holds my hands. He tells me to make an effort to rid myself of the child. While I struggle I know it is my own being that I am trying to force out of myself. I am certain that my insides are torn out of me, disintegrating, and I wonder at my head which, as I dimly perceive, keeps alive all to itself.

It has to go on. My mind is white, still, and separate. It is conscious of itself but of nothing outside. The pressure against my spine continues. My mind continues forever, parallel to my hurt but unconnected with it. It is terrible to have such a living mind. I hate it. I want it killed, because it goes on and on so brightly and is so meaningless.

John tries to relieve me by tying a sheet around me and lifting me away from the bed in that. The pressure is just as merciless and I feel the tired ache of his arms beside.

All at once I scream. I am startled, humiliated by the unconscious sound which has come of itself out of my throat. I am on guard against the scream. I won't allow it to come up again. I ask John to apologize to the physician. I screamed without intending to. I despise women who give way in situations like this.

Doctor Januario, with a faint shrug of astonishment

at my inexplicableness, acknowledges my excuse by a slight smile. I yet feel that he has never seen me, that he never will. If he and I gazed with the same eyes we should perceive different things. And I resent his perpetual suggestion of another world, a world in which nothing that I am is included. I want him to accept my reality, to come into it, or else to take himself away from me forever.

John had pled for the use of chloroform, but Doctor Januario has refused. I don't want chloroform even now. I don't want to relinquish my will utterly to the will of the physician. I must save myself from those cold shallow eyes. I cannot bear to relinquish consciousness to the hand that plays with the emerald watch fob and smothers the fastidious yawn of the full bored lips.

JOHN said the baby was a boy. I was glad. John elevated my shoulders and I saw the baby lying there on its stomach, naked. Its conical head was lifted uncertainly and its blue eyes, fixed, without even inquiry in them, stared at me with a blind look. I had nothing but a head. There was chaos between me and the child who was stretched out near the place where I once had feet. The room seemed to me quite dark and I wondered that I could see the child so distinctly.

Doctor Januario's stony regard passed over me politely and he spoke to John in Portuguese. The heap of instruments clicked together as they fell into the bag.

When the physician had gone I relaxed in the inertia which I craved. I had become huge, passive, and undefined. I was without contours, as wide as the world. The baby wailed indistinctly. I heard the cry almost without responding to it. Nothing could touch me. I was outside time. I was rest.

I FOLD my eyelids against the brutal light. Little pains understood in the darkness are more beautiful in delicacy than the coarse limbs of a goddess—a goddess white as mountain fire in the sun. My little ugly ones, your eyes are lovelier than the eyes of the strong that are cognizant only of distance. There is more love in you—in me—than in the hearts of all the gods blank as the cosmos. Weak sensitive fingers, feeling things to cling by, strangle me with secrecy. But their touch is kinder than the cold palm of Deity. The strong gods are blind gods. Their sandals are of iron. The foreheads of the gods are clouds above the darkness, but I can see the night and they have never seen it.

OUR windowless bedroom contained an iron bed, the makeshift dressing table on which the lamp stood, and between the wall and the baby carriage there was just room for a chair. A soiled diffused light fell over the shadows.

Dona Amalia, who lived across the street, had come in to wash the child. She begged me to preserve the navel cord and place it in a little bag around the baby's neck. She was burning dried lavender flowers in a dustpan— the invariable ritual of a native birth.

John asked me how I was. I felt well but I was certain I could never again pass through the same experience, because no human being on earth would have the strength to endure it twice.

ESCAPADE

I closed my eyes so that I need not converse with Dona Amalia. The aromatic smell of the leaves was sharp and sweet in my nostrils. I wondered why the birth of a child appealed so little to the imagination of the artist. Why were all the great realistic novels of the world concerned with only one aspect of sex? This surely was the last—the very last—thing one needed to know before one came to conclusions about life.

I could hear the slosh of water in the basin, the baby's weak fretful intonation, Dona Amalia's high nervous voice. The wings of a moth made a thin whirring sound as it circled the stillness. Dona Amalia had borne fifteen children. Without glancing at her, I could see her wide pale face, her small stooped body, her large belly. I knew that she was enjoying herself. Her husband often beat her. She did not know how to read or write. She believed in herself as every creature believes in itself simply by continuing to exist. But she had never been able to express what was in her heart. The words of educated people confused her, and she retreated in her humility. She was wrong, she was always wrong. She admitted as much. But in what concerned childbirth she was timidly self-assertive.

WHEN Dona Amalia had gone home, John washed the baby all over again—especially his head which she had been superstitiously afraid to touch. And John also removed the little woolen cap which Dona Amalia had put on our son.

I was surprised that I could not move, even to turn

ESCAPADE

on one side, but I was content. I felt that I no longer
needed an obscure justification for my existence.

JOHN swung up a hammock against the wall. He lay
there and we talked. Every now and then, to reassure
me, he got up and looked at the baby, quiet in the
carriage.

Once he brought him to me. I felt the child's still
eyes upon me and was astonished by the movement of his
lids. His body had a faint pungent odor that enchanted
and disturbed me. I wanted to hide my face against
him. My senses were marvelously, voluptuously agitated.

I was pleased by the movement of his bowels, which
occurred toward morning. My fastidiousness had disappeared. I enjoyed, without any restraint, everything
which is designated as purely physical.

He was too young to want milk but I held his face
against my breast. In all my desire for him I was conscious of a heavy sensuality, a massiveness of appreciation.

JOHN could not remain for more than one day away
from his sewing-machine store and his books. Maria
Magdelena took care of me and looked after the small
house.

It was always dark in the bedroom. I lived in the
long contemplation of a blank wall, of a pale violet
light that fell across me as it penetrated the blinds of
the sala window which was opposite my door. The
baby lay beside me. He seemed fragile. I was heavy
with response to the new indescribable smell he gave

out. I had been close to babies before but I did not recognize the odor as anything familiar. I had found something which I had needed for a long time. I knew now what I had needed.

When he drank of my milk, all of me was arrested in the sensation of his soft clinging touch. I was mindless, beautiful. I wanted to be like that forever and ever. I let him drink too much. His head fell back and the white milk trickled warmly from between his parted lips. His mouth was loose and red. He half closed his eyes and I could see the delicate pinkish veins in the thin lids. He looked drunken with himself, and I was drunk also. We were in a relaxation that was almost a debauch.

Once a bat came into the room while we were alone. I was terrified of bats, but I got up and put a mosquito net over the baby. I had a sharp painful pleasure in my fright, in my sense of bondage to my child. I would always belong to him. I would always think of him first. My abandon to him was humiliating and sweet like abandon to a lover. I thought, It is my body I give to him. And I was surprised in recognizing this. I had imagined maternity as something thin and ideal.

A GREAT many persons—old women and young girls —whom I had never seen before, or did not remember having seen, came in to visit me. News that the foreign senhora had a baby went up and down the block.

The old women, entering my bedroom, took the baby up, held him loosely so that his spine curved and his head wagged on his limp neck, and rubbed their lean dirty fingers inside his mouth as they discussed his prospect of teeth.

I was rebellious against all this intrusion, but Maria Magdelena, satisfied with her own knowledge on the subject, only smiled at my protests. She arranged my food to suit herself so that I should eat nothing but chicken with pepper. I must not have salad, and, until John interfered, she would not give me any water for a bath.

She was tall, black, with a grotesque face and a cunning, understanding smile. When she was at work she wore a loose calico wrapper that dragged the unswept floor. Her legs were bare and she thrust her feet into chinellas only when she went into the street. All of her gestures were awkward and indolent. Her only facile motion she made when she spat. In the beginning she spat everywhere, but when I had reprimanded her several times she began to pick out the darkest corners. Every time she went by my door, she pulled it a little closed, spat behind it and swung it back.

MADEMOISELLE, whose dwelling adjoined ours, came to me with apologies—because I did not know her—and offered me a baby cap she had made from the scraps of lace and silk which her trade of milliner provided. She was thin, not old—twenty-nine perhaps—and pretty in a severe way, though gossip was that she had been a prostitute in Rio before adopting her present mode of life. She wore spectacles on her neat little nose, and her straight black hair was piled high, not at all in the fashion. Her dress, however, though of cheap material, was cut in an ultra mode. She spoke Portuguese badly and occasionally lapsed into French. She stared at me curiously a long time, and her dark gray eyes were quite tragic. She told me that, on the night the baby was born, she had heard me scream. How old was I? What a shame! So young! To Maria Magdalena she spoke of me as "cette pauvre femme."

I thought of her drunken lover and wondered for what she pitied me. Perhaps for my respectability. Perhaps because she saw in my plight something which resembled her own experience.

MADEMOISELLE is on one side of my house, but in the room adjacent to my bedroom the sick man lives. Jackie is twelve days old. John has been obliged to leave me, and when I am alone at night those terrible groans are like the articulation of my own vague fear.

But today at noontime, one awful guttural shriek as if terror had been born in some tangible shape. Then a ponderous quiet that submerged everything. A quiet that permeated the walls, that flowed over me like a sea of heaviness.

I waited in blank expectation of some horror. When the smell of incense and the burnt greasy odor of candle wicks stole through the walls, above the silence, I understood what had occurred, and I was glad for him. Poor people may challenge God. They may challenge the Devil. But when they cry out, Death is the only one of Three that will listen to them.

ESCAPADE

MARIA MAGDELENA squats on her haunches in the courtyard, her buttocks swinging, her skirts tucked up so that her bony brown legs are exposed to the hips. Between her broken and blackened teeth she holds a pipe. Her hair, plastered with lard and cocoanut oil, stands out in a woolly ruff about her face. She chops the meat for dinner on the floor itself and distributes little particles of sinew and gristle to a circle of stray cats that have crept over the wall to watch.

When she has finished her work and wants to cool herself, she removes the two garments she wears and pours libations from the water jar over her scrawny hips and emaciated breasts.

I know that she is stealing from me and that she despises me because I am unable to prevent it. She has a little girl, almost white, who is, I am sure, treated very badly. The child comes here for dinner in the afternoon and, though she is only nine years old, is also smoking a pipe.

MARIA MAGDELENA has left me. I am exhausted. The housework and the care of a heavy child are too much for me so soon after leaving my bed. My nerves are too vivid, exhausted by responsiveness. I feel as if I were dying already of too much life. I am in terror of my fatigue which is strong and impersonal—stronger than I am. I pray to something or other, beg myself to go on, beg the baby to sleep, to give me a little rest.

When the baby cries in the night I get up in the dim relaxation of despair and talk to him. "Oh, baby,

ESCAPADE

I can't bear it any longer. Please go to sleep. Please
go to sleep."

He has a lovely round face flushed with pink, an
unsteady head covered with silver-gold curls, his eyes
are dark blue, clear and intent. They observe everything yet seem to take nothing into themselves.

WHEN I go into the courtyard to cook my breakfast
the sky is coral-colored. In the narrow enclosure, only
a little protected by the overhanging roof, nothing can
be seen but the white plaster wall that rises beyond
me, and the golden and rosy wall of the east. An enormous star which the daylight has blanched scintillates
pallidly among clouds that have an ashy texture. A
palm tree in the next garden shows a ragged fringe
of leaves from which the morning drips somberly, like
moisture. The palm fronds, shaking above me in the
stillness, make a papery rustling sound.

When I hear a knock at the street door I know the
man has driven the cow to the curb and is waiting there
to milk her into my cup. I am excited by the smell
of the coffee I have put on to boil, by the quiet, and the
feeling that everything that is enjoyable in the world
belongs to me. My nerves throb. My senses respond to
my surroundings as through a muffling of wool. But I
am happy.

I take advantage of my security. The baby is asleep.

IF John knew that I was out of bed and doing everything for myself he would be tortured by anxiety. He
is in the interior, a three days' journey on horseback.
I try not to think of sending him a message to return,

but I have begun to have frightful pains when I lift anything. I feel as if there were knives implanted in my navel. My back aches. And the baby is merciless. Yes, sometimes I am so tired that I long for the irresponsibility of insanity in order to escape.

DONA ROSA, a fat old woman with a hooked nose and small impregnable eyes, is the owner of our house. She is the widow of an Englishman, a man who embezzled from a London firm and came here to hide himself, and she is also the daughter of a priest. I hate her pious ways, her perpetual curiosity. She left some plants in the courtyard and today she came and reproached me for letting them die.

With her slow, flat-footed walk, she went about the house, looking into all our poverty with her keen unkind eyes.

When she left me I carried pail after pail of water out and poured it over the roots of the plants. I was resentful of my responsibility for them. I knew I was hysterical with weakness but I wanted to hurt myself, to kill my own incapacity and feebleness.

Now I have given up the luxury of protest, I hate only the pain. I won't give in to it.

WHEN I saw John again I stopped struggling. He made time seem long and easy to bear.

If Doctor Januario had come back to examine me and had told me how torn I was this would never have occurred. John has been obliged to neglect his work. He is frightened of losing his position. If the Company become dissatisfied I don't know what will happen to us. John knows enough of surgery to understand the operation I need, but Doctor Januario is the only physician available. He has a sort of hospital here. John visited it and described it as a horrible place.

If Doctor Januario comes near me again I feel I'll kill myself before I will endure his touch. If I am about to die it will take a great deal of kindness to bring me back to life.

THE operation I require is a major one. It will be very expensive. We have no money to pay for it. I realize now why Maria Magdelena groaned at the idea of calling in a doctor when a midwife was at hand. Yes, I would rather have the dirty old woman I have seen, who at least has borne children herself, than that man with his cold professional ignorance.

Doctor Januario did at last come to the house. He wanted to make an incision in my abdomen so that the lacerated ligaments could be sewed up. He pursed his lips at our anxiety, and shrugged. He said, "It often happens like that with a first child." And he went on smoothing his mustache with his plump delicate hairy hand.

I pretended not to understand him and refused to answer his questions, while I wished that he might be subjected to some kind of torture. In his ugly little face turned toward me there was not a symptom of feeling. He could surely feel for himself. The Devil is what we fear. He is the Devil. I am afraid of him. As far as he is concerned I am a mere *thing* on which he wants to operate.

Then he began to talk to John about money—about

how much it would cost, and his features became suddenly animate. His black eyes glowed slightly with repressed interest.

I WAKE in the middle of the night and think of Doctor Januario's neat Parisian clothing, his small hands playing with his fob, the hard self-containment of his face. Over and over again I feel him victorious against me. I have exhausted myself with resentment.

JOHN found another house for us to live in. It is far out on some sand dunes by the sea at the edge of the town. Because it has been deserted for some years and is falling to pieces for lack of a tenant, we have it cheap.

THROUGH the window of my new room, I can see, while I am in bed, the sea spread out below me. It is thick green, like milk into which has been stirred a pallid radiance. I am impressed by its indescribable heaviness. The wind crisps the harsh surface, and pools of violet light rest in the hollows of the swell.

When the rain comes the sky is a transparent shadow, like a curtain, and it advances upon the land. We have to close the blinds over the glassless window openings. Then the house is almost pitch dark. The wind makes a dragging noise along the eaves, and the rustle of the water is accompanied by the sound of trees scraping and brushing their limbs against each other.

TODAY the sand dunes flow away from us like rippled silk, and the surf smokes and flashes along their edges.

ESCAPADE

The long gray sea disappears on the horizon as if within itself.

The American ship that called yesterday is going out again. In the white air the smoke looms brown. The squat funnels are heavy against the mist. I can make out the rows of decks. The ship moves away and away from us. The drawn line of the wake pulls me with it. The slow bulk fades. On the broad colorlessness of the sky, the green-white monotony of water, nothing remains but a faint bronzed stain the smoke has left.

I hate what I have just seen, but even the hate is precious. Something I don't wish ever to lose.

ABOVE the blind quiet of the sea a green-white star opens and sheds itself in glistening elongated tears. Hills are frozen violet. The clear color of the sky is like yellow ice. The track of a little fishing boat in the water makes a long welter of satin, like a turquoise scar.

THE rain is over for a time. Since I have a servant again I can enjoy rest and I got up today and walked about. Back of the house I see red clay hills, mudhuts tumbling crookedly along them. The wind sweeps in clean strokes from a speckless sky, and against it are tall rows of palm trees twisting and flashing. Prickly pears in the grass are fat with spines like moles in green-gray flesh, brown-green moles with the yellow hair of blades. Grass all around has spikes like stiff yellow paper. Grass makes an ugly dead shiver. I see a man walking over the hill. Man has a pale shadow, man is separate. Birds flying shake air. They vanish. The bush they have flown to rocks.

THEY pass the house endlessly, refugees of the secca, the great drought up country. Old men can scarcely walk. Young girls have children on their backs. Their tongues are swollen so that when they ask us for bread or water they can barely speak. Their eyes are terrible. I imagine they see something that I don't see—the thing they have left behind.

This morning Petronilla told me of a donkey that had been found wandering without a master about the churchyard. In one of the panniers fastened to its back was a starved baby, quite dead.

Every day the people congregate in the square before the church, in front of the cross. They are praying for rain. But here it is not so bad. A few drops have already fallen. I can imagine the quiver of fear, of joy, that the refugees must feel when the first moisture touches their faces.

Petronilla is not upset by the secca. She has seen it before. She says that in the place she came from the people were without rain for two years.

OUR few pieces of furniture make little islands in the emptiness of the house. The lamplight is scarcely anything. When I hear the thud of something small and soft descending from the tiles I know that a tarantula has dropped from the roof.

A gebôa lives in the kitchen chimney, but Petronilla asked me to leave it alone. It kills rats and will bring us good luck. It is a wonderful snake with a long thick body and a rich deliberate movement.

In the field all around us where there are dwarfed-looking cajú trees and mangaba trees with gray leaves, the marmosets abound. When I step outside in the dark, I can hear them rustling the foliage.

*

*   *

WHEN the refugees went by today I couldn't help thinking that the streets in the city, those in the country, and even the paths to sea, all had the same end.

NANNETTE is coming to visit us. Uncle Alec has secured the money at last. She is going to pay us board and perhaps that will make our financial situation less difficult. Her letter had the tone of a conspiracy and at the end of the last page she instructed me to burn it up. I had simply forgotten the fact that John and I were in danger of the law—that we were being pursued by Louise.

But I am afraid all the time, afraid, I think, of my own helplessness.

THE shadows keep flying over the little town, droves and droves of shadows with the rain and the wind behind them. Over the tiled house tops, the thatched huts,

the church tower covered with lichen. The bronze
church bell sleeps Sunday after Sunday. Padre Antonio is dead. Petronilla believes that this fact is responsible for the weather.

I KNOW my country is not here around me where the
pale light through the banana leaves is thin and poign-
ant, nor there, where the palm trees sway like young
girls dreaming after last night's dance. But as the
endless undulations pass the shore—the endless surf,
the endless sky—I feel that it is somewhere, and that
They, hurried and frightened, are searching for it too.

NANNETTE continues to play romantically with the
idea that I am a writer. I have just received from her a
magazine of poetry, the first I have seen since we were
in London. Someone discusses in it the advantage which
would come if art were not commercial, if the artist had
no financial remuneration for his work.

I think of an old cow herder John told me about who
lay ill on a straw mat in a mud hut for ten years of his
life. His son killed ant bears and planted enough mandioc to make them meal. This was in a bad climate
where mosquitoes were a pest. I feel as if I had heard
someone say, over and over, "I am Life. They pay
good blood for the poems that live in me. I am Life!"

PETRONILLA'S brother is darker than she is—nearly
black. He goes out every day on a jandaia. I can see
him down there on the water, clinging with his bare toes
to the dripping logs of the raft above which a torn sail
flaps. He is naked to the waist. The sea, the color of

lapis-lazuli, is as hard as stone. There are sharks all
around him. I recognize their exposed fins.

I FEEL sometimes as if Death were holding me softly
in a feathered palm, feeding me with the white blood of
sorrow. And I think of a lost bird flying toward a
gray horizon it will never reach, above the broken mirrors of marshes and the gray fur of reeds, endless!

MR. AMES has come back to Natal. He came to see
us and talked about the war which has taken hold of
Europe.

Germany and England—I see some names on a map
and have a feeling of dream, of everything moving. This
is the unreal world of which I have already too intimate
a sense. Chaos. The contradiction of astonishment.

Mr. Ames came into the bedroom and sat down near
me. He glanced at me once, sympathetically, but looked
away again. I suppose he did not wish to overemphasize
my changed appearance. I can scarcely bear it when
people think that they are kind to me in *overlooking*
something. If anything about me is unpleasant I had
much rather come to the point at once. I won't be conde-
scended to because of my illness. The attitude of everyone has a faint complaisance which I find absolutely
maddening—everyone, that is, but John.

JOHN goes every day into the surf. This morning I
put my clothes on and walked down to the beach with
him. When he was in the water I took off my shoes
and stockings and ran after him. He begged me to
keep back, but it was intoxicating to imagine for a mo-

ment that I was well. The waves were enormous, translucent like swelling glass. They were cold however and broke against my breast with such force that I could scarcely stand. The effort of withholding them made me feel all at once sick and weak.

This afternoon I am in bed again. I feel frightened. I don't think of the pain I suffer as any ordinary illness which has attacked me from the outside, for as long as I lie perfectly quiet I am well, I am hungry at meal time, and interested in life. But the moment I indulge my energy I am reminded how enslaved I am. When people become broken, maimed, they ought to be put out of their misery. To let them live amounts to an injustice. Everyone they come in contact with is unconsciously superior to them. John is the only person who doesn't make me feel this. And I have a sense of guilt in regard to him. It is as if I were reducing him to my level. If he were not so genuinely good to me I could be proud.

WHEN the pain dies away from me it is like a great sound fading. What is left is a happy silence. But I am lost in the silence. I wonder what I am and if I have actually ceased to exist.

I see some trees on the hillside stirring their branches, and I am in the branches. I am the movement and the stillness. My own dizziness is the oscillation of sunlight on the grass. The tall dried grass is violet-colored. The fresher grass is yellow with a bluish tinge. I know all these things, but I no longer know myself. I haven't any self. And what sickens me is the effort to recover my personality, to get back what

ESCAPADE

I have lost. If I could only relinquish my being to a world without contours, without relations! If I could only go on giving myself to the motion of dizziness which is like an endless yet disintegrating rhythm! But I can't. I must gather this huge thing together and re-arrange it in its old form, even though I am so fatigued with it.

The tiles over the bed are the color of pink hyacinths. There is a giant black wasp, a solitary, a tarantula hunter, crawling through a space where two of them overlap. His body is diamond-black and his delicate wings, trembling against the glare, have a rich blue-purple lustre. I am not afraid of him. The thought of his sting doesn't frighten me. This is a gorgeous death of happiness. The ugliness will only begin when I try to cut the soft color with the bitter glassy edges of myself —with clothes, food, responsibilities, my relation to other people—the hard little facts that make up the routine of individual life. There is nothing frightening about death, I am sure. The horror is in being forced to come back to old things again. Having destroyed the illusion of the personal, one has to recreate it with terrible effort.

The air is warm and rich with inertia. The sea is still. When the trees stir, the leaves stir, a blade of grass rocks, I know it is only the motion of the dream. (A cherry orchard back home. Nannette had on a lavender organdy frock. Her eyes were large and bright. She smiled at me when I shook the tree and the cherries fell off. There were bees in the garden. Everyone smiled.) Smiles. The light is a smile. It belongs to no one. It

74

is my smile. I can feel myself smiling as I sleep—smiling and sleeping in the dream that is endless.

The lean cow that strays under the tree is the smile also. She crops grass in the smile, in the smile—she crops grass, endless. Endless boats, endless white sails, endless smile on the sea.

But when I hear Jackie cry I have to come back, and that hurts.

JACKIE is so healthy and beautiful that I can regard him only with humility. He ought to have no one about him who does not suggest positive energy, happiness, life. But I recognize humility as false. It is drama, a mechanism with which I relieve myself in a situation from which there is no release.

JOHN has gone down to Recife for the Company and he is to meet Nannette, who lands there. He will bring her up here by tomorrow's boat. I dread seeing her. I know the things she will tell me will make me angry and I haven't the strength to resist any more assertions that John and I are wrong, that the world is right.

WHEN I greeted Nannette I felt she must observe that I had become utterly different. But she seemed not to notice any change in me. She is terribly nervous. She says that she is much distressed about my illness.

I used to think that Nannette had beautiful eyes. They were large and gray. At the least excitement the pupils dilated and they looked black. She had dimples, too. And her plump small figure somehow made me think of a Frenchwoman.

75

ESCAPADE

Now she is thin—lean almost. The dimples are lengthening and suggest tired lines on either side of her sensitively precise mouth. She and Uncle Alec are very poor this year and Nannette's clothes are much simpler than the ones she wore a long time ago. But among us here she really looks elegant. When she came into the house she had on a small black hat with a tilt that was subtly chic. Though she has only the severest street clothes, after what we have been accustomed to seeing. they appear to be beautifully cut. Heavy rouging doesn't conceal her haggard expression. Her cheek bones are prominent, and her beautiful long hair has become, since I left her, faintly dusted with white.

She has the strangest manner. She talks about happenings in the United States and half whispers all the time as though there were danger of Petronilla understanding what she says. Nannette wore a thick veil when she got off the boat. John told me that he was obliged to introduce her to the consul and that her manner with him was mysterious also. When she sat down by my bed Petronilla brought her a cup of coffee. Her hand shook so that in handling the cup she spilled half of the contents on the front of her immaculate blouse.

She recounted an incident regarding an Egyptian gentleman on the boat who, it seems, followed her about continually, and was always taking her hand or arm and pressing it. Nannette does not admit her age, and a faded aroma of sexual attractiveness yet clings about her, but I cannot imagine that she would really have had any difficulty in ridding herself of the Egyptian if she had cared to impress him with the dignity of her years. She must be forty-six or seven at least.

ESCAPADE

Uncle Alec is very broken. He has undergone frightful anxiety on my account. I remember the emotional
struggles I went through when I was at home. At that
time Uncle Alec, in whom I always wanted to confide,
kept me at a kindly distance. He could never bear to
have me serious with him. If I tried to talk about myself
he made a sympathetic jest of my ideas. Then he gazed
at me, smiling, patted my head and was wistfully humorous about life. Life was too much of a muddle. Better
not attempt the impossibility of a solution. He wanted
me to be happy. I know now that his sense of responsibility in regard to me related only to my virginity. This
is what I always felt. The love of those among whom
one has been reared is usually not love at all. One can
die inwardly without any of them being aware of it.

Nannette has been over all the details of my "dis-
grace," much more elaborately than she wrote them to
me. She talked about the weeks and months when she
did not know where I was and her eyes darkened in that
blind expression of pain which I remembered so well
and had dreaded to see again. But Nannette is utterly
lacking in any sense of proportion. One thing distresses
her as much as another. She has the same look when she
discharges a servant. I have seen her like that when a
seamstress spoiled a dress. She is kindhearted to a fault
and yet somehow not kindhearted at all. No amount of
unhappiness is apparent to her unless it is thrust upon
her attention. Then, if one's finger even bleeds it makes
her ill.

When she was recounting the unpleasant things that
people had said to her and her fear of the newspapers

as they came out with one insulting story after another
—stories she was not able to contradict because of her
own uncertainty—she began to weep. I can see, however, that her tears are only for herself. She knows
that I was almost insanely miserable at home, but
she simply cannot imagine that the agony of another
equals the pain she herself has passed through. Over
and over she said to me, "I thought I was going mad.
Louise pursued me with insults and reproaches about
John, and you know I was the one who pled with you
not to do anything rash. I did not know there was such
injustice in the world!"

She has worked very hard, too. She and Uncle Alec
have for some time been reduced to dispensing with
servants and the house is large. She showed me her
hands, coarsened by water. She has even, she says,
been doing the family laundry.

And that is why she cannot realize that John and I
are very poor. Our house is nothing but a great brick-
paved stable with an unceiled roof and has in it only a
table, a couple of beds, and a few chairs, but I have a
servant and lie in bed most of the time. Nannette
evidently considers illness a luxury. I know that she is
fighting her satisfaction, yet she commiserates me with a
little malice. She considers John responsible for my
decision to leave home and my poor health is a proof,
to her, that his grandiose plan has failed. He is the one
person, so she would have it, who has reduced me to
my present condition.

Absurdly mingled with her antipathy to John is a very
real comfort in the distinction which he achieved in the
past. She has justified him to other people by recount-

ing his accomplishments. If matters could have been satisfactorily arranged I might have married him with her approval. As it is he has become a "monster." This is the appellation which others have used which she constantly repeats.

It is the usual indignity. If I had been older I would have been called a "vampire." As it is, I was "seduced." In any case I am not to be allowed any decent self-responsibility for my acts.

NANNETTE is at me continually. She believes that Louise will ultimately secure a divorce in order to remarry.

Nannette tells me that if I had remained at home and suffered all that she has been obliged to undergo I would alter my decision to continue legally just what I am. Louise has said to Nannette that she will never rest until John and I have been punished for everything she has innocently endured. Louise yet hopes to invoke the Mann Act and to have John sent to prison.

And I continue to reflect on the moral value of sacrifice. Of course, Louise has suffered, and she would only have been satisfied if John and I had suffered more. Louise's deepest happiness has not been involved—only her vanity. She did not love John. She admitted as much. But even if she had and John had not loved her —well, I know that real pride could not have survived the falseness of unwilling constancy.

I dread conclusions that appear self-righteous. I

don't wish to be tricked into self-justification. We behaved as we did because we wanted to—and if we die because of it and everyone else dies I shall never regret it.

I really don't understand regret. Life simply *is*. Every sort of reasoning is merely a mechanical contrivance through which the ego, impelled absolutely and inevitably, justifies itself in relational terms.

NANNETTE certainly interferes with the privacy of life with John. In an old house like this which has really only one room—for none of the partitions meet the roof —it is impossible to exchange any kind of confidence without the danger of being overheard. And she is always watching us, furtively: hostilely, as regards John; apologetically, as regards me. Her attitude recalls my impression of Doctor Januario's gaze. She sees us, she observes facts—mostly facts which she construes as inimical to our relationship—and she is entirely oblivious to our actuality, to our true being, to the subtleties of our dependence on one another. If I express dissatisfaction with our poverty or with my compelled invalidism, dissatisfaction with the slavery of John's employment, I know I only confirm her self-righteous spirit. She is continually stressing her devotion to me, our congeniality in the past, our common interest in music and books. Really Nannette has not, for a long time, had any interests of her own, though she has always responded in a feeble manner to everything with which I was engrossed.

When I suckle Jackie in her presence I am conscious of my breasts and of an immodesty in the act which I never realized before. She is very guarded in her references to sex, but she evidently considers me initiate in a something or other which must only be referred to vaguely.

I am astonished when I hear Nannette place so much emphasis on the current incidents of gossip at home. Did you know that Mr. and Mrs. Henderson were going to separate? They have tried their best to conceal the true condition of their affairs but such things will out. And—oh, yes—Grace Henderson married a German, a Baron Something. None of the family approved of the match and now that Germany is at war they feel justified in trying to get her home again. You remember Gerald DuBois who inherited such a fortune from some relative in England? He has a magnificent place now out at Cedar Ridge. Everyone says he is interested in Lucy Stone. It seems hard to believe that he would marry her.

Nannette's gossip is not deliberately malicious. She merely has a blank excitable way of repeating what she has heard said. Why doesn't she understand more! Her body seems to me to have suffered, to be marked with life, but nothing it knows is ever admitted to her mind.

She is more contented here than I should have supposed. She has a perpetual vague interest in her environment, in our future, in the possibility that John and Uncle Alec will reinstate us in the material surroundings which, she believes, belong to us by right.

I sink into sleep like a stone into a pool. Who can tell the dreams of stones or the dreams of men. My illness is like a long sleep. But I do not wish to awaken from it. If only the pain were not so hungry. I can't feed it enough. Yet there is always more and more of myself to give to it.

NANNETTE regards the life about her with an utter lack of conviction. The Brazilian people have, for her, a lesser reality than the Anglo-Saxon people. That is why she is so little shocked by our poverty. She does not believe in it.

She is an utter fool about finances. I find it impossible to leave any responsibility in her hands. If she has anything to do with the spending of money I see we are going into debt. Her attempts to speak Portuguese are half-hearted and hopeless. She says that she has no motive for learning it. The Portuguese never interested her. They have no culture, no literature of importance. Apparently it never occurs to her that if she mastered Portuguese it would be a help to me.

Just the same, Petronilla makes me angry with her insolence to Nannette. Whenever Nannette addresses her she chuckles maliciously—unless, of course, she observes me watching. And Nannette, very rightly, becomes indignant. When Nannette is angry she is particularly helpless. Her eyes turn velvet-black and have a startled hardness. When she comes to me there are tears in them. Her little gouty hands shake. And as a defense she always says something that is utterly stupid and pointless. If Nannette looked as she did fifteen years ago her vexation would be charming. Now, it is only pathetic and grotesque. To "take down" Petronilla, Nannette talks to me in French, halting

ESCAPADE

French like a high-school girl's, very badly pronounced and very exact. And as my familiarity with French is less than hers, I often find it difficult to reply.

After all, Nannette is close to me and my pride relates to her protectively.

NANNETTE laid twenty milreis on the table and went out of the room for a moment. When she came back it had disappeared. It was all the money we had to buy food with for a week. I can tell by Petronilla's look when it is spoken of that she has stolen it.

And I am such a coward that, because of the bare possibility of condemning her unjustly, I hesitate to make any broad remarks on the subject. However, as inconsistent as it seems, I am going to dismiss her. I am too helpless to endure her presence now that my faith in her honesty is shaken. I can't afford to use my energy in nursing suspicions.

I understand now when ruthlessness is weakness. However, anyone who feels himself invulnerable is really living at the expense of someone who is more afraid. In the beginning I was less afraid than John—less cautious. And he has slaved to supply me with the luxury of noble gestures. I hope I am through with them.

WHEN I told Petronilla that she had to leave, a curious guarded expression came across her face. She drooped her cautious lids and a few tears gathered slowly and trickled down her flat, broad cheeks.

She glanced up at me and her eyes—usually dully veiled—were hard and bright. But her voice, when she spoke, was suave and conciliatory. She said, "Por amor de Deus, Senhora, do not send me away. I am in great trouble and I have no people—no place where I can go." The words were almost theatrically tremulous.

I watched her fixedly, not intending to be unkind, but she couldn't bear my look. She covered her face and began weeping with ostentatious violence. I knew somehow that, though her abandon was so complete, she was keenly aware of herself and of me. When she regarded me her eyes said that she hated me. I was disconcerted by the involuntary expression of a secret resentment I had never suspected. But why not? I was stronger at that moment than she was and I had a certain power over her. Hate is only the most positive phase of the instinct to preserve one's self. Hate seems to me very honest and worthy. Humility and Christian love are a hypocritical sneer at life. If one truly loves one is defenseless, and as long as one defends one's self against what menaces—call the psychological gesture by any name you will—one really hates—rejects the being who opposes one.

I said, "What is the matter, Petronilla? Are you ill? Has anything so serious occurred? Why didn't you tell me? I might have been able to help you." In my heart I felt hot and confused and anxious to extricate my vanity from the appearance of injustice.

Petronilla began to draw marks with her thumb nail on the foot of my bed before which she stood. When she finally faced me she seemed quite determined. Her eyes were dark and glistening, without any intelligence of observation, but with a suggestion of mysterious inward cunning. She is short and stout and appears robust, and, because I was weak and unable to move, I felt at some obscure disadvantage before her. I was angry with her. I resented her hostility. I pitied her. I wanted to be comprehending, but not to pity, as pity seems to me a falsified contempt which should be nobody's privilege.

She said, "I am going to have a child." And became sentimental at once. Her voice quavered. She called on all the saints. She had no mother to care for her welfare. She had given herself to a soldier who had professed to love her but had abandoned her immediately she told him of her condition. The facts she stated were simple and I was convinced of so much of her truthfulness, but the insincerity of her manner insulted my benevolence. I wanted to tell her that I was unaffected by her moral eloquence. Her sexual morality didn't concern me. All that commanded my response was her evident material difficulty and her need for help.

When I tried to talk like this, she became bewildered. Her distrust became more apparent. She looked at me almost cruelly. Finally she did realize that I intended to allow her to remain. I said, "I don't like the way you do your work and I don't know what arrangement we shall come to later, but until your baby is born you can stay here as if it were your home and I will find someone else to cook. I don't think you should do housework in this state."

I was romantic enough to imagine that Petronilla would be proud of having a child and glad to take care of it herself. I asked Nannette to get out some of Jackie's dresses that I had made and give them to Petronilla for her baby.

ESCAPADE

Since Petronilla has no work to do and is assured of her position here her manner to me is unendurably suave. She calls me her "querida patrôa," and is always telling me how pretty I look. That is really ghastly and I feel it in my heart as an insult I can't forgive her. I don't want to be blinded as to what has happened to me outwardly since I have been ill. I am trying very hard not to dislike her, to see her cunning, her distrust of my kindness, her deceit, as pathetic only. But she is becoming almost repulsive to me.

She has smooth fat hands. Her fingers taper delicately at the tips, and her long unbroken nails are always dirty. She spends most of the time squatting outside the kitchen door with a pipe between her teeth. Occasionally when I get up and walk about I go out to the room I have given her at the end of the house. She sees me approaching and pretends to ignore me while she begins at once to grimace as if in pain and to groan to herself. She is growing very stout—huge—with enormous pendulant breasts. She is half Indian, but her skin is unhealthily white. She has a low brow, heavy cheeks, and her nose is coarse and flat.

I feel a continual obligation toward her—an apology that I am not able to overcome my repugnance to her.

Glancing out of the window by my bed, I was attracted by some men passing in the road. They were soldiers in khaki uniform braided with red. All three of them were short, two were coffee-colored and one quite black. They had little mustaches curled at the tips, and they wore their small caps rakishly. They were like thousands of other soldiers, but I watched them because they hesitated in front of the house and used lewd gestures to solicit the attention of someone out of sight. Their bold laughter offended me.

Then I realized that it was Petronilla they were speaking to. She had advanced out of concealment and was responding broadly to their overtures, beckoning them to come in through another way. I suppose I was shocked, but my greatest irritation was aroused by the men who were evidently oblivious to her condition or took no account of it. Her homeliness, her ill-health, her distorted figure made the proceeding hideous to me.

However, I did not wish her to know that I had taken account of the incident. I lay in another position so that I could no longer see her. The men remained in my imagination; the hot, still road behind them, their dwarfed figures—the negro was short but very heavily built—their oily, coarsely amused faces.

Theresa, the new cook, is a beautiful creature, tall and strong like a brown Viking girl. She is as large as John. Her features are heavy, suave, and indefinite. She has just enough white blood to shadow her cheeks with red. Her eyes are translucent brown, clear and bright, and her sharp, quick glances are innocently cruel. She is maliciously humorous, but good-natured. In the kitchen she shouts, screams, sings, and, if I correct her for any mistake, she giggles, tears come to her eyes, she doubles up like a jacknife and throws her apron over her face.

Her judgment of Petronilla, whom she dislikes, is unimaginatively exact. "It suits Petronilla very well to be ill. She always has the same disease, the disease of the lazy. But the senhora must not believe all she says about the baby. This is Petronilla's third child— always by a different father. If she doesn't want to get in trouble why doesn't she leave men alone—married men, too!" Then Theresa is frightened because she has expressed herself so freely. I say, "I am sorry for her just the same." Theresa stares at me, giggles stupidly and rushes out of the room.

Theresa also has a lover. He comes every night to see her and they meet in the petanga bushes just beyond the house. And she vies with Petronilla in flirting with the men who go by on the road, especially with soldiers whose attraction seems the greatest. I was astonished to observe that it was Petronilla who received the warmest response to her solicitations. Theresa is a virgin and all of her little tricks and glances exhibit a mixture of timidity and daring. She has the bold gaucherie of a colt. She does impossible things and the moment after is terrified of herself. Besides, she has an old mother who comes almost every day to see her and asks me if Theresa is behaving. The old woman is thin, stooped, and has a poverty-stricken neatness. Her vague eyes are cold, tired, and perfectly relentless. She is always assuring me of her respectability and says that she has a match arranged for Theresa, that Theresa is going to be married next spring. I do not reply but I wonder if the lover in the petanga bushes is the bridegroom-to-be. I can't bear to think of Theresa ever growing old, ugly, or ill.

THERESA told me today that she was sixteen years old. I can see through her calico dress that she has beautiful long legs, rounded hips, and firm breasts, heavy yet delicate. When she goes to the well for water she runs down the hill full tilt and up again with the big jar poised on her head. She sings continually. She has a powerful nasal voice, the high notes almost unbelievably shrill. Her singing isn't beautiful, but it has an exciting quality. From somewhere she has learned a little American ragtime set to Portuguese words, and she fairly screams it. She behaves most of the day as if she were mad with vitality.

She likes Jackie, and, of course, that adds to my predisposition in her favor, but she is cruel and unkind to old people. I had to speak sharply to her because she was so open in ridiculing an old beggar woman. To Theresa, who has never suffered anything, weakness is absurd.

Petronilla is as hostile to her as one would expect, but always in a veiled way. "I do not wish to speak ill of Theresa, she is so inexperienced, she doesn't know— but I thought I ought to inform the senhora—" And she tells me, watching me slyly, of some error Theresa has made. When I see them talking and laughing together it is almost unbelievable that they hate each other so much. Today Theresa smoked Petronilla's pipe. When she saw me looking at her she giggled in delighted embarrassment. I wasn't shocked as she had expected, but I felt that a pipe was a very intimate object to exchange like that.

PETRONILLA has a horrible sore on her huge breast. She showed it me today. She had covered it carefully with the leaves of a medicinal bush, and as she drew them off one after another her gesture, for some reason, indicated that she was proud of her disease.

Nannette, who was in the room, was nauseated by the sight, and did not conceal her disgust. But Petronilla was not humiliated in the least. Her narrow black eyes glistened with amusement. She began to chuckle. "Dona Nana finds it ugly." She laughed thickly and unpleasantly. I was feeling very sorry for her and her humorous attitude disconcerted me. She went directly up to Nannette, pulled all of the leaves away, and said, "Look, look."

Nannette was furious and left the room with her handkerchief to her lips. I tried to find out why Petronilla did such a thing, but she wouldn't answer me —only kept on laughing.

JOHN brought home some peroxide and an eyedropper and I washed out the great hole that seems to go straight through Petronilla's flesh to her heart. I scolded her for not having told me sooner. Suppose it had been something that she could have given to Jack!

There are three other sores in her breast, smaller ones. Whenever Nannette comes near her Petronilla makes some apparently casual gesture which will expose that horrible place, and she chuckles as she observes Nannette's determined inattentiveness.

Nannette is very frightened of disease and has asked me to send Petronilla away because she may have something contagious. John thinks the sores are the result of malnutrition and unhealthy conditions in the past, but Nannette takes no comfort in his opinion. She has a hunted expression when Petronilla enters the room.

ESCAPADE

The sickening thing is that Petronilla had some man with her out under the trees last night.

WELL, I have meditated over it a great deal and decided at last that in some inexplicable fashion Petronilla is absolutely beautiful—beautiful in spite of her ugliness. Her face is wide and flat, her brow is low, and her yellow-white skin has an unhealthy appearance. Her mouth is large, with thin pale lips, and their expression is delicately sardonic. Her eyes interest me most. Under straight heavy brows, they are narrow like a cat's, opaquely black, and when she smiles coldly and cunningly they have a wonderful hard luminousness. Then she also displays the whitest and most exquisitely perfect teeth.

Her figure is squat—very broad for its height. With every gesture her huge breasts swing, and she walks sway-backed in order to support the weight of her protuberant belly. Her clothes are unspeakable. She has made them herself. A red-and-white-sprigged dressing sack and a ruffled skirt. She goes barefoot and moves very securely on her short, prehensile feet. Although she is hopelessly slovenly in most of her habits, her crisp waved hair is always immaculately combed like the hair of a madonna, and I never saw anyone who could wear a rose with more provocativeness.

WHEN I woke up this morning Theresa came in great excitement to tell me that Petronilla's time had arrived and that she was very ill. I went into that bare little bedroom to see her. She was lying on a straw mat on the floor. Today she wasn't beautiful. She was hideous.

ESCAPADE

Her hair was in disorder, her face looked coarsely unintelligent, and her eyes shone on me dully with their old hostility. She refused to have a doctor. She had already sent word to the midwife, she said.

With a feeling of loathing for the whole affair, I yet wanted to offer her my bed, but John would not allow it. It was somehow horribly degrading to me to have to leave her lying there in such a condition. To say that the women of the people are accustomed to it doesn't seem to me any excuse. We have no money to buy her what she needs.

THE old midwife, filthy, almost in rags, with a lined face seamed with dirt, squats on the soft clay floor, a pipe in her toothless mouth between her puckered lips. She has grimy claw-like hands that fumble with her tobacco. She rocks herself, sways on her sunken haunches. Her old eyes are leadenly intent.

She has fixed two boards over some carpenter's horses and Petronilla, covered with some thin sheets I have given her, is lying on them.

It is raining. The swishing drops sift continually through the interstices of the moistly darkened tiles. They have closed the glassless window. Some strong herb tea is warming on a brazier. The cold air is weighted bitterly with the fumes of charcoal and the odor of the drink.

The old woman looks at me without saying anything. I notice that her eyes are red-rimmed and the inner corners appear as if scalded by the constant exudations of the tear ducts. Petronilla tosses her stout arms above her head and groans. Her face is swollen. All the modelling is lost. Her glistening eyes, fixed on me blackly, are quite expressionless.

THE most startling thing about the delivery was the way the midwife tore the navel cord from the child with her bare hands, without even asking any scissors of me to cut it with.

I never saw any creature so utterly repellent as the emaciated newborn baby with its crimson face, bleared eyes and huge gaping mouth.

While I was in the room Petronilla talked to it caressingly, but her glance was always furtively on me, and all of the sardonic cunning had come back to her face.

When I got outside the door I stood still for a moment and listened. I could hear her cursing it.

THERE is no reasonableness in blaming Petronilla What one needs to blame is the stupidity of Nature. But in spite of all my attempts at detachment I am indignant. Theresa says the child is starving to death and I can easily believe it. If I don't keep after Petronilla she never feeds it, and she is deliberately careless in her preparation of the milk. The child had to be taken from the breast. I have heard her call the baby "o diabo," and I am almost certain that she strikes it, small though it is.

Why shouldn't she! For her it represents an added burden to her penury. And of course the maternal instinct, even when it is strongest, only modifies the individual without altering her predilections in the least. Just the same I hate Petronilla for her stupidity, her unkindness, her lack of imagination.

ESCAPADE

I try very much to be fond of the poor ugly little baby but its appearance revolts even me. I gave it a bath and it yelled terrifically all of the time. Petronilla asked me to name it and stand madrinha for it. I think Elena is a beautiful name, so I have called it Elena after Elena in Turgenev's "On The Eve." I could weep and laugh at once, the appellation is so inappropriate. But Petronilla seems satisfied. She told me the name was "muito chic." Of course I must give it a christening dress.

THAT poor hideous little baby had spasms in the night and this morning it died. Petronilla pretended to cry, but she could squeeze out only a few tears. She made a great deal of noise and wanted me to believe in it.

I suppose she feels that at last she has got to the end of an annoying experience. And there will be another dead baby next year, and next, and the next. And reformers, of course, would set about the hopeless task of making an admirable mother of her instead of somehow putting a stop to this waste of energy and suffering.

She has on clean, stiffly starched clothes and has refrained from placing the usual rose in her hair. Her manner in my presence is woodenly decorous. Just the same, while the baby, like a little wax image—its face faintly mottled with violet, its transparent lids closed thickly across its sightless eyes—was stretched out in that pathetic room barren of anything comfortable or decent, I caught Petronilla at her old pastime, exchanging signals of invitation with the low-looking men who were idling in the street. Her figure has relaxed and is less obviously grotesque, but her breasts are large and flaccid and her belly remains slightly inflated. She is furtive with me, but her carriage with men is very proud. I never realized until I knew her that shamelessness could be so magnificent.

I resent her, I know, because she is able to ignore moral obligations and I am not. She lives at the expense of those who are weak enough to assume responsibilities to others, of those who are vain enough to be kind.

ONE thing that made me behave hypocritically, as if I were fond of that pathetic little baby, was Nannette's unconcealed aversion to it. Whenever I held it out to her she made frightened gestures of repugnance and never once did she touch it.

And soon Nannette will be old. When one becomes physically repellent all of the attention one receives is a condescension. I want to begin now to live alone.

A BLIND fiddler stopped here today. He had sunken eyes and a calm unseeing face. He played only the gayest music—old waltz tunes and festival songs of the people. I thought of Orpheus, his enchantment broken, and of the beasts that would come to rend him.

I feel sometimes that if it were not for the warmth of bodies, of people's hands, I should die of fright. We are like blind kittens left in a gutter—poor little animals snuggled together—giving birth to our own mother, Death. Love has silver hands, fire wings, quivering wings futile in the darkness.

ESCAPADE

Nannette is very much depressed because she has had no letter from Uncle Alec for such a long while and because the money he promised to send her failed to arrive.

I was depressed also but when I stared out of the window my melancholy became pleasant. The water today is Nile-blue and the dull light trembles in it with a quick stillness. The sky, without a sun, is a formless solution of light, and the horizon rises against it and is flat like a wall with a deep-colored steel edge. Straight up over the house, clouds, dull purple, move across the zenith with vast unhurried rapidity. The sun bursts open the sky. On the cold ocean it makes a pool of hot glass. The horizon line, momentarily illuminated, is thin like white-hot wire stretched taut. Coldness is through the shriveled currents, green-blue, gray. Hot greased sunlight sizzles in the coruscations above the brown-red shadows of rocks.

John worries continually about my health, and because he has not found any way to have me operated on. In the last nine months we have saved up fifty odd dollars, most of it accumulated while Nannette was paying board to us. John wants me to go back to the United States, but I am not strong enough to endure a third class passage alone, and there is the war to be considered. We have no passport yet. I am really glad. I feel that if I left John and Jackie down here I should never see them again.

After all the war isn't surprising. One kind of suffering is so much like another. The war astonishes people because it presents the customary struggle in nature more dramatically than it has ever before been presented. It calls attention to cruelties in the scheme of things which comfortable people can usually ignore.

Perhaps, as long as the war continues, it will be impossible for us to leave here—impossible to secure a passport. I feel as if we were surrounded by a huge invisible wall too high ever to be scaled. Probably it has always been there, but until I put my hand out in the dark I did not realize it.

JOHN telegraphed to a mission station in Pernambuco where the minister is also a doctor of medicine, and asked if they would take me in there and operate on me. They replied, with a great show of reluctance, that they were not accustomed to receiving patients from a distance, but that they were willing to make an exception in my case. John stated that he could not pay well for what they were undertaking.

Now I have decided to go, Nannette thinks of nothing but of being left here alone. I don't know what she imagines will happen to her. Her eyes grow wide and terrified, like a child's, as she talks to me about it, and I can see a pulse beating in her thin neck.

There is a ghastly kind of instinctive coquetry in Nannette's appearance. She wears nothing that is in positively bad taste. Her clothes are very simple— almost shabby now—and might be suitable for persons of any age, but she makes such a depressing effort to dress appropriately for every occasion, to change her clothes for our dinner of feijoâda and mandioc meal, to keep her hair perfectly arranged, and to take good care of her complexion. For hours every night she uses lotions and creams. Her poor little hands are thin, mottled, and dark, and her fingers are twisted with gout. Her throat, that used to be charming, has a meager, withered look. Her chin has sharpened and her small face seems all eyes. About her lips are drawn pencilings of repression and frustration. It is only now and then when she forgets herself for a moment and becomes suddenly animate that she looks faintly pretty—something of the self she used to be. Then that sick perpetual confession of fright is, for the time, wiped out.

Her life seems to have no aim, no end, no beginning. Without requiring opulence, she has always been interested in pleasure, in being amused. Her absorption in art—in "culture"—represented just that. She cannot understand why Uncle Alec has stopped writing to us and she is alarmed. I feel worried too, but it is principally on account of the money. When she and Uncle Alec are under the same roof they are, in a profound sense, quite oblivious to each other. They don't share anything.

WE have nothing to read here. Nannette brought out some old French books, Daudet and Pierre Loti and Anatole France, which she knows already by heart. Every night, by the light of the only lamp we dare to burn, she pores over them until her pince-nez slips off the end of her nose and I understand that she is asleep. It humiliates her to realize that she is dozing in her chair like an old woman and I pretend I haven't noticed it. She snores. Except for the small choking noise she makes, everything is quite still. There is the continual rush and reverberating descent of the sea, but the sound is so monotonous and unceasing that I take no account of it. It is very cold here in the rain and we are wrapped in our old coats. Sometimes an agitation of the wind loosens a tile over us and rattles it. The house is filled with brown and black scorpions. They run along the floor ready to strike whatever they encounter, their tails raised over their heads. To keep out of danger we have to elevate our feet.

Yesterday Nannette found a snake under the lid of her trunk. It was harmless but it frightened her very much. She says this is a horrible place. Her manner is growing strange and secretive again, and she groans terribly in her dreams at night. I sometimes wonder if what she has gone through has deranged her mind. She is more cowardly than I am. She simply can't do anything for herself, and is always calling on John. Poor Nannette! She was born with a gold spoon in her mouth and she doesn't understand what has become of it.

Nannette and I spent our early childhood in the same house. It was large and somber looking with enormous pillars in front. In the dark old parlors with their exaggeratedly high ceilings were cheval glasses with consoles, marble mantels, banal statues, and huge majolica vases. There were also many dingy paintings in massive frames, "masterpieces" they were considered, which my grandfather had purchased in Europe. When Nannette married Uncle Alec she gave up, as she explained it, every luxury but a riding horse.

ESCAPADE

We kept Dandy for a long time and his name was the first word I said. When he had to be sold Nannette cried so much that I cried too. I felt that Uncle Alec did not realize how serious Dandy's loss would be—that he did not understand Nannette. Incidents of this kind made Uncle Alec take up all sorts of semi-gambling enterprises. He was certain that, no matter what else was lacking, he had to be rich.

Nannette used to tell me long stories of riding to hounds and of another horse called Robert-the-Devil on which she used to exhibit herself in the most daring feats. I always found it difficult to associate Nannette with daring, but the stories were interesting and threw into relief our changed estate.

THERE is one automobile in Natal and John secured that to take me to the boat. I was carried on board the dirty little steamer in a chair. As we passed people turned and stared with dim curious interest. "Aquella mulher está doente?" I heard them asking one another.

I felt unpleasantly my distinction from the rest. For some reason not to be able to walk made me ashamed. I resented having to feel like that. I wished I had had a veil over my face and I tried not to see any of these individuals clearly. The sense of shame is a physical impression. My body was bare and hot. My clothes couldn't cover me. I wanted to get away from myself—the self that was at the mercy of everyone else.

It is only when the distinction is one of power or superiority that it is agreeable to find yourself different from the group.

ESCAPADE

THE bunk in the stewardess's stateroom—which was all we could get—is on top of the linen chest and there are no springs under the thin mattress so that to lie on it aggravates my discomfort. All night the porthole had to be closed. I could hear the water splashing against it and trickling away with a full sound. When I turned on the electric lamp, the glass was covered with opaque silver drops that spread out slowly like silver vines growing against the gold-violet light. The cabin smelt of soiled linen and I was roused more than once by cockroaches running over my face. The floor—everything in the cabin—kept rising up before me with a stiff motion. As we were close to the engine room, it was very hot. Some sailors talked for hours in the passage. I could hear them cough, laugh, and clear their throats when they spat.

I was very ill. My pain and I were caught together in the movement of the ship. It was as if my pain were begging for rest, but the waves, making the steamer pitch and jerk, kept shaking it. Jackie was on the sofa. He cried and I was too ill to do anything for him. John had to sleep on deck.

DAYLIGHT. The sea, on the other side of the glass, rises up to the level of my eyes, gray and cold and weighted. The spray, striking the massive porthole, sounds like a shower of sand. The waves are of lead and oil. The water gives forth cold sharp sparks. The sun fades out. Great colorless drops, elongating on the pane, obscure the world.

My pain moves the quiet. There is nothing but the

ESCAPADE

bright agitation of suffering, bright in the dark, and the pale agitation of a ponderous ocean, too far to understand. Back and forth, back and forth, to the ends of the world, like a shuttle moving, like the weaving of a shroud—draw it close, draw it close.

PART III

DR. BEACH is sixty-five perhaps. He is tall and strong looking and walks with a heavy stride, his clerical coat flapping. He has white hair, a clipped white mustache, and a stern face full of coarse hard reticence. When he stares at you with his impenetrable blue eyes you somehow imagine there is a veil between you and him, an impalpable obstruction to communication. His hands are heavy, covered with gray-blond hair, and to indicate his medical profession he wears, on the first finger of the right hand, a large emerald ring.

When he met us at the boat I was in such pain that I felt it would be impossible for me to board the train and go on to the mission station, but he was impatient, abrupt, and matter-of-fact. It had to be done, he had come down to take us there, and I had just as well make up my mind to it. He did not offer to give me anything to make me feel the pain less.

FOR miles along the track the mangaba trees were covered with vultures, still as sphinxes. Not a wing of their huddled shapes ruffled as the noisy train slipped past. In the distance I saw new white stucco houses, gay green window shutters mellowed by the sunshine. A vine-grown chapel on an eminence darted the last beams from a gilded cross. In the meadows hundreds of cattle were browsing.

ESCAPADE

A stench of blood was borne to our nostrils and a few moments later, in its commanding situation, overlooking everything, the huge slaughterhouse—The Slaughterhouse of St. John, as it was called—came into view.

A PLAIN covered with scrub grass and the endless brown cones of ant nests. A solitary rider in a leather hat. A small gray monkey runs close to the track and cocks his head sidewise as he stares at the flashing windows of the passing cars.

THE thin foliage of the bamboos is like green smoke. Their plumes ascend behind some deserted huts, the doors sagging in the frames, the walls of unbaked bricks cracked and sunken at the sides. Dr. Beach says we are going higher and higher, and I am sensible of a chill stealing upon us. We are chilled with our own being, with the strangeness of our surroundings, with our fear of what we are.

The train drags and rocks. The wheels under us make a flat clicking sound. There are all kinds of rattling noises, and the lonely churning of the engine suggests that someone is being suffocated. On the bench opposite us a countrywoman in a ragged dress has gone to sleep. The landscape, through the blurred windows, seems entirely deserted. Trees flop loose curved branches. In a stagnant pond water twinkles, throbs, hot-cold, cold-hot. A guard goes through the car and, striking match after match, succeeds in lighting some swinging oil lamps that give out a strong smell of kerosene and make reflections like dim sparks—will o' the wisps—in the gray-blue glass. The train, the people inside, everything is as if submerged in the vast quiet of the abandoned hills. The cold has covered us up. We are numbed, still—as if already in our final sleep.

When we draw up at our station we have been twelve hours in the coach. Besides the shed before which the train stops, there is not a house in sight. Only a pale road, lost upward at the first turn, and, as there are no carriages in the country, two boys waiting with a chair stretched on poles to carry me to the mission.

"We never expected to have any white people on our hands and until the hospital is built to take care of them they'll have to put up with what they can get." Mrs. Beach's tone is cold and blunt. She is stout, dark, with white hair and an aquiline nose. Her manner is frigid, but tolerantly humorous, and her precise gestures are somehow full of self-congratulation. She tells me immediately that she is a Southerner and, I can see, means me to infer that she is an aristocrat. From a recent habit of secretiveness I fail to retaliate by informing her that my grandmother came from Maryland and that my grandfather was a Virginian. I am trying to take her attitude lightly, but the atmosphere she creates leaves me very much depressed.

John helped me to bed in the back room of the guesthouse next to a cavelike sort of apartment where the coffee from the plantation is stored. Mrs. Beach sent me in tea on a beautifully arranged tray. It is ridiculous how exciting it seemed to drink out of fine cups and use really exquisite napery and to have a bunch of fresh-cut roses beside one's plate.

ESCAPADE

THE partitions are very thin. In the night I was awakened by groans, and one thin scream that startled me so I felt it had been torn from my own throat. John told me that the young wife of Dr. Beach's son was in labor, bearing her first child. She had chloroform, he said, and could not be suffering as much as her groans indicated. I wonder if this agony of birth is really all there is—if it is life—the basic thing—and if everything else is irrelevant.

JACKIE has to be weaned. When Dona Inez comes near him he screams, kicks at her, and pushes her away with his fists. It is only after dark, after he has fallen asleep, that we can rouse him and persuade him to take her breast. The candle flame sheds a dim trembling lustre on his plump rosy face, paled a little in slumber. He half opens his eyes and accepts between his moist parted lips the bronze-tipped golden globe she offers him. And he goes on sucking, his fat arms thrown upward in a gesture of abandon, his lids drooped, his lashes heavy against his delicate cheeks. It disturbs me in a strange way to see Dona Inez so close to him, her sloping shoulders bent above him, a smile on her thin dark face, her black mysterious eyes glistening with reflections.

WHILE I was preparing for the operation I was left alone with the three men—old Dr. Beach, young Dr. Beach, and John. Young Dr. Beach has red hair, a gross mouth, and a red mustache. His eyes have never yet met mine directly. He is good-natured, slangy, and humorous in a fashion that shows his cowardice.

ESCAPADE

John took my nightgown off and the two doctors examined me. I didn't like them. I felt cold and helpless and antagonistic. I was very conscious of being looked at by men—not doctors, and I knew they were conscious of it too although they were trying to pretend otherwise. I thought of Mrs. Beach's excessive modesty, her constant stressing of propriety and the uncleanness of the flesh. Taking off one's clothes strips one of so much mental covering. And I can't abide the conventions of these people with their pseudo-Christianity. Whenever I gazed at young Dr. Beach he turned his head away and coughed slightly. I see where hatred of the flesh comes from. It is through the flesh that you are at everyone's mercy.

Dr. Beach says that he is going to perform a temporary operation which will serve until we return to the United States. His equipment is so crude that he is afraid to make an incision in the abdomen and sew me up as he ought.

Mrs. Beach came into the room when the men brought up the big scarred table. The table had appliances at the end to fasten the legs and keep the patient in the proper position. Mrs. Beach had a glass of wine for me. Her manner was casual and important. I felt that after all I had rather have men with me when I was helpless. Something in the atmosphere of sexual difference softens the circumstance.

I suppose I was frightened but I was conscious only of a calm elation. When I laid down on the table I was amused by the whole performance and wanted to laugh. My hands were very cold and shaking slightly.

John said, "You are beginning beautifully. Don't be afraid."

The very suggestion of fear was ridiculous to me. I giggled outright. It was as if, in an intoxicated moment, I were contemplating a leap from a very high place. The room was still. It was sunny out of doors. I could hear a hen clucking to her chickens. The white sash curtains swept softly back and forth. In the tiling over my head the glare twinkled and made black stars outlined with fire.

Mrs. Beach had brought Dr. Beach a large cup of coffee. She remarked that he always took coffee before he began to operate, and she indicated that the ordeal was much greater for him than it was for me. He was looking at me for the first time with real interest. His face was a deep brick-red, his eyes were bright and keen, and he kept nervously biting at the edge of his mustache.

"Well, she certainly is an excellent patient." He pushed my sleeve back. I had not observed anything in his hand but I felt a long sharp prick in my arm as he held the morphine needle in place. "I'm giving you this so you can go right off."

Morphine. I was curiously quiet. I waited to know morphine but I was too far away from myself. My own body was irrelevant. I asked them if they were going to strap my legs apart on those awful rests. They said yes. The room detached itself from me. I saw it accurately but as if I were outside it. My skin was excited. It prickled coolly, separately. I could feel a tide of life flow through me, beginning at my ankles and ascending my body in lengthening waves. The light made dark flakes against my eyes. I was lost in a storm of intensity, in an onrush of being.

Young Dr. Beach put something over my mouth. The smell was thick, sweetish, and unpleasant. They weren't giving me enough chloroform. I tried to tell them. My tongue was soundless. My blood thickened. My fingers closed on a full intangible softness. This was vaguely disagreeable. I sank into a muffled world and realized suddenly that the blood was choking me, that I was in it like a river. I was the river and it was my own blood which made pain through me as it flowed. I was a dark horror and the agony I was suffering was red. The red ran through me under the black in a long thin stream. My red self rushed on terrifically all blended with the black. There were figures moving in me that were not me and it was from them I wanted to free myself. I wanted to get them out of myself. I struggled hideously to expel these monsters from me. It was of no use.

Then the pain flowed away. Silence. I had disappeared from myself altogether. The emptiness was formless. The darkness had gone and I had gone with it.

As I waited blankly for becoming, my lids lifted and I gazed into John's face. He was bending over me. I had been two hours under chloroform, he said. I began to feel ill, nauseated, and to be conscious of different parts of me and of pains that bound me like aching threads. I tried to reach up to John. He told me I could not move. I had to lie on my back.

ESCAPADE

JOHN had to return to Natal to resume his work. Dona Inez took charge of Jackie. I was left to myself. I lay on my back hour after hour while I was waiting for someone to come and turn me over.

When I groaned to myself it was not in agony, but because I had to hear something beside my own monotonously agitated silence. The sounds I made distracted my attention from myself. I used to listen to these strange noises and wonder at them. I pressed my teeth against my wrists and enjoyed the small ache which brought a little meaning into my world. Such surface pains related me to my body, diminished my formlessness.

It rained continuously. The room was very bare and clean. It contained no furniture other than a chair, the washstand, and my bed. On the worn brick floor was an old faded rug, torn near the middle. Above the drawn curtains I could see the thin flag of a banana plant. A long red-purple spray of Bouganvillea, swung against the glass. The rain with its subtle motion on the window frequently obscured everything. The downfall in the tiles suggested the minute rattling of pebbles. Occasionally a fine spray came through the roof and fell with a cold sweet smell on my upturned face. The tiles were black-pink like mother of pearl and glowed dully with a secret look. Sometimes I heard voices. A cart rumbled along the road. The wheels squeaked, and, hearing the driver's shouts, I knew he was prodding at his oxen with a long pole. But we were in the country and for the most part everything was very quiet.

Dona Inez came in several times a day and attended to my bodily needs. I relinquished myself to her and tried not to think of my helplessness. It seemed to me that, no longer able to do anything for myself, I had escaped life.

THE light in the room is black-green. I feel as if an imperfect glass had been laid against my eyes. When the curtain floats back I see the mission house drifting against the thin still air. A rooster crows. Sounds beat dully against a clear flat surface, transparent day through which I can see the night. A bird flies past and I have the impression of a steel arrow drifting. The day stretches and stretches. I am conscious of the stretch—life spread out on a rack. My life. The bones creak. Suffering falls into suffering as rain into a pool. The heart of God one fathomless gray agony, one passive ear tortured with sound, one constrained tongue receiving the words of others. All the agonies of man must be immortal in that horrible eternity.

The rain drips. I am frightened of the whiteness of the sky, of the noiseless motions of the trees

AT night I am alone in the guest house. The sacks of coffee crowd high above the partition that imperfectly divides my sleeping place from the storeroom. During the day bats hang inertly over the moldering bags. As soon as dusk begins to gather, before my lamp is lit, they rush into my room. As many as eight or ten of them fly round and round my bed. Their wings have a hushed sound, like velvet brushing the air. Sometimes they are so close to my face that the stir of their motion sends a cold glow across my forehead. When the lamp is burning, their quick successive flight makes a rotating shadow between me and the wall. Round and round, a cadence of monotony. My nerves respond curiously to their eternal restlessness. I have given up being terrified of them, but the ceaselessness of their agitation is almost unendurable.

I lie on my back in a rigid attitude, waiting for them to circle nearer and nearer. Their rushing is the silence, the stillness more vivid than motion. A wing fanning me relieves me through an ecstasy of horror. Night after night I lie there wide awake until the slats of the window blinds are marked horizontally with cold pure shadows of light.

DR. BEACH, in sewing me up, took twenty-four stitches. Seven of them came out. I had to take chloroform again and, though the repair was trivial, I felt as if I were repeating the first ordeal.

He gave me only a little chloroform. I could hear everything that was being said. I even tried to lift my hand to show them that I was awake but it hung toward the bed with a terrible weight. My feet were stones dragging remotely at my elongated legs. The darkness in my eyes dilated thickly and was like black wool through which it was impossible to discern anything. I heard young Dr. Beach say that the job was a nuisance. Then the blackness got into my ears, and they were filled with words that had only a sickish vagueness.

ESCAPADE

When I came to myself I was far more upset than on the previous occasion. Dr. Beach made no effort to conceal his impatience. I was an hysterical woman and had no excuse for being disturbed by such an insignificant experience. His expression was of deliberate inattentiveness to all I said. As soon as he could get his instruments together he left the room.

Mrs. Beach came in and remained with me for a time. In a harsh voice she told me that my fright about myself was ridiculous. The doctor had just amputated the gangrened leg of a patient who could not take an anesthetic and the man had gone through the inconvenience without a murmur. Immediately afterward he had even drunk a cup of coffee and joked.

Mrs. Beach has a cold tolerant manner. She is a little afraid of her husband but in his absence she refers to him as if he were a child. She is continually telling me how much responsibility she has on her hands. The native women come to her for every kind of advice. She has no respect for any personality but her own, except where fear inspires her. In approaching John she is wary but intensely curious. As to what I say, she always brushes me aside with good-natured contempt. In order to shame me, I fancy, she described the two operations she had undergone, and gave me the details of childbirth on the five occasions she has been in labor. Four of her children are at school in the United States. She fortifies all her opinions with quotations from the Bible, ignoring of course the mystical element in Christianity. She enjoys her importance, but beyond that mission work doesn't interest her. She is constantly ridiculing the Catholic people

113

and the Catholic faith, and even her comments on other protestant missionaries are barbed with malice.

Christianity is the naive poetry of despair. Its heaven is so simple, so childlike a fulfilment of all that life has denied. And I hate Mrs. Beach who has survived so admirably and articulates without feeling this transfigured expression of defeat. Actually there can be no such thing as a successful Christian.

IT seems that any sort of continuous moisture is likely to rot the stitches. Dr. Beach told me I must drink as little water as possible and go without relieving myself as long as I could. I soon thought of nothing else. When he used an instrument on me it only made me worse. The stitches have been replaced a third time. He is very angry and says that he is utterly disgusted with my lack of restraint. I am the very worst patient he has ever had to deal with.

I have got over caring what happens to my wound if I can only be left alone with it. I am not grateful any longer for what is being done for me.

The bats persecute me more than ever. When they rush toward the bed I want to shriek, but as I had rather die than be heard I smother my moans under a pillow.

DR. BEACH came in today and in a tone of condemnation—as if the fault were entirely mine—said that I was doing very badly. He asked me if I were *really* in great pain. I felt degraded by the necessity to defend my suffering, to argue about it, and I hated him for asking such a question. I wanted to tell him that I was all right. I want to ignore him in the same way that he seems to be ignoring me.

He said, "You are placing me in a position where I shall have to give you morphine. I consider that the worst thing that can be done. I entirely disapprove of it." Then he tried to force on me the responsibility of deciding whether or not I should have anything for my relief. He hates women, though he says a good woman is the adornment of her husband's house. He told me that if all women were like Mrs. Beach the sex would be justified. And they live almost entirely apart and have really nothing to say to each other. Since he has discovered some of my opinions on art, politics, and religion, I affect him with a constant irritation and he feels that he is wasting his time in doing anything for me. I have more real sense of religious significances than he has, but he told me Darwin was a fool and a monster and left the room when I asserted that Darwin was a fine and courageous individual. All these cross-currents of antagonism stir him whenever anything comes up as regards my health.

He stood there staring down at me coldly and evasively, and because I said I wanted morphine if he was willing to give it to me he evidently regarded me with suspicion. "If I did as I thought best I should never give morphine at all. By giving away to your emotions and deliberately making yourself worse you force me to act against my better judgment. I want to tell you that *you* are making me do it. If you exerted more will power it would be unnecessary."

He bared my arm and, handling it as though it were

repulsive to him, pricked it with his needle. I was nauseated the moment the needle touched me. My mind seemed to me rigidly calm. My body was dead yet vivid around me. Morphine stimulates me but it gives me none of the blurred impressions of intoxication.

Of course these people dislike me because I have failed to play the part that John advised and conceal my attitude toward life. I realize the folly of the half truths I have told them, but it is too late to repent. I've often felt as if nothing mattered to me so much as being able to relieve myself of the burden of an hypocrisy in which I shall never succeed.

AFTERNOON: the thin slivers of sunshine, thin as paper tongues, lick under the tiles, under the eaves of the roof. The sunshine is spirit-yellow. The light is pierced by the thin green arms of the young leaves. My thoughts, foreshortened, float in tiers, one above the other, rich like the foreshortened figures by Veronese hovering against the ceiling of the Doge's palace.

Houri, beautiful positive to captivate my negative, slide your warm arms about me, slithering as leaves in the wind. Let me rest in you as in a cradle of air. As a shadow rests in the arms of the wind—as a shadow rests in the light.

MY brain pulls, stretches, tears; but cannot open wide enough to see. Always at the agonized point of conception, but never conceiving. Always giving birth, yet never born. What is it I am to conceive? To what must I give birth? What is the question I cannot answer that must be answered? What is that blank face I must fill in with features?

Golden tiger never halts. Slow marching he comes on feet of emerald satin. Golden tiger has a smooth velvet tongue, drips blandness like the light of a crimson moon. Loves the feel of bone, clean as stone, smooth as milk. Loves the brittle ache of bone he has caressed. He came out of a night like powdered blue plush. He lashed me softly. His eyes glowed into mine. He was a sun at midnight.

LAST night I was violently ill. My retching disturbed everyone. I wanted to die.

Mrs. Beach came in here to find out what was the matter. I closed my eyes to keep from seeing her. I heard her say to her husband, "Just what you prophesied! A very good lesson for her. No more requests for morphine after this!" Her satisfaction sounded vindictive to me.

I didn't care what happened. I had no desire to control myself. For the most part I kept my eyes closed and groaned loudly. What I vomited was blue from the medicine they had given me. I saw stains on all the sheets, on all the bedclothes, on the floor, the towels that lay about. And in spite of the warning that I would break more stitches, I threw myself wildly from side to side of the cot. I hated them all and I wanted to show it. When I allowed myself to be quiet for an instant I saw faces in the dim light—young Dr. Beach's red mustache, his father's eyes, Mrs. Beach's severe carriage and her reproving fastidious mouth. I wanted to spew blue all over them, to contaminate them with my dislike.

DR. BEACH is very ready to let me sit up. I can tell by his manner that he and his wife are extremely anxious to get rid of me. They keep making little casual remarks about expense. God knows I have no desire to stay here longer than necessary. I wish I had a thousand dollars to throw at them. If people are unkind to me I want to get away from them. I can't beat them at their own game. Something in me protests too violently. I want to insult them and leave.

Today one of the mission employees, a tall hand-some man, half Indian, carried me to the big house, to the veranda, and I sat there in an armchair while the family ate. I was very self-conscious in the big man's arms, particularly because I knew how pale and exhausted I was and that from his standpoint I was probably absolutely hideous. It pleased me to admit a sensuous pleasure in submitting myself to his strength —pleased me principally, I suppose, because my very thought would have been an impropriety to Dr. and Mrs. Beach.

A Brazilian who has just qualified for the ministry is visiting here with his wife. He is tall and thin but looks like a Japanese. His eyes are dark with an obscure expression. They remind me of grapes in hoar frost. He has beautiful manners and when he delivers himself of a Christian sentiment he is eloquent. He is very attentive to me. Evidently, despite his call-ing, he is willing to have me think he has a way with women. The Beaches are paternal toward him. He has two small children. When I look at his pretty shallow little wife with her faded vivacity—the atmosphere she conveys of mingled coquetry and fatigue—I resent him intensely. I should like to say something to him that would hurt his vanity forever.

It has been raining and while the group were at the table they suddenly laid down their knives and forks and began, in a doleful manner, to chant some hymns. They sang well and the music, full of the passion of the cross, disturbed me with its incongruity. I gazed at the dismantled roast, the well heaped plates, and I felt that human beings were indeed mysterious to themselves. The plantation is very isolated. I could see nothing anywhere but abrupt hillsides covered with coffee trees, and beyond them, high and dim, sequestered mountain peaks.

Dr. Beach has a full strong baritone. Doctor Galdino, the Brazilian, has an excellent tenor. Dona Perola sang what is generally called "second," and Mrs. Beach carried the melody in a sweet soprano voice. Young Dr. Beach and his wife—who is nicknamed "Chick"— were the only ones who seemed to think the performance a joke.

A Mr. and Mrs. Andrews are also visiting here. Mr. Andrews is a stout man with handsome features, black hair, and large indefinitely sweet blue eyes. His wife, of Norwegian extraction, is from Minnesota, blond, tall, and, without being fat, shapelessly robust. He depends on her utterly and she is very kind to him. I feel somehow that life has hurt them and that they have a simple right to belong to the church. From a worldly standpoint they are unintelligent and ignorant, but they have been through some kind of an experience in themselves which has convinced them that there is an end to things. They believe in death, and to that extent they have the true vision of poets. They have the psychology of all ecstatics, an aspiration toward self-abandonment, toward a negative solution of the universe. Religion alone permits the male a passionate assumption of irresponsibility. It allows him to assume toward God the sexual attitude of the female. Jehovah is the male spirit in Judaic religion, while the female element was supplied by the advent of Jesus.

WHEN I tried to walk my legs melted beneath me, the earth lifted itself and began to sway, and I felt I was being swung in the vortex made by the flowing trees, the rocks that sank under my feet. But I am determined to get away from here. Today Mrs. Beach said, "I do hope some day when we are too old for anything else the doctor and I will be able to enjoy a little family life. As it is, if we don't have divinity students visiting here, we always have some sick person or other on our hands."

I can't eat much but I go to table with them. Sometimes Dr. Beach prays for a long while before the meal can begin. They have prayed for me, for the recovery of my health. I feel hypocritically uncomfortable when I hear my name mentioned in a pious context. They have been ridiculing a fanatic who goes about among the country people preaching non-resistance as the doctrine of Christ. Dr. Beach laughed coarsely and heartily. He said, "I asked him, since he believed in non-resistance, if he would have any objection to killing a cockroach. He says he wouldn't even kill that." Dr. Beach cut himself a slice of mutton and, while he was masticating, passed his napkin carefully along the glistening under edge of his mustache. I thought of the lion lying down with the lamb and wondered how they adjusted themselves to such phrases. I remarked that I had once been a vegetarian. Mrs. Beach said, "Well, I think we ought to accept God's laws without questioning them and enjoy freely all that he has given us to enjoy." From what she has told me on other occasions I suppose this remark applys to food but not to sex.

Since the conversation about Darwin I have learned that they regard monkeys with a venomous dislike. They have a little black monkey, given them in all innocence, by a "believer." I can see the monkey from my window as he gallops back and forth, back and forth, at the end of his chain under the breadfruit tree beneath which he is tied. He has sad yellow eyes and a small disconsolate face. If he catches sight of me he stands upright on bent legs, elongating his thin disproportionate body and catching at his chain with his dry sensitive hands. Then, wrinkling his brows in a mournful grimace and showing his teeth slightly, he rubs his stomach to indicate that he wants something to eat. João, the Indian, is the only one who ever feeds him. Mrs. Beach told me that she thought monkeys were "digusting things," and she added, "so hideous and so useless."

A NATIVE woman was brought here yesterday, half dead, her body completely gangrened. There is no hope of her recovery. It makes me ill to imagine what she has suffered. She was carried in this condition thirty miles in a hammock. Those who suffer are those who are compelled to submit. No kind of suffering which is elected really needs to be commiserated. No one can renounce liberty, for renunciation also is an expression of freedom. Life breaks us when our wills become subjugate.

DR. BEACH must be troubled about something. The room next me is vacant and he goes in there every day alone to pray. For as long as an hour at a time I hear the steady monotonous sound of his voice, sometimes calm, sometimes broken with feeling, sometimes lifted as if in exhortation. Since I have listened to this I feel more sympathy for him, but I can't attempt any approach. His religion is stern, heavy with the sombreness of Judaic prophecy, unmodified by Christ. His wife, apparently, is unaffected by his mood. She told me this morning, almost unctuously, that her husband went to God for his strength and that Dr. Beach's strength was as limitless as his belief. I think him a monster, but at least his inhumanity is artistically of interest.

I LIKE sitting in my doorway in the wonderful silence. The sunshine in the afternoon has the late color of bruised apricots. In the air there is a soft agitating quality and the faint smell of flowers. We are face to face here with a very old mountain. It has a blunt peak, seamed sides, and the mist that stirs delicately around it is woven with the wings of some large birds. Olympus, Ararat, Sinai, Calvary—mountains are the

altars of the gods. I think now of the last wine squeezed
from the old press, a kind of bacchantic dusk. The
enigma of myself is the failure of romanticism to sat-
isfy a being fundamentally romantic. Physical timidity,
mental accuracy, a sense of justice, and a too complete
identification with the case of others is responsible for
my paradoxical state.

Oh, these terrible Christians! Venus, Clytie, Mercury
are flung down from their pedestals in the museum,
and it is as though the lives of little children were
being broken at my feet. I don't believe it possible
for an adult to be, at the same period, virtuous and
innocent. Sometimes the wreath of rose and laurel
becomes the crown of thorns, but in either case the
same longing is expressed. The statue tries to break
out of its rock, the poem out of its language, and sex
out of the organs of sex. Somehow, strong like a
hunter, I shall tear my way through. At least that is
what I like to believe.

THERE is a great deal of talk about the war. Dr. Beach
uses pompous words, clears his throat, and Mrs. Beach's
eyes fill with tears. Each enjoys his own sensitiveness.

After thinking about the people who are in the
struggle I have decided that the Latins have vanity,
the Anglo-Saxons pride, and the Germans conceit. That
is to say pride is weakest in the Latin, most insane
in the Anglo-Saxon, while German complacency is due
to a limitation of the imagination.

When I do not join in the orgy of vituperation of
"the Enemy" they all look at me blankly with the
resentment that arises from their confusion. They

regard my lack of patriotism as a species of ingratitude. Ingratitude for what? The war itself is less
hideous than the comparatively unrelated emotions it
has loosed. I read today in an old newspaper of a
clergyman in a small town who was tarred and feathered
by the populace because he refused to subscribe to a
doctrine of hate. Dr. and Mrs. Beach and even gentle
Mr. and Mrs. Andrews thoroughly condone the action
of the mob. I realize now that deep down in everyone
is an instinct of being, unaffected by the values which
consciousness imposes. This being is impersonal, undefined, a mere gesture which asserts life and takes no
account of obligation or consequence. I want to be
saved from myself, from the terrible self from which
all my secondary life proceeds, the self which goes with
closed eyes toward its own end.

Life, the ultimate thing, to which all our prismatic
vision can be reduced, is sleep, is sightless. Always,
always sleep. And there is no awakening. The atmosphere of the dream is the spirit of the dreamer who
will never rouse. I felt this in a picture of a foetus
I once saw, its oneness with itself, its terrible actuality,
its darkness. It was really the monster who created
Frankenstein, the great blind sinless monster who is also
the father of all we call beauty.

Dona Perola, the wife of the Brazilian convert, came
in to pay me a visit. She is very pretty, with a thin
white face, dark blue eyes, and hair that is black,
fine, and straight. She is proud of her husband's learning, his association with Americans, and the degree of
divinity which he has just taken. But she is bored and

exhausted with poverty. She told me of the gay time she had when, before she was married, she visited an aunt in Rio, and she described all her clothes to me. Her thin cheeks glowed. Her eyes hardened with a far-away look and her little figure was poised with the self-confidence her retrospection inspired. It seems a man—other than her husband—at that time wanted her to be his wife. He was of a bold reckless temperament and when she refused him he threatened to kill her and himself.

She had her baby in her arms and while she talked she opened her matinée and put the child to her sagging, pear-shaped breast. Her skin was almost transparent, dazzlingly fair, but her throat and shoulders appeared emaciated. I remembered that Mrs. Beach had told me that Dona Perola was threatened with tuberculosis and was taking Emulsão Scott. This is her second child and she has had a misplaced uterus since she bore the first. I watched the delicate baby sucking avidly, folding and unfolding its hands. The mother's vanity, so much gratified in the mere recollection of admiration, has been sold. The life which is so strong in her imagination has already gone into her child. It was like an enchantment to listen to her. She was a young girl with the independence of a virgin. As for the woman I gazed at, Dona Perola did not recognize the existence of that person with her attenuated throat and bosom dragged down by the suckling of young.

I felt dream all around me. I was deep, deep in Dona Perola's dream. Perhaps in the last moment, when the darkness is growing white, her lids will flutter a little, the pain of vision will be hers for an instant—

then go out. Her hands are thin, tired, and move helplessly, but they are dream also. They cannot see themselves and their fatigue.

JOHN has come back. We are leaving. I have dressed
very carefully to go to the train—at least as carefully
as my wardrobe will permit—and I have put some
rouge on my face. The hat I got in London still looks
rather smart, black velvet with a white pompom at
the side. My old blue suit is shabby but it fits me
well. I feel protected in this costume. My personality
has been too much exposed by illness. I enjoy the
security which comes in being reduced to a type. Dr.
Beach refuses even to look at me. Mrs. Beach regards
me with more profound antagonism and greater respect.

I see now how little I want honesty, how undesirous
I am of presenting myself unadorned to the crowd. My
face is neither pretty nor ugly—sometimes one, sometimes another, always a little of both. I have a straight
nose, well modeled at the tip, a full mouth, delicate
and sensual—ugly almost and at the same time fine.
My skin is sallow, without any color, and my hair,
gray-gold. All this serves very well for make-up, for
the subterfuge of an appearance. But when I look
into my eyes I am grateful for the stupidity they must
confront—gray eyes that remind me somehow of rocks
and pools that the tide forgets, eyes filled with a sad
and brackish protest. I am twenty-two years old but
I can tell by those eyes that something strange has
happened to me. I am like Dona Perola. The self I
remember ceased to be even while I was thinking of it.
My breasts sag. I have no more milk for Jack. I no

longer feel my flesh opulent. And I know my body so well. My round throat that is not so round as it was, my square thin shoulders, my narrow hips and plump firm childish legs. I suppose I look young, faintly attractive, and rather pathetic. But there is a gauntness in my whole being that youth disguises a little. I am so convinced in my emotions of age and ugliness that I want to be old and ugly at once. If I could really renounce youth it might be possible to slip into age without any of the ghastly incongruity of spirit which I see displayed by Nannette.

THE train was moving through darkness. Beyond a window glazed with reflections the water showed an oiled mark—a stiff vertical line that, wavering in its rigidness, was longer in time as the train passed. Hulks of houses had vacant panes in which there were lights like seeds. A street, illumined: wiry flowers swayed and elongated on stems of shadow. At a crossing, a lamp. Rays of light like hairy legs struggled with darkness, pushed it frantically back.

A factory. They make cacao there. Cocoa, grown in Bahia. They send it to the United States. The factory chimneys are three strokes of iron against the twilight. Smoke one with the sky rolls away and away. Little flames of factory fires dance in the glass.

The bay reappears and reflections, wriggling through the oily depths, shudder and sink aside.

Train, low moving now, swings beside another train: a hollow shadow filled with light. Inside, in liquid glass, men gambling with cards, women asleep with babies in their laps. Train, roar dulled, drags its sound—soft, dies flattened. Sound flat. Silence more heavy than sound. Silence, following the other train, lies ponderous along the track.

In the car squeaks of woodwork, a squeaking hinge. Thump, thump, a sharp thud, spreading as the wheel turns. Unattached voices speaking a strange tongue, dangle with the limpness of confusion. Voices climb shrilly and slip down an invisible cadence. Voices cackle and drone: voices without bodies, without words. In the bench beside me a girl asleep leans on her arm, heavy, overweighed with an inappropriate reality. A man walks along the narrow aisle, sways from his feet —a wooden swing. He braces himself stiffly.

Clangor of hell. Train sobs, chokes. The distance suffocates. The floor of the car swings at an angle to its sides. Sides rise and fall. Shakes. Shakes. Sound stumbles after itself.

American car. It the ceiling one light encased in a dull glass globe burns like an illumined shell. People's heads jerks. A swarthy fat girl has blondined hair sticky with light, amber. Short hair—here the mark of her profession. She crosses her ponderous legs and ogles the train guard as he goes past. A man's bent head, bald and pinkish through his meager hair, bobbles. Englishman. Recife is filled with English. With stupid intentness he stares before him, and seems transfixed with motion.

THE station, after my country experience, seemed to me enormous and brilliantly lighted. John asked for the name of a cheap hotel and a chauffeur drove us to one in the lower part of the city near one of the wharves. We crossed a bridge. A surface car went along with us, flickering a chain of light. In the purple-black water, a fan of light, barred waves of gold vibrating, streams of gilt flowing over a field of onyx. The city was dim. We could hear the train behind us, a hearse snorting. A boat moved woodenly, floated deathly into land. Loud voices came from the boat and a seepage of reflections. As the steamer drew near the heaviness of the wharves sank into the water like iron into flesh.

The office of the hotel was not on the ground floor, and when we had mounted to it and asked for a room we learned that the only one available was on the top story, reached by three flights of stairs. It was twelve o'clock at night and we had to take what was given us.

The room is long and narrow, furnished with two iron beds, a washstand, and a stand on which there is a carafe. Two high windows with heavy blinds admit us to a balcony which overhangs the street.

THE harbor is at the end of the street. A new building of stucco, large and boxlike, makes dead angles against evening. A boat whistle, hoarse and strong, tears the stillness—fades—and is thin. The shops are closed for Sunday. The houses are cold with quiet. Motor car over the cobblestones. Click, click of motor. Reverberation of rubber tires. There is a luminous glaze in the shadow over which it passes. About the lamps that are slowly ascending their light, insects swing in diaphanous motion. The car passes under a lamp and a delicate shadow swerves forward in a semicircle and shrinks before the advancing wheels. Shadow of barefoot man following also swerves and shrinks.

A pharmacia across from us. On the second story the proprietor and his wife have a housekeeping establishment. I can see into the sala—crayon portraits in gilt frames, mirrors also surrounded by gilt and draped in pink tarlatan to keep off the flies, severe lines of chairs facing each other as if in readiness for a ceremony of some kind. The huge fat woman in the lace matinée sits there all alone, fanning herself heavily with a palm leaf. Sometimes she rises, comes out on her balcony, and gazes dully up and down the contracted distance. She has been there all day in the same contented ennui—the same idleness.

Latin women continually astonish me. I envy their fatalism and their indolence. Yonder in a corner is her saint, all gold and blue in a huge glass case. Her emotional needs are no doubt supplied when she prays to him. A gentle sentiment already prepared for every occasion, coarse food, accumulating fat, stupidity.

JACKIE has the croup. About one o'clock last night I realized that he was breathing hoarsely, and a little later he began to choke, cough, and almost to suffocate himself with screams of fright.

John had to get out of bed, dress himself, and go across the way to rouse the pharmacist. While he was absent Jackie became very pale, his lips took a bluish tinge, his lids drooped so that only the whites of his eyes showed. His fat little hands, tremblingly clutching the bedcovers, were cold with moisture. I suppose I

lost my head utterly for I picked him up and began
to carry him about. This morning the same pains like
knives thrust in my navel, the same thin tension of the
nerves, the same curious disturbing aliveness of sensation in my spine, the same feeling of helplessness and
of unbearable weight. John had to make a mountain
of pillows under my knees to hold up my legs that
seemed to me massive and were as if suspended limply
from my hips.

Jackie is wan and fretful but very much better.

THE boat trip was uneventful. When we reached home
Nannette was waiting for us at the gate. There was a
high wind up and down the deserted road and the blown
sand stung our faces. Nannette was excited and relieved. She was bareheaded, her hair all disheveled.
When she saw that I was being carried in, her thin face
quivered, her eyes darkened, and I knew that she was
about to cry. I longed so much to cry myself that
I resented her grief.

I felt somehow that in coming home like this I really
was disgraced. I thought of thin breasts bared with
a simple gesture, offering their ignobility with a shudder. Beauty is generous now. If she hated me I could
bleed pity, but she is as bland in her degradation as
any saint.

I could suckle many children, or, I fancy, as many
lovers. But the children grow up, and the lovers will
find the drying teats filled with a bitter liquid. Who
is there to drink? No one will save an old woman the
pain of the overladen. There are the poor of course,

and those hungering for new creeds, but the fountain
is poisoned by the fever in the breast.

Jackie, once you were my darkness. You were of
me, the darkness in which we both went. With the
opening of your eyes my eyes opened and the walls
of my bedroom descended around me. And after that I
began to see walls everywhere: walls of sea; walls of
sky; walls of eyes. Come back into your prison. Or
perhaps you will build another wall of blocks, sur-
mounted by a cotton elephant without a trunk. The
wind has taken the leaves from one of the trees in
front of the house, and the stiff branches, spreading
like a fan of lacquer, brush at the sky. We can look
at that.

PART IV

JOHN, Jackie, Nannette and myself climbed down the long ladder from the steamer and seated ourselves in the small boat. Dinah, my dog, stood beside me, barking and jerking at her chain, her body taut and strained forward, her muzzle lifted. There was a glassy silence over the big bay, broken a little by the drip of water from the oars and the soft dragging undercurrent of the outgoing tide.

Bahia. John has gotten his promotion. The houses climbing the hillside rigidly, pink, golden-blue, worn red, are warm-colored among black trees. The dawn sky, wide and bare, is like lighted stone. The steps of the wharf are old, lustrous, dripping dimness.

In a motor car we mount a long precipitate street. Walls tower above us. The neglected garden of an old church. Among crumbling violet-green stones, clusters of aloes. Blue rays of leaves—black-blue—like huge dark stars bursting with light. A century plant has a single delicate spear of blossom, tall and gold-feathered at the top. Clumps of prickly pear, blue-violet, have a stiff, frozen appearance, the leaves, flat as palms, spined as with nails, like crucified hands.

In the square some black women in sleeveless camisoles and wide flowered skirts, red and yellow shawls knotted under their arm pits. John says that the black women in Africa knot their shawls like that.

ESCAPADE

From the hilltop now we can see the bay stretched before us in azure stillness like a congealed lake. Sail boats move with harsh suavity, their submerged keels cutting through an unbroken crêpe-like surface.

THE pensão is at the corner of a poor street, the huge plaster church of the Franciscans in the square opposite. When I lean very far from my window I can see the enormous monastery down the hillside. A great many monks go past. They wear beards, brown robes, and sandals. When the church door is open I have a glimpse of a dazzling interior ornate with gilt, and, near the entrance, the statue of a black saint in a Moorish costume.

On Sunday there was a religious procession: little girls in blue and pink with angel wings on their shoulders and silver paper crowns on their heads. The church dignitary, in a yellow robe like a mandarin's coat, walked under a purple and white canopy hung round with lace.

EASTER EVE. In front of the churches the rockets go up, and at dawn, from the row of mud houses behind us, emerge women and children beating on basins, old tin cans, buckets. Palm trees blowing against a pearl-colored sky twist their fronds in distorted shapes. Christ, Our Lord, is risen! Shouts, cheers, yells. The women at the fountain stop washing to shout. The lame shoemaker in the shop next door leaves his bench with his awl in his hand. Christ, Our Lord, is risen! The ragged boys in the square take up the cry ecstatically. A military band on a passing tram car plays, with

strident joy, the Grand March from Aïda. Clouds of
incense mingle with the smoke of bursting fireworks.
Christ has risen!

MONDAY morning. Down the gay street with its blue-
and-white tiled housefronts, its animated shops, a fat
asthmatic matron with a basket, wheezing as she stoops
to extract her roll of savings from her stocking in order
to make a purchase. A pious whore goes by me on
her way to church.

Then—far-off music and excitement. Faces at the
windows. Naked yellow gamins begin to dance. Clerks
with scented hair and oily scented mustaches, no coats,
and brass watch chains delicate across the fronts of
their cotton vests. One wears a pink-striped shirt,
check trousers, and linen suspenders. They step out
of doors and ogle curiously the unrevealed distance.
The half-breed drunkard on our step draws a single torn
garment across his nude chest and rises unsteadily to
his feet.

The Rogue's March. Between the ranks of titillated
onlookers and the bands of soldiers in full regimentals,
the man who has been stripped of his uniform, walking
slowly, hands tied behind him, head bent. His drooped
lids conceal his eyes, his sneering lips twitch. Blank
baffled face, expressionless with caution.

Down the square the procession goes, followed by the
music, turns a corner, and is lost. The gamins leave
off dancing. The clerk in the pink-striped shirt smiles
with complacent pity and shakes his head in satisfied
wonderment. The ragged drunkard, smiling also, sinks
back inertly in his former attitude of somnolence. Along

the cobblestones the heat waves undulate palpably in a quivering tide of transparence. Blank silence— blanker even than the face of the man condemned. Above the cries of a water carrier and a sweating charcoal vendor abusing his donkey, echoes, like the shadow of a sound, that strange jerky tune of two bars, repeated over and over.

AT the fore of the funeral procession comes an old negress in a sleeveless camisole and a flowered skirt. She has a bold humorous face, the features of a man. A red shawl, caught in a fold under her armpits, blows loosely about her generous hips. On her head she balances a wooden tray filled with flowers in coarse confusion—orange, red, purple, blue. The wooden soles of her tamankos beat the pavement with a jerky rhythm as she trots along in a running walk. She calls over her shoulder to some passerby, chuckles to herself, and spits. Behind her the pallbearers swing lightly the box covered with red cheese cloth, a box only long enough to contain the body of a child.

The tall mulatto woman that follows must be the mother of the deceased. She has red eyes, listless hands, a dragging step. Her figure is bent with fatigue and with the labor of maternity. I notice her loose breasts, her distorted belly, her soiled clothes. And I read in her eyes bitterness and envy of the dead who are able to rest.

I know the poor people's graves in the Campo Santo; yellow clay mounds marked with black wooden crosses on which hang the moldering wreaths of gilt and silver flowers. I can imagine the white empty church, the shuddering sound of wings as nesting birds are disturbed by the entrance of the party of death. The old priest will wear a soiled lace robe over his greasy soutane, and the acolytes, without any kind of vestment, with their coarse black hair smoothed hastily into place on their little boys' heads, will perform their offices in the striped cotton suits they wear all day.

Soft clay mud, spreading where it falls. Earth on the coffin lid. The clots follow each other and mingle as it was in the beginning. I want to think that Death also is a dream. I will not believe in it.

THERE is an old church close by with a garden that overhangs the lower city and the bay. I walked there with Jackie and Nannette. The garden was filled with beggar children, and sometimes, in their games, they ran in and out of the big bare edifice. Their thin cries echoed in the dimness and silence about the altar that I could see, alight through the open door.

In the twilight the penumbrous sky seemed withered by the quiet, and in green acidulous vapor shrank away from the earth. The water was pink-amber. The boats on it were black, stained with lights. The wind and waves together made a tearing sound like silk, a noise that died away faintly in the blurred rocking of the trees. A pronged palm branch above me twanged like a harp.

Realizing that, of necessity, an ill person is unsexed, I try to wring a cold mental harmony out of life, but, instead, I find myself sucked inward, my intellect smothered as by a voluptuous and nauseating rhythm. What I most long for is to be able not to desire anything, for I think of all life as gradually and eternally becoming nothing.

THE church and the houses of prostitution are nearly opposite. Before one of the houses I see the proprietress, a Creole, in a blue silk dress appliquéd with lace. Between the sagging blinds of a window above, leans a broad-faced Indian girl—from the upper Amazonas—and, behind her, inside a room, a pink china lamp is visible, a sofa with "tidies," an alcove for the bedstead, screened with a torn curtain of Nottingham lace.

All around the square, other windows, faces. From the hollow of a doorway an old beggar woman, taking refuge there, looks out from eyes ageless with pain. With a dumb gesture she holds forth her strained trembling hand and I observe the distorted knuckles, the veins knotting her wrists. "Uma esmolha, senhora, por amor de Deus." Her sunken mouth mumbles other words that have no meaning for me. Certainly it is through the senses that individuals approach each other and make an exchange of their experience.

Up the hill, donkey carts in a long procession. The whip falls unceasingly. Blood and sores on a furry back, as the donkey drivers, iconoclasts, flay our benignant God to death.

ONE of the brothels is a very elegant establishment. The prostitutes are from Rio and very "chic." Mademoiselle Juliette, reclining on the balcony, is draped in a long pink negligée. She has a tired thin face, little eyes full of ennui and cunning, and white exquisite hands. Most of her day is occupied with manicuring her nails. The tall man who visits her most frequently is a Scotchman. He is obviously embarrassed by being seen with her, but he cannot resist. I have been near when they met at the front door, and his eyes, dim with sensuality and emotion, followed her gestures with an avid look. Mademoiselle, I am sure, despises his plastic stupidity, his gullible admiration for her little tricks. I respect her for she shows me that she has very few illusions, either as to her profession or the men she meets.

Mademoiselle Fifi is not French at all, but low class Brazilian. She is tall, stout, of a voluptuous appearance, and there is a kind of dull sensuality in her face. Her features are classically regular, and her hair, combed severely away from her brow, gives her the appearance of a popular madonna. I have never seen her dressed for the street. Her entire existence seems to be passed in a blue satin kimono embroidered with gold, tarnished and a trifle soiled, and in red mules with high gilt heels. The impression I have of her is that she is repellent and indescribably depraved. She is so obviously stupid and unimaginative. Mademoiselle Juliette, by contrast, convinces me that there is a certain definitely moral virtue in intelligence.

Sin offers continual variety in experience, a duplex mingling of enjoyment and fear. The worldly minded do well to preserve the sense of sin while sinning. Thus they can continue pleasure indefinitely and avoid that irrevocable termination, that new beginning, which is socially so dangerous. Really logic is no more impartial than sense. Its business is to *prove* the sentient end. There is a positive to every negative, therefore the self-contradictory phrase, the paradox, is likeliest to approach the truth. I am going to give up the absurd attempt to justify logically my way of living.

Nannette is shocked by the brazenness of the prostitutes, but she is quite as interested in them as I am. She watches them furtively. Observing them in their profession stirs the dim fleshliness which propriety has submerged. Her shame only adds nuance to her appreciation.

"I LEFT Chicago thirty years ago," Mr. O'Malley told us. "I suppose there is quite a difference." His vague blue eyes misted a little in his lean red face, and he rubbed one dry small hand along the grizzled beard on his chin. He has an engenho—a sugar plantation—not far from the city, and once a year he and his wife come in here for a visit. She is a tall Indian woman with gaunt features and a stern but kindly presence. Mr. O'Malley's son is at the University of Illinois. He speaks of the boy. The English words come hard to him. He hesitates, embarrassed, and gives me a bewildered interrogative look.

IT was a new experience to have tea at the Pensão Inglez and meet some people of my own tradition. Mrs. Wilson, the doctor's wife, has a large flat figure, straight red hair, a big thin mouth with pale lips, and heavy tired eyes behind glasses.

Mrs. Donahue is a Spanish woman married to an

Irishman. She has a narrow youthful countenance, small rat-like eyes, and a curly black bang. She is wrapped always in the vagueness of emotion. She is timid and, in detail, rigidly formal. She says: "My fadder—my gran'fadder ees in de diplomatic corps. Eet ees what you call tradeetion in de family. My fadder meet my mudder firs' at a ball. Dey love at once. Eet ees ve-ery romantic." Her gaze dims with tears, and, demanding a response, she regards Mrs. Wilson fixedly.

Mrs. Wilson's voice is dry and her manner quizzical. She says, "That's nice." Her nasal American intonation is marked. She is disconcerted by Mrs. Donahue's naïve seriousness and defensively regards it as a joke.

"My fadder ees not Spanish. He ees Italian. But we are reared in Spain. We are Spanish. In Spain eet ees different from here. Servants don't have dees ideas to be democratic. Housekeeping eet ees ve-ery different. My mudder always gifs de butler—everybody—t'ree litre of wine a week. No my husban' he don' speak Spanish. We talk togedder in French. Eet ees good fo' him, vee-ry bad fo' my English."

Mrs. Nelson arrives. She has cold straightforward blue eyes, fine color, and a wisp of blond hair unbecomingly arranged. "I am late for tea I know but the English mail has just come in. No one who isn't acquainted with our dear old England can realize what it means to spend one's existence in a place like this. Nine years. Oh, the green of English fields! My heart aches when I think of it."

Mrs. Wilson purses her lips facetiously. "Even Americans are afflicted with homesickness."

ESCAPADE

Mrs. Nelson realizes condescendingly that this is wit, and smiles a cold far smile that frigidly illumines her eyes. "Yes, I dare say. I suppose you are."

The large room, with its straw mats and wicker chairs, is redolent of the warm odor of tea and the scent of baking bread that steals in from the kitchen. Through the glass doors one sees the garden, the mango trees, a flame tree in bloom—a tent of scarlet blossoms without any leaves. The breeze that comes to us is sweet and tepid and smells of rotting fruit, and the air, like soft, lukewarm water, is faintly disturbed. The women sip their tea and are passively stimulated. A melancholy satisfaction possesses them. Sky, hot blue, quivering with light. Sentimentality. Indolence. Mrs. Nelson, with a large lonely gesture, appropriates a cup. "Alas, these little gatherings are about all we have to console ourselves with."

THERE is a hospital here and even a medical school, but they are badly organized, there are only male nurses —these untrained—and Dr. Wilson says that, because he could not get the necessary remedies and supplies, he has more than once endangered a patient's life. He agrees that this is not the proper place for me to be operated on, that everything possible should be done to get me back to the United States. John, in order to have something to show the consul, wanted the doctor to sign a document saying that my life would be in jeopardy if I were forced to remain. Dr. Wilson was unwilling to commit himself to an extreme statement, but he did say that as my physician he advised me very strongly to return to a temperate climate.

ESCAPADE

John went today to visit the consulate. Mr. Harris, the consul, was polite but gave us no satisfaction as regards the future. He says that we should never have come here without the passport, and that in war time he has to be very strict in issuing them.

JOHN has been to the Consulate three times. His clothes are shabby but he assumes a confident air. He says, however, that he would secure more attention if he appeared prosperous. We are obscure, almost unacquainted with the small group of British and Americans here, and that makes everyone suspicious of us.

Today, while John was away, a strange man stopped in front of our house and stood there for a long time, apparently gazing directly at our windows. He walked away for a quarter of an hour, came back, and his scrutiny began as before. As Brazilians of the educated class never smoke pipes and this man, smoking a pipe, was very well dressed, I decided that he must be either American or British. And I at once concluded that John's persistence in regard to a passport had aroused the consul's suspicions and that we were being watched. John returned home very late and I was imagining all of the time that he was under arrest.

For two hours that man stood there keeping his mysterious watch. I wanted to go down into the street and ask him what he was doing. Anything seemed preferable to suspense. But when John appeared the man was gone. We have not heard anything since. I am uneasy. I can't find a satisfactory explanation of the incident.

ESCAPADE

Nannette has been with us more than a year and she came expecting to pay us a visit of eight months. She cries all the time. She cannot understand Uncle Alec's vagueness in regard to money, his failure to answer her letters. When I left home I should have left everything behind me, as John did. Nannette is so ashamed of her bad clothes. When I am not strong enough to go out, she remains indoors, and always I have difficulty in persuading her to go into the street. Her face is become perfectly colorless, without even pigmentation. Dr. Wilson says this is the result of malnutrition and a neurotic condition. The function of pigmentation has been arrested. My hands have the same appearance. They are large, with broad palms, long spatulate fingers, and thin wrists. This pallor that is overcoming us suggests leprosy to me. Nannette wears a heavy veil to hide herself. She is almost ill with anxiety about her looks.

Uncle Alec has divorced Nannette. I don't know when it was done and I, of course, can't blame him for doing it. When I was fifteen years old I realized how things were between them and tried to persuade them to separate. Then I used to feel crushed by the misery that surrounded me. Uncle Alec was worried by my strange attitude toward marriage. He often told me that nonconformity was a symptom of youth, and that he believed I would outgrow it. If men admired me too pronouncedly it was unpleasant to him. He thought that my mind was virginal and he could not understand my intuitions in regard to sex.

Uncle Alec dreads emotion, and Nannette lives by it.

ESCAPADE

She is responsive to every suggestion and she assumes every phase of feeling. Formerly she was only stimulated by an outbreak. Now she seems to be exhausted by one.

I don't want to feel bitter, but suffering overcomes one's sense of justice. And besides Uncle Alec is dishonest with himself. He has no money, he has imposed on John a horrible responsibility, and he insists on writing to me that his devotion to me has not diminished. As difficult as it is, I must defend myself against his endearments. He has really ceased to be our friend, but I can respect an honest enemy. There is something decent and straightforward about hate. I want to overcome my present sense of confusion, of having been somehow tricked.

Nannette will not believe in what she calls the "cruelty" of the divorce. She threatened to kill herself, walked out to the beach, and remained absent for hours. But she came back after a while of course. Her eyes were hard and bright and strange. She says it is all the fault of John and me. If I had remained at home Uncle Alec would never have contemplated anything so humiliating and so desperate. She believes now that she would have been perfectly ready to accede to a legal separation.

John says that he sympathizes with Uncle Alec's attempt to escape the bondage of an unhappy marriage, but that he cannot forgive Uncle Alec's sentimental lies to me. When people speak of being "broken by life" they mean that their behavior, however morally unjustifiable, has been inevitably precipitated, and that they are helpless any longer to explain themselves to others. What is, in an inner sense, must be, and we must resist our despair of consequences. I, at least, have nothing to bewail. When I met John I had nothing.

NANNETTE'S hair has grown quite white. Her eyes have a fixed expression of bewilderment. She goes about with a weak, baffled look, suddenly remembers her troubles and begins to weep. Strangely enough she will not allow any condemnation of Uncle Alec. She blames John entirely for the horror of her situation. John's manner to her is kind, but underneath he is irritated. He says she has no consideration for my ill health and burdens me unbearably.

She has a wealthy sister with whom she quarreled years ago. I am trying to persuade her to write to this aunt of mine, and ultimately to leave us. But Nannette does not wish to leave me. My aunt is also my enemy and if Nannette went back to her we should need, for our own safety, to conceal our address. There is always the chance that Louise may discover us.

THE worst of John's present employment is that he has to be away from home so much—sometimes for six or seven weeks together. He has to go up in the interior on long horseback trips and everything is much as it was when we were in Natal. But there is no escape from the situation. The American and English companies, for the most part, send out their own men, and there are no other positions that pay even a living wage for four people like us.

One of the Americans in the office has been dismissed

and is going back to the States. I think of the three thousand miles between here and New York: seas like oil, waves sapphire hard and sapphire blue, second class passengers, bored and heat-weary, stretched in scant steamer chairs, fumes of fried onions, dull games of shuffle-board, comforting tinkle of glass in the bar. And Pagliacci, the flashy little American who has written boasting letters home, fired—without a penny. If only he had the nerve to order a bottle of champagne! But he will drink beer and go on lying half-heartedly.

At any rate that isn't before us. It is perfectly definite now that our passport application has been refused. We've tried to become naturalized Brazilians—even paid a little to the lawyer we had to consult—but people of warring nations will not be accepted as citizens by the Brazilian government.

On Saturday night I felt able to walk again and John and I went down the hill to the Baixa Sapateiro where there are some poor people's shops. Everything was very gay, the narrow street well-lit, and there was the usual week-end crowd moving about. We went into a shop where I wanted to buy hairpins. As we emerged an electric car passed us and we noticed some soldiers running down the road after it. The people around us hesitated as we did and gazed stupidly after the running men. Just then, from nowhere, a scream, men talking in loud confused voices. A mob began to collect. The shopkeepers let down the heavy iron shutters in front of their establishments. John and I, realizing that something unusual was occurring, were in great haste to get away. I was too unwell to make much progress.

ESCAPADE

John pushed me through an open doorway, just as the door was being closed.

Darkness. An iron bar clanged. With our hands we felt along a cold wall—blank. The air was acrid with moisture. A passageway in which several individuals unknown to one another had hidden themselves. The faint odor of their breathing disturbed the small silence removed so little from the tumultuous noise of the street. A man, whom we could not see, told us that a revolution against the new governor was fomenting.

"I live here. There is a ladder back there. João, a ladder." The ladder was dragged forward with a stealthy scraping sound. The pale figure of a youth mounting it was all at once illumined above the iron-grilled transom. Sighs of anxiety stirred the shadows. "Nossa senhora, miseracordia de seu povo. Jesus, piedade. Tenha compaixão, meu Deus!"

The clatter of horse's hoofs, slipping, crowding the cobblestones. No words. Voices. Shots exploded separately. They were muffled in the obscurity which also enveloped us. A woman in the passageway cried out sharply, inarticulately, and I had the feeling that she had covered her mouth with her hand. Santa Maria, Santa Theresa, Sao Antonio, nos salvem. From the wordlessness of the mob outside a scream of agony. Nothing to answer it but the impersonal sound of the cavalry passing, the constant explosive tinkle of descending glass. "The shops are being broken into! The crowd is rifling the shops!" Once there was a pounding at the door behind which we stood, but John and two other persons pushed it back while it swayed against us.

148

ESCAPADE

This is a revolution for food. The crowd want meat. One thing is as beautiful as another if it is overpowering, and if it is actual it overpowers us—we belong to it. The hunger of our bodies is as living as a tree.

Two hours have passed. The clamor has dwindled. The boy, descending the ladder cautiously, glides downward as if along the moonlight which shines torpidly against the iron grill. The invisible bar swings inward, grates the door frame. And now not only the sky is disclosed but the street also, deserted in its confusion. The lamps burn on an unconvincing quietude. An old woman peering out at us from the half-concealment of a wall, has uncombed hair and bright eyes, dangerously still in a face haggardly excited. Her skirts are torn, her chemise has fallen from her shoulder and her lax pouch-like breast is exposed. One hand, strong like the claw of a bird of prey, holds a threatening bottle by the neck, ready to hurl at us if we should pass.

We left our hiding place for an opposite direction. I turned once and glanced back and she had turned also and was silently, carefully watching us—moveless —watching us with an eager look of death.

On Monday the streets were lively again, but somewhere, about eleven o'clock, a terrible explosion occurred. I learned afterward, that a mob of people had collected in the square in front of the governor's palace; that the governor was courageous enough to come out on a balcony and begin a speech with which he hoped to pacify them; that an aged negress, almost insane with excitement, ran toward the sidewalk threateningly, her arms uplifted; that some of the crowd followed her; and that the palace guard was given the command to fire. Thirteen unarmed people were killed at once and many more wounded.

I found it impossible to remain indoors. The unusual atmosphere made me feel strong and calm. Men on the street corners, talking excitedly, paid no attention to me. O povo, usually so subdued into respect, were enjoying themselves thoroughly. They were afraid but they enjoyed their fear. The martyrs lost to the government stimulated the dramatic sense of the people. I walked out to Graça, to the hospital. On the way, three or four funeral street cars passed me, ominous in their transcience, and in front of the large building of bleak windows, was a black enclosed vehicle in which bodies were taken to the morgue.

There was rain in the air. A cool stillness pervaded everything. Under the opaque sky the trees of the gardens scarcely moved. Death was an immanence in my own being. When the shower descended, the threads of rain, nearly invisible, suggested a stiff trembling of the atmosphere. From the iron balustrades of the houses depended crystal globules of coldness. With my umbrella over me, I sat down on a bench from which I could watch the bright twitch of lengthening drops, the frondlike foliage of a tree, bitter green with moisture, giving itself, with a flowing motion, to the almost imperceptible wind.

Somewhere, laughter hoarse with stupidity, bellows, shouts. In the hospital the tinkle of a telephone, thin and shrill, had a white sound of protest, and rang on interminably as if enraged with its littleness.

ESCAPADE

The funeral car, going by again, jerked and swung along the track. Its black was a sealed color into which nothing I imagined penetrated. The motor driver on the front of it looked grotesque. I know and I don't know. Death is like the unknown lover to whom the child, in infancy, is already dedicated.

WE are in a little house in the Sête Portas. I am glad we no longer see any of the English or Americans who regarded us suspiciously. Estephania has come to work for us. She has the yellow face of a skeleton, bleared romantic eyes, a flat nose with enormous nostrils, and pale negroid lips. Her woolly hair is light red. She has a short waist, long helpless arms and hands, pendulant breasts, and sunken buttocks. At work she goes barefoot. Her feet are huge, but the toes are contorted by the pressure of the patent leather slipper in which she walks into the street. In spite of her savage genre, her penchant is for elegance. She has pink and blue blouses, sheath fitting skirts, and large paste pearls like the blisters of a scald which she wears in her ears. She is enchanted with Jackie and calls him alternately her little saint and her prince. Today she told me he resembled the picture of the baby Jesus which she has on her wall above the straw mat where she sleeps. Her grief is that we are not more prosperous. She says that before she came to us she thought all foreigners were rich. She persists in her belief that we are of noble origin and that some picturesque misfortune has brought us to this estate

We have to eat the food of the country but she is "Bahiana" to the finger tips, and her preparation of native dishes is not to be excelled. Vatapá is a mess of fish and corn meal, peppers, cocoa nut, dried shrimps, and palm oil. It seems to me really delicious, but Nannette is always ill when she partakes of it.

Nannette complains less vociferously than she did. She goes about in a kind of hypnotic obliviousness. If she talks at all it is of things that occurred a very long time ago. Her gaunt eyes have a perpetual pale expression of astonishment. She seems relieved when John goes away. When he is about she is silent and her manner is secretive. She is very nervous—pathologically so—and goes into a panic at the least suggestion of an unusual happening. There is no way to discover, without endangering our safety in revealing our whereabouts to others, whether Uncle Alec has lied to us or not. He has almost ceased communicating with us, and the only link with him we have is the address of a postoffice box.

Thank heaven, there is a bare plot of ground around our house and a high wall encloses it, for we almost never go into the street. I have been less well lately and Nannette stays at home because of her shabby shoes. In the afternoon I sit out of doors and look at two royal palm trees on the summit of a red clay hill. Their fronds, whirling against the blue wind-swept sky, are green like swords.

John has brought me a toucan that drags about with a chain on its leg or sits in a huddled plaintive heap at my feet. The toucan has beautiful eyes, soft with anxiety, violet in a pale lemon-yellow setting. The unmanageableness of its huge beak as long as its body aggravates its timidity and it seems continually afraid of being hurt—in spite of the fact that it is tame. It has almost no tail but some dusty red feathers show under the edge of its black coat and its soot-gray vest. It plucks feebly at my ankles, the hem of my dress, the buttons on my shoes; and makes a small whining noise like a child, objecting to my inattentiveness.

DINAH is dead. When I went out to see her today she jumped up and ran forward to meet me. All at once her legs stiffened, she swerved, and described a kind of half circle toward me. Her eyes fixed in glazed appeal. She made two or three circles around me, dragging her paralysed feet, her whole body twitching. Then she fell over on one side and lay there woodenly. In an instant she had stopped breathing. The focus of her gaze disintegrated. A clotted stream of blood trickled from her nostril on which a blue fly had alighted, rubbing its legs. She has left nine puppies to be nursed. I have sewed her into a ragged dress and John has buried her very deep so that nothing can dig her up.

I HAVE a new dog. When I found her she was in a corner of the yard beside the gate. I offered her a bit of bread but she was too weak even to lift her head for it. After long persuasion I got it into her mouth. She felt stronger and followed me on shaking legs. She is so small and thin that I thought at first she was only a puppy, but I see now that her great teeth are worn—those of an old dog—and that her muzzle is gray.

To love something is not to condescend virtuously to another creature but to indulge one's self in luxury. If I could have John and Jackie always I would be satisfied to live without the companionship of any other human beings. My love is a kind of benevolent tyranny and I can indulge it best with pets.

We have two sariemas, beautiful birds with slender exquisite legs. They hold their crested heads high and step with a delicate and fastidious awkwardness. When the mornings are cold and the mist has made them invisible, I hear them on the roof which they have mounted from a shed, and their antiphonal cries are like the cries of wild and rapacious spirits.

I KNOW that really I haven't the least democratic feeling. I treat people of all classes with perfect equality only because I imagine myself so superior to everybody that on my part graciousness is a case of noblesse oblige. Jackie has been quite ill and as no doctor would come to him through the rain—though I sent Estephania after three—and John is out of town, I dressed myself and took him to the hospital to the charity clinic. In a long bare room old women and children, mothers with babies were waiting humbly and patiently in attitudes of dejection. I sat down with them. An interne came in whistling, hesitated, looked at them curiously—me among them—twirled his little mustache, and went out again. I don't know what was happening in the operating room but the old women waited and waited.

The rain was passing and a hot pale glare glossed the walls and floors. The window panes were spaces of burning emptiness against an uncolored sky. Some of the old women sat with their gnarled hands in their soiled laps fondling a rag or handkerchief in which a precious object was enfolded—money perhaps. When-

ever an interne came to the door they glanced at him
furtively, timidly, but their lids immediately drooped.
One old silent woman was crying. Her face was
puckered in a thousand wrinkles and the tears slipping
along them wetted her grotesquely contorted lips. A
mother had a baby with a bandaged head. It fretted
weakly and scratched at her breast with its burrowing
hands. Her face was heavy, stupid, almost expressionless. I was secretly pleased when Jackie screamed,
kicked at me, and threw himself about.

My irritation against my surroundings intoxicated me
with egotism. I got up, walked brazenly out of the
waiting room, and wandered along the corridors until
I found an interne. Then I told him in broken Portuguese that his hospital was disgraceful, that I was a
person accustomed to receiving courtesy, that I had
been waiting there more than an hour, and that I
must have attention at once. If consideration had to
be bought I would pay for it. And I held out to him
twenty milreis which was for the time being all of
the money I had in the world. I was gratifyingly aware
that I talked very loudly and that I stamped my foot.

The interne was first amused, then alarmed. He could
comprehend very little of what, in my excitement, I
said to him, and I don't know yet whether he thought
me a mad woman or a very great lady. At any rate
he went immediately to find a doctor for me, and he
succeeded. The humiliating climax to my grandiose
gesture was the doctor's refusal to take any remuneration. When I went out of the place I was cold and
trembling and my forehead and the backs of my hands
were covered with sweat. What actually frightened me

was that money and money alone could, in the world
at large, command for me respect. I was able to defy
these people only because of having once been on an
equality with them, and with continued poverty my
capacity to do so would be more and more reduced. God
save me from the quiescence of fatigue which enabled
those pauper women to sit there hour after hour!

In the house next us with her daughter and granddaughter lives an old madwoman. The madwoman is
hideous, short, brawny, with uncombed white hair and a
kind of fierce stupidity in her heavy florid face. The
daughter and granddaughter are washerwomen. In the
morning, when they go out to the fountain, they lock the
old woman in the house and we hear nothing all day long
but her shrieks and curses and her assertion that they
are starving her to death. When none of them come
to her she calls her daughter "filha de puta" which is
rather funny as it is really herself whom she is insulting
by the epithet. I have inquired about her of all the
neighbors and am assured that she has enough to eat.

However yesterday it was the screams of the granddaughter that disturbed me, and so unendurably that I
got out of bed and went over to the house to see what
was happening there. The place has one window and
a sagging door on which I knocked. As my solicitation
was ignored I simply walked in without waiting any
longer for a response. The room was very dusty—
dust on the window—dust on the floor in which my
chinellas made an imprint. An old wicker sofa slipped
limply forward on a broken leg. There was no other

furniture. In a heap crouched the granddaughter, fifteen years old, and the mother, a strong black woman, was beating her with a wooden shoe, beating her terrifically. The crazy one, excited by the girl's cries, huddled in a corner crooning to herself, her eyes half closed, an expression of sensual delight on her bold wrinkled old face.

At my outcry the black woman suddenly let her huge hand fall and turned on me a frightened gaze of vindictiveness. "Porque veu aqui? Aqui é a minha casa." I was so angry that I felt happy. I was conscious of a cold strength in all of my body. I told her I would find the police if she dared to strike the girl again.

And I stood there until she had capitulated utterly. I was bold and virtuous, but underneath a little sick from the hideous scene I had witnessed which I thought I should never be able to forget. The black woman never for one moment realized her cruelty. Because she was poor and I was a senhora delicada she was afraid of me. Poor people are accustomed to be dictated to and they are afraid of everything. They understand their sin—the sin of failure, and that the world is always against them without regard to the justice of their case.

Opposite us live a man, his wife, and two small children, and the man has the habit of beating his mulher so severely that she is frequently confined to her bed for several days on account of it. I shall interfere with them also and the atmosphere will be identical.

Estephania shrugs her rugged shoulders and says, "E como Deus quizer." It is as God wishes.

ESCAPADE

First Estephania was ill, then I fell ill of over-exertion as is always the case. I can't, when I am at my worst, so much as lift my arms above my head without feeling as if their weight were dragging something out of me, and without succumbing to severe pains through my navel to which the ligaments inside seem secured by arrows. Later I am violently nervous and my whole organism is disturbed. I think illness is disgusting. I feel as if we were all killing John, smothering him with our dependence. And my love for Jackie, like all maternal love I imagine, resembles a fatal disease. Because I know myself physically helpless in a crisis I am always anticipating one. I feel as if I were being consumed by my child's remorseless weakness and, without being able to behave otherwise, I realize the morbid completeness with which I abandon myself to his most trivial desires. Maternity provides an irresponsible condition. The mother, the individual, has no longer to decide what is best for her in life. Instinct indisputably arranges her existence.

Yet I long for another child more than for anything on earth. I can't understand myself. It is like longing for annihilation. And it is not the ideal conception of a child which appeals to me but the sensual experience, the feel of weak hands upon me, of eager lips at my breast.

Jackie is ill with croup, and Nannette is ill also. We have only one bed and, because the position assumed in a hammock gives me great pain, I need to sleep comfortably. Nannette in her bare room with the hammock humiliates me indescribably. If I could only

supply her with luxuries I should not need to carry so
continually the burden of her unhappiness. Then I
would not be obliged to think of her so often and to see
always before me her vague startled eyes, her blank
brow, her drawn bewildered mouth.

I telegraphed for John.

It took John three days to return to us, and when he
arrived he was broken with anxiety. John is rather tall
with a beautifully shaped head and a well-made slender
body. He has fine eyes, deep-set blue gray and a still
look of determination. His nose is large, well-modeled,
and his mouth is sensitive and rather small. He man-
ages always to convey the impression of imperviousness.
But on this occasion he looked almost old. When he
greeted me his lips trembled slightly and his voice shook.
Bahia is undergoing a double epidemic of yellow fever
and bubonic plague and in spite of the care with which
my telegram was worded it frightened him very much.
He says that he is going to pieces nervously, that he can
not endure leaving me any more. He wants to resign
from the Company, draw out our guarantee fund, buy
some government land he has seen and stock it with
sheep. He would need to pay only for the measuring
of the land and the purchase could be completed within
five years. He will begin by asking a leave of absence
on account of my health and in that way he can keep
his salary until we have moved and are actually in the
vicinity of the ranch.

At carnival I was feeling better and went out with
Estephania, Jackie and Nannette to see the maskers in

the streets. There are yellow fever quarantines on all sides. A street car decorated with butterflies went by us and a moment later the huge bargelike conveyance in which the dead are taken to the Campo Santo. One of the men in John's office was buried yesterday having been ill altogether less than a week. And the devastations of the plague are really terrific. I am afraid of the rats that prowl about the yard and upset the slop pails even in the daytime. I think all of us are afraid— not of any particular thing but of our physical weakness, of life, of our inability to cope with it. Nannette is afraid, I am afraid, and John is afraid of our fear. If John fell ill that would be the end, for we have no one to turn to—not a friend on earth. The people we knew at home have already forgotten us. Though I realize that I could not endure submission, I understand very well why people refuse to rebel against the machine. Now that we have attempted to build our own world nothing is left which we can cling to with any sense of permanence, nothing but our love for each other. I am astonished by the human beings among whom we live— the prostitutes, the old man who plays a French horn for a living, the little boys with dull satisfied faces and ragged clothes * * * the matrons, large and passive, who leave readjustments to others. Life spewed everywhere and in everything the immanence of death.

Three little men in uniform, a workman accompanying with a ladder, come to our house and peer into all our concerns: into the water jars, into the toilet, into the bath house where Estephania washes clothes. They want to see if we have any receptacle that is breeding

mosquitos, and in the ditch below our walls the wiggle-
tails propagate undisturbed.

I AM so tired, so tired. Fatigue is like an appetite, a
rapacious possession. I have nothing to give to it.
The yellow fever is next door and across the street.
The granddaughter of the madwoman has died of it.
Estephania is not perturbed. She lost a brother and a
sister through it. But it is all "como Deus quizer." She
does not believe in our precautions. With her huge
bony hands she tells her beads reverently and is in
perfect peace. And John has the plague on either side
of him. In the two buildings adjoining the office of the
Company they have been carrying out bodies at night.

For myself I am too ill to care, but I stimulate my
own anxiety in order to ease my conscience in regard
to Jack. Sometimes when I am utterly exhausted I
find myself with a terrible hatred of everything dear
to me, of everything I am obliged to love.

PART V

A DULL day. The train is crowded with country people: women with babies, men in tight cotton pants, celluloid collars, and little straw hats. The men are small, dark-skinned, and have silky mustaches. All the married women wear negligée, even on a journey, and do not trouble themselves with hats. The window glasses are dirty, smeared, and have a bluish look, and smoke and sand, drifting through the open doors at either end of the car, cover all the agitated people as with an opaque silence. The train moves very slowly, rattles, jerks, rattles.

When we cross the Ribeira at Itapagipe we can see the bay. The wind, dragging in its hot monotonous passage, shakes the glass slightly. A newspaper blows from a man's hand. The woodwork creaks. The shore line is covered with a scrub growth of flying green, and trees with exposed roots like talons, sink themselves into the dun-lilac rocks. The white clouds, descending soddenly on the horizon, are huge damp masses of inflated cotton. Almost imperceptibly diffusing in the bluish-purple atmosphere, they are as if motionless. In the hollow of the swell the bottle-green water, glossed with reflections, shows the light of a fire on a distant silvered expanse. White caps continually uncurl and, spreading fluted crests for an instant, widen with an inward heaviness. Very far off the open sea looks like a flaked river of turquoise marble moving across the world in an undeviating current.

Later the water fades out and the landscape becomes bleak and abandoned with almost the character of a desert. And at night the train halts in a vast clearing. Visible through the transparent twilight are the station house and one large barnlike structure marked Hotel.

WE spend the night at the Hotel. Many of the passengers, unknown to one another, are crowded in the same rooms but because we are estrangeiros the proprietor concedes us greater delicacy. Estephania sleeps in a hallway but John and I occupy a bedchamber with Jackie and Nannette. There is only one sheet on each bed and we have a cotton blanket apiece. We are very cold. We hear one another stirring in the heavy darkness. The air has a sharp smell of drenched grass, of flowers and dew, a thin atmosphere of all that is remote. The bedbugs will not allow us to rest. Through the fragile partitions we hear yells, songs, groans, and coughs. An old man has a nightmare and cries out suddenly in a horrible voice. The sounds suggest the cattle cars on the siding of a railway at home where I passed the night in a Pullman berth. With dull panic I realize that the exertion of the journey is going to prove too much for me, that I already have twinges of pain which can be expected to develop into something worse. John has given me wine to drink and my mind feels thick with excitement. I am annoyed by my own stupid aliveness, by a brightness of being that blankly illumines the hours.

ESCAPADE

At four o'clock in the morning the train whistle blows outside our windows, a signal for us to rise. We get up and clothe ourselves. Our limbs are weighted and numb. Jackie is drunk with fatigue and, his eyes tight shut, allows himself to be dressed. While the train is waiting for us we go into a vast room furnished with bare tables and benches and have some hot coffee and some pão de ló.

The sun has not yet risen. Gold clouds in a palely lighted sky suggest a frozen storm. The moon, transparently dissolving, is a sliver of ice. Slow-rocking half wheel of moon sags, dims—dim and mellow in dim sky. Roosters are crowing. In the distance a dog barks. Still we can see no houses. Only low hills covered with brush, a few paths disappearing nowhere, and a small boy, half naked, driving some gray humped cattle into a field. The moon drifts torpidly, drags earth, drags sky in its torpidness.

In the gray quiet the passengers climb back into the coach, sink wearily into their seats. Then all at once the sun bursts the horizon and shatters cold pure rays against the windows. The whole car is filled with an orange light so that even the faces and hands of the people are tinged with it.

If I could only abandon myself to pain, but the car, with its insistent rattle and swaying motion, is a counter irritant. I am jerked this way and that, between something inside me that numbs my legs and makes my spine throb, and that torturing uncertainty of the train which jolts me continually about. The benches are of cane, very narrow and upright, and there is no possible way of lying down on them. When I feel myself about to vomit and go back to the toilet room, I find that the country passengers, unaccustomed to convenience, have left on the floor a lake of filth that slops over my feet and darkens the edge of my dress. * * *

Back and forth the car sways. Back and forth pain drags me with it. Outside there is nothing to be seen but desert—endless unbroken desert. The cacti are as tall as trees and their spiney arms are outstretched in rigid attitudes of torture. The sky is granite blue, and the landscape, the inside of the car, every object on which the eye turns, send back with merciless clarity the reflection of the light. The faces of the men and women, pale with brightness, are dripping with sweat. Jackie frets weakly. Nannette complains of being faint and pulls at her veil with trembling hands. In Estephania alone the stimulus of drama has survived. She has on her pearl earrings and a shrill pink blouse and she sits bolt upright, preserving her dignity in the new experience.

Except for the Itapicarú River, at Santa Luzia, there has been no relief from the parched scenery, the wide horrible silence of a country without any animal life. True, these are cattle lands and occasionally a steer breaks through the bushes near us. We see horns wide as antlers, a moist black muzzle, and soft alarmed eyes.

There are a few small villages where the train waits for a minute or two: some plaster and adobe vendas, mud and wattle houses, a street in which pigs run and children, the color of the soil, wallow nakedly amidst the blanched refuse that gives out a sour hot stench. At

ESCAPADE

one place an old woman whose features have been entirely consumed by syphilis thrusts forth a palsied interrogative palm and makes a hissing noise, attracting our attention to her plea for alms. A little girl in a ragged chemise has tangled black hair, rust-burnt by the sun, and large dark eyes vacant with astonishment. John buys some hot goat's milk from her, and she runs along by the already moving train, reaching frantically for the two-hundred-reis piece that he is holding out.

IN the afternoon John requested the train guard to allow me to go back to the caboose where the benches ran the length of the car, and I could stretch myself out. The boards were cushionless and unyielding. In a torrent of quivering fixity the rayless sunlight poured through the uncurtained windows. The toilet for the trainmen was close to my head and the door, without a lock, kept opening and swinging back. The car, brilliant with motes and dancing light, held closely the foetid odors * * * from this room mixed with stale smoke. I tried without success to lift up one of the glasses. I wanted to throw myself out. But when I looked backward at the gliding track glittering with salty sand crystals and at the endless glassy landscape over which the purple shadow of a cloud moved like a shadow over a sterile sea, I was more frightened of what I saw than of the pain I felt.

At seven o'clock in the evening we arrived at Villa Nova da Rainha. White houses, low and vague. On the only height, a cold white church. In the distance roads winding and a great isolated peak growing purple in the dusk.

ESCAPADE

WHILE John was in the mountains measuring our land, Nannette, Estephania, Jackie, and myself, lived in a small dirty house that belonged to the telegraphista. Only two of the rooms had windows, but the doors at the back opened into a small overgrown garden with a high mold-green wall around it. I felt lonely, separated from everything, like a sword pointing up, as if, in the pain of isolation, I were piercing heaven, piercing the world. For some reason I imagined John had gone away from me forever, that he would never come back. I could, for the first time, see him whole, like an immortal, unbroken by words. Unable to send a message to me, he was gone three weeks. His silence seemed to me beautiful, finished, but I wanted him again. I wanted to destroy his perfection with intimacy.

Coming up to Villa Nova my finch died in the baggage car. Grind, grind, the noise of the wheels. The shadows must have swayed with the swaying of the monotonous wings that struck the cage bars. Back and forth across the cage the little wings struck the bars to find a way into the dark, away from the lamps, the noise, the light. And when he was brought to me his feathers were loose, white like the hair of the aged, and his claws contracted, gripping the emptiness.

It rains continually. From my windows I see the big peak starting up sharply from the whiteness of the mist. In the heaviness of the rain the wind is not wind at all but an enormous movement of the stillness. The whole landscape lifts itself quietly and there is a perpetual rush of small cataracts sweeping before us down the sandy street.

In the damp, chill weather the young girls wrap them-

selves in shawls. Some of the girls are very lovely, barefoot, water jars or kerosene tins carried levelly and
proudly upon their shrouded heads. Their ivory faces
are obscure—dark unconscious eyes, glances timid and
defiant.

One morning a missionary from the United States
came in to call on us. He has been stationed here at
times and, passing through, he heard that there were
foreigners in the place. He was a gentle, nervous little
man with an intense gaze and, at the same time, a great
diffidence. He was very curious to know why we had
come up here. I lied to him, spoke of John's leave of
absence from the Company and about my health. The
doctors said that the high altitude would be good for me.
Mr. MacGregor watched me. He had a frightened
interest in all I told him. Fortunately, he was leaving
the town immediately for a long inland trip. He
promised to come back. I knew he was puzzled by the
appearance of the room in which I received him. It was
almost unfurnished, though John had improvised some
necessary articles from kerosene cases.

JOHN is satisfied with the land he has measured, six
hundred acres. There is water on it—the head of the
Itapicarú River—pasture land, and wood. A negro
man who will work on shares with him is going to help
him build a mud and wattle hut. The railway is just
now being extended to Lamarão and if we can go to
that village with John he thinks he can find a place for
us to live until we have shelter at the ranch. The fore-
man of the gang that is making the road told John we

could go up on a switch engine and flat car with which
supplies were being moved.

I HAVE seen a bridal procession. The little girl could
not have been more than fifteen years old. She had
large unconscious eyes, sombrely lustrous and full of
fright. Her skin was pale gold, as if from somewhere
it had caught an amber reflection. She wore a white
dress, very short in the waist and full in the skirt, and a
sleazy limp pink sash. Her hair, combed close to her
head, was oiled until it appeared varnished, and in the
knot at the back she had placed a small red rose. Her
slight bony hand rested heavily and unsteadily on the
sleeve of her husband's coat.

He was being very polite to her, for, though the sun
was coming out, he held over her head a torn umbrella
that had some protruding spokes. About fifty-five years
old, he was attired in an ancient green-black Sunday
suit, but not even in deference to the occasion had he
removed the grizzled stubble on his chin. He walked
ponderously and loosely. I noticed his sagging cheek
and his coarsened wrinkled neck.

The old woman—the mother-in-law—her feet dragging in chinellas that were almost soleless, her dressing
jacket of calico clean and very faded, followed comfortably behind, her rugged cunning old face expressing
completely her satisfaction in what she had just accom-
plished. With quizzical eyes, she watched the bride, her
daughter, and the new-made husband, and every now and
then, removing her pipe from her lips with a gesture of
indolence, she spat. Two little boys, encountering her,
raised their left hands, palms facing, and asked for her

blessing, and almost as if she were the Pope she replied to them, "Deus lhe abençoe, os meus filhos. Deus lhe mande saude e felicidade."

NANNETTE, Estephania, Jackie, and myself sat on some chairs placed on the flat car. With me I had Sally, the dog, the toucan, and some parrakeets. The few articles of furniture we owned were piled up behind us and John kept hold of the heap to prevent it from falling. A strange negress in a wide skirt and a shawl was our accidental traveling companion and she sat on a little trunk at our feet. The landscape was a sea of darkness, impenetrable, over which the moonlight flowed silken in an arrested torrent. The grass and the bushes, faintly silvered, quivered fixedly with the silence of the wind. Without ever coming any nearer, the mountains approached us continually, an encroaching heaviness.

Once or twice the engine slowed down and the train crew, descending, went off into the bushes for purposes to be guessed. The engine gave out long thin whistles, piercing and shrill, and the glassy echoes were thrown back to us. Sally, trembling with excitement, began to bark and strain at her rope. When she found it impossible to escape, she pressed her belly to the floor of the car and a moist shadow spread darkly around the old black woman's feet. I was touched by the old woman's humanity. "We have all been in tight places," she said.

Through the main street of Lamarão the train went undeviatingly. White huts, tightly closed, not a ray of light through the cracks, through the blank faces of the massive wooden blinds. The thatched roofs reflected the moonlight with a lilac tinge. And across the white sand the bluish shadows were finally and terribly marked. A donkey, grazing on the track, leaped aside before us with a clatter of hoofs amidst dislodged stones. He was a small shadow galloping away through the palpable quiet. A flat rattle as of jangling metal; the train came to a standstill. The voices of the men were loud and sonorous, awful voices breaking on a sleep. Though they were so close they came over the mountains from infinite distance. The voices hung and floated like floating stones, ponderable in the diaphanous stillness. We were cold, very cold. Our numbed legs scarcely enabled us to alight. Jackie had an old blanket wrapped around him and Estephania held him close in her ape-like arms. All at once the parrakeets began to shriek. Their small harsh cries excited us vaguely. The toucan, as he allowed me to take him up, gave a subdued whine and stirred his feathers. From the frozen-looking earth the milky fog floated under our feet and made translucent spirals above the icy grass that the dew had drenched. The water of a brook, shrunken with light, showed a surface harsh as tin. Near shore silver-gilt blobs palpitated—darkness throbbed. Wonderful inflated moon bore down, low with light.

ONE of the train men went with us to a small house —of the few in the place that had tiles on the roof— and knocked heavily for a long time without getting a response. The door vibrated to the blows, but when the sound died away dully the chill lifelessness of the atmosphere seemed more pronounced. Finally a sleepy voice asked who we were. There was the scraping noise of a match, a hiss, a sputter, and the glow of a candle flame showed through a crack. It seems that Senhor Alberto, the proprietor of the "hotel," has political enemies who are threatening to kill him and he is very careful to whom he opens his door.

We were admitted to a kind of barroom. Senhor Alberto was suspicious of us and greeted us with dry politeness. There were no sleeping rooms in the hotel so we passed the night stretched on some benches in the long sala where the visitors eat. Of course, we had no privacy. When we waked in the morning, before we had even risen from bed, we found children, a few men and some bold-looking women who had come to stare at us.

Nannette was ill with dysentery, brought on by weakness and bad food, and she was ready to cry with the humiliation of having to attend to all of her wants under the eyes of people she had never seen before. The latrina was a hole in the ground with a barricade of straw about it.

John had some difficulty in securing a house for us, but at last he has found one, a tumble-down dwelling almost a mile from the hotel at the very end of the street. The gossip is that we are rich people who have come up here to buy land and improve the country, and our half a dozen pieces of machine-made furniture have excited a great deal of comment. We are really very poor, for our entire capital of seven hundred dollars will be used up in planting the land and in buying sheep, and we shall have nothing to depend on until our investment brings some return.

This house has floors of natural clayey soil, the tiles

are cracked so that the rain drips through, and we have nothing to cook in but a pot suspended over a heap of sticks. Thank heaven for Estephania, whose devotion to Jackie has brought her to a place like this!

DONA ISAURA, my neighbor, coarse and big with stupid antagonistic eyes and dark red cheeks, came today to sell me a turkey. She asked too much for it and I refused, though John has advised me to purchase a little poultry to take up in the mountains to supply food for Jack. Dona Isaura was quite drunk, staggering slightly, and nervously drawing her shawl across her breast. She talked loudly and insolently and, with an uplifted fist, advanced toward me. Before anything serious occurred, Estephania interfered. Estephania calls these people "taborel," considers them foreigners, and is always disturbing them by references to the elegance of the city. All of the women here drink heavily. In fact, they drink most of the time. I am annoyed by peering drunken people coming to the door and looking in and sometimes lying there until they fall asleep. At night they dance in the street. The bean rattle and the accordion are kept going until nearly dawn. The men beat the women, who fight and screech terribly and the pandemonium in the distance is nearly continuous.

None of the women I have talked to know either how to read or to write. They are strong and ugly, with bold eyes, coarse features, and discolored teeth. A great many of the very young women are toothless already. Some of them have syphilis, and their only remedy for all their ills is the herb tea which they drink.

ESCAPADE

WE have been here a month. John goes up the mountain once more on Monday, and on Saturday night he comes back. Our shack is built and some of the clearing is done. He is exhausted by the unusual manual labor, but he keeps telling me that he doesn't mind it, that soon we will be together *all the time,* which is certainly what we most desire in the world. We will live somehow until the war is over and then perhaps we can get back to the coast and, without a passport, return to the States. I will be glad to leave here. The people are hostile to us because they are afraid. We are the first foreign women they have ever seen. They don't understand us. They ask us every variety of question, and as the doors have no locks we can't keep them out. They even come inside and watch us dress. Yesterday some boys began to throw stones at the house, but when I went out as if I didn't care and spoke crossly to them they ran away and hid. Nannette has the wildest theories as to what will be done to us. There is a feira every Monday and at the last one two men, crazy with cachaça, stabbed each other. She considers that a portent of our future. I confess it is the drunkenness that frightens me the most.

Estephania walks a long way to a spring to get our water which she brings in a jar on her head, so it is very precious and we have almost to dispense with washing ourselves. She cooks our meals in a little dark corner of a room under the eaves, and when I go in there I see hot sticks glowing on the floor and find the atmosphere so heavy with smoke that breathing is difficult. Estephania, with a cloth draped over her head, squats down beside the panella, stirring its contents with a wooden spoon. She looks like a witch.

ESCAPADE

The heat in the daytime is terrific, the landscape all about here uninteresting and dry. But the big still mountains are magnificently irrelevant. They are like the gates to the garden of paradise. I feel already as if they were between us and escape. I wonder if anywhere in the world there are people who understand us, whose language we speak.

AT night the tin lamp casts a wavering rust-red glare on the white walls. In the unceiled tiles above us we can hear the squealing of rats and the quick patter of their feet. Jackie is in bed. We are very still. Nannette has lain down in the hammock with her clothes on. The light is on her faintly. Her face looks gaunt, hollow, awfully asleep. I remember when Nannette wore gray and lilac frocks, violets, and her feet were small to me unbelievably. Nannette coming out of the cold—the way her fur coat smelled and the veil on her face, a kind of dry sweetness, powder and wood-violet perfume. I hear footsteps, muffled in the dust of the road. Footsteps. Quiet. The door, divided in the middle to swing outward like a window, leans crookedly on its rusty hinges. In the crack between the upper and lower segments, eyes. Eyes gaze at me steadily, eyes encircled by pale yellow flesh. I force myself to look squarely at the eyes and the eyes, unwinking, gaze back. Eyes— vision in which the hostile darkness concentrates itself.

I wanted to cry out, but I only sat there, listening to Nannette's heavy breathing. She slept like an old woman, abandoned, her mouth wide open, loose and helpless. In the room behind me Estephania was sleeping also. To get away from the eyes, to pretend I did

175

not see them, I walked very slowly over the dirt floor. I walked into the room where Estephania was. I wanted my feet to make a noise, a sound more substantial than a look. But I was gentle like a shadow and could only imagine an echo of the movement I could not hear. The rats had climbed on the crib and were dragging away at Jackie's sheet. At my entrance they scattered. I saw them glide into the corners and observed the rigid attentive quiver of disappearing tails. Even the blind tails were conscious of my approach. There were more eyes, rat eyes, spying on me from the roof, eyes filled with a bright stillness. The screech of the rats was the screech of silence because it said nothing—nothing to me who wanted a word so much.

I went back into the front room and sat down again. The peerer outside must have gone on, for in the crack of the door there was only a vacant line of blackness. I sat very straight in the only chair. The lamp flame flared and my hands in my lap were greenish orange. They were heavy with the strange smoky light that crept over them. They were asleep. My whole body was asleep. But my eyes refused to close themselves. My eyes were stone-wide, like the eyes of a dead woman. Nothing could shake my unbroken gaze, colder and more enduring than the quiet and the night. I saw everything.

Wind sucked dryly at the stiff grass that grew about the house. I felt the mountains that surrounded us. I knew them invisibly, blacker than blackness. I went to sleep.

When I roused I realized that something smooth and white like a blade had slipped under the doorway and lay along the floor, something cold and piercing slipped into me. Needles of glass penetrated the cracks in the massive blinds, needles of emptiness. I got up, threw back the shutters, and, through the window space, saw the long road, the smoke that came from a fire in front of a group of huts.

The sky sent its colorlessness into the bleached thatch of huddled roofs, and they radiated a glistening pallor. The trees, black, shuddering, detached from the sky, were clouds of polished darkness blown upward from the vague earth. As the sun rose behind the heavy edges of the mountains, an acrid smell of damp dust blew in my face, a warm smell, harbinger already of the heat and miseries of the day.

ON Thursday, the thirty-first of August, nineteen· sixteen, we made our momentous journey to the ranch. We were ready to leave at seven o'clock in the morning, with seven animals and ten men. Half the village witnessed our departure, and when I unbuttoned my old divided riding skirt and threw back the front panel a murmur of shocked astonishment passed along the group of shawled women and barefooted men. Nannette, on a man's saddle, was mounted sidewise on the mare, Boneca. John and Estephania came on foot. Jackie went part of the way on the shoulders of Cecilio Gomes, but at last became frightened of the half-naked man with the wide black beard, and John had to carry his child the remainder of the distance. We had a bed, Jackie's crib, a native cot, a sewing machine, a table, a camp chair, a few pots and pans, some parcels of clothing, and a dozen books. Our trunks were left

behind, for the way was steep and narrow, the journey
long, and the animals could not be heavily loaded.

As I rode, I awaited the pain that took possession of
me whenever I exerted myself. But I felt no pain. I
was held against the bright wideness of the sky, against
the spread-out fields covered with flowers. Nannette,
afraid of falling from her horse, clutched at its mane.
I could see her tense hands, her slightly distorted fingers,
the skin to which ill-health had given the mottled appearance of age. I wondered if, nowadays, Nannette ever
thought, if she had any idea what was happening to us.
She wore an old panama hat, tied with a black ribbon
under her chin. Her chin quivered. Her anxious eyes
had a blind expression.

The mountains went straight up before us like a wall.
No path was visible and, for our guidance, we depended
on the sure feet of the pack mules who walked in front.
When we lifted our gaze a wild sky of blue iron oppressed us with its weight. Jackie, utterly panic-stricken
by the strangeness of his surroundings, began to shriek.
His thin little cry ran sharply through the vast lighted
quiet in which the voices of the chattering mule drivers
were murmurous and dull. "Jackie," I called, "Jackie,
don't be afraid. Here are father and mother and Nannette, and isn't it fun to climb a mountain?" But Jackie
drowned my voice with his own screams and John had to
go back and take him up. I looked down, down, upon
one mountain falling away from another, to the bluish
desert over which transparent plum-red shadows floated
with huge outstretched wings. John ran up a gentler
declivity and, panting beside me, asked me if I felt very
tired. He was bareheaded, coatless, and to save his only

shoes he had strung them on their laces around his neck. He seemed cheerful, elated almost, but his eyes, as if concealed from himself, had a sharp worried glint. His forehead was branded with sunburn and glossy with sweat. In spite of his graying hair, he was strong and determinedly young. I liked his bare arms and his strong small hands grasping Jackie's waist. As he went on I gazed after him from the great distance of my excitement.

On, and on. John now far ahead. At the tiptop of a mountain a high plateau laid back the rocks. The grass, choked with the red of flowers, grew as in a meadow, and bent ever so softly with the heaviness of the light. Down one side of the plain ran a crumbling stone wall that marked off land which had once belonged to a priest. Cows grazing behind it were warm and quiet also. They lifted slow heads and moist black nostrils dilated with inquiry. I tried, out of my giddiness, to make my mind reach back to them.

I saw a white eagle on a boulder. Its eyes stared without recognition at the moving objects that approached. It was very still. When it rose leadenly and wheeled above me the sky was pale with feathers and I felt suffocated by the sound of wings beating the air thickly—or perhaps it was the sound of my own heart beating thick. I could no longer make out John. Nannette and Estephania were behind us, small creeping things half lost in waving foliage, in the precipitation of a great depth. I was too much alive. There was too much light about me, too much space. I longed for the definiteness of pain to draw me again into a world of littleness.

PART VI

THE sun was yet high when we arrived at the ranch. I looked about me at the circle of mountain peaks: one, to the left, had a delicate conical shape like some virginal breasts I had seen: the other, the largest, curving itself in a vast low line, invited to repose. I thought that the most magnificent appeared comfortingly maternal.

The hut which John had built seemed enormous. Really there were two huts joined together over a roofed-in space between. The palm thatch was green and fresh—green bronze—and its stiff spikes shook gently in the bigness of the wind. I had never known a wind that came carrying with it such an atmosphere of distance, big wind with a wide sound, endless, swift. With its intensity the wind darkened the sky. Its sound was dark blue like stiff water. It came from the very edge of the world, dragging the mountains with it, and the mountains were more terrible than the wind. The mountains were the world falling down over us, crushing us under their weight. Quickly and slowly the mountains revolved. The mountains were the earth.

The sun began to set. The long light rushed over the bending grass tops and stained their edges with the pallor of agitation. The light and the wind ran together under the grass. I could see the pass where the trail descended. Nannette on Boneca. The gray mare seemed to be walking like a fly on a perfectly vertical plane. Nannette's calico dress made a bright moving spot, like a moving fire among the lilac-colored rocks. When she came up to us, Senhor Januario, squatting on his hams in front of the earthen pot of beans, was ladling food into our tin plates. His long thin hand, brown and sensitive as a monkey's, withdrew from the fire.

Nannette slid awkwardly from the horse. Her hands trembled with fatigue, and on her blank quivering upper lip I could see little beads of sweat. "I thought I would never get here! Up hill and down dale! Did you ever see such a path! I thought every moment that I was going to be killed."

Helpless. Nannette helpless. "Isn't it a beautiful place, Nannette?" Staring all about her, she said yes. She had a pleasant voice with a light timbre and her enunciation was careful, ladylike. Her pale, disturbed gaze, like the eagle's, traveled over the landscape without recognizing anything. Her gaze was lost in the wind that shook out her skirts, wind that was already darkening the valley. Twisted mangaba trees pull against themselves, disappearing sun lost in their faded leaves. All lost. The emptiness was too quick for any of us to keep pace with it.

When Nannette learned that John and old Januario had built the house she was duly astonished. I walked inside with her, into the dim interior sprinkled with the sky that came through the palm thatch, with the vaguer whiteness that entered through chinks in the mud and wattle walls. She turned to me and her eyes—always wide now—widened a little more, and her pupils were dark like those of an animal responding without consciousness to an instinct of terror. "How do you suppose

181

we will get on without any windows?" I told her that
some day when we had money enough John was going
to cut some spaces in the walls and bring up a few
pieces of glass from Villa Nova. Nannette was excited
by the suggestion—pleased almost. The wind of iron and
glass, in a perpetual agony, drew itself toward us. It
was a beautiful twilight. Through the doorway were
stars and the placidity of the mounting slopes.

On the second day after my ride I went to bed again.
And I had to lie quietly. I wanted to move softly in
the depths of my being so as not to awaken the pain that
would master me. Secretly, when I was not disturbing
it, I was able to enjoy an unusual amount of freedom.
My mind, for instance, ran up and down the four mud
walls that surrounded me. My mind investigated all the
little crevices, the pale stars of light that scintillated in
the cracks made by the drying of the earth, the interstices
of the roof where, through the thatch, there were spots
so brilliant that they burst against my vision like an
explosion of diminutive rockets. I enjoyed the feeling
of being enclosed by this dim quietude, and defying
the daylight, the wind, the tide of sunshine that was
beating against everything outside.

To be truly ill and helpless permits one an escape
from the limitations of material existence. I could lie
here safe in myself, in a universe on which nothing
impinged. Time disappeared. And this was not only
because John's watch was gone and all of the business
of making a ranch out of the materials which Nature
offered crudely had to be conducted according to the
ritual of the heavenly cycle. I felt as I lay there that

life indeed was endless. My heart was still, was a grave. The hastening feet were rushing to destruction. There was quiet under sound. There was a star, and a star, and another star beyond that. There was my face and there were a trillion trillion faces unseen. Whiteness—nothing.

And the strange thing was that, without any stimulation from the contact of other being, I was conscious of a peculiar sentience. Somehow, out of emptiness—out of darkness—I had a tactile feeling of warmth, of the warmth of my own being which surrounded me, and I lay in myself, sleeping while I was awake.

JACKIE comes in. He is two years old. He wears a ragged little dress. In the dimness I can just see his face as he stumbles along the uneven surface of the floor on which some tiny hillocks of drying grass have been left. When he runs toward me his arms make a gesture of flight. Jackie says, "Mala, I am plantin' sour. É bonita, não é?" And I examine the bits of stone he holds in his tightened fists and wonder what "sour" is. "Sim, Jackie, é bonitissima. É com isso que vae fazer jardim, meu bem querido?" Oh, Jackie, Jackie, I love you! I draw him to me. A vague unpleasant excitement stirs me and warns me that I do not belong to myself, that my pain is jealous—jealous of Jackie, jealous of John. I drag myself up, support myself on my elbow, and hold Jackie closer. He struggles instinctively against the too-much feeling I have for him. "Oh, Jackie, Jackie, forgive me!" I want to apologize to Jackie because I have brought him into a merciless world against which I am helpless to protect him. I pity myself and am conscious of a degradation in such pity. My pride struggles. In order to make my helplessness bearable I convert all of this confusion of sentiment into hatred of a society which has brought us to such a pass.

But I also hate my body, which I cannot control, hate it because it cannot rebel utterly. There is a time when pain is everything, when it has taken me so completely that I have not any longer the knowing of consciousness, and I think more than anything of being left alone, of peace, of a kind of extinct quietness. I do not wish to know any longer. I know too much already, and I am burdened with understanding a world which is mine only. I cannot draw into this horror those whom I love who have already too little happiness. But I wonder how it is possible to go on forever carrying with me an unshared experience, the most profound that I have ever met.

The worst of it is that my body, which has betrayed me, also obliges me to exert myself in its behalf, and as there are no toilet facilities other than a large tin bucket, I have to drag myself to it. Then I understand that I am really not alive at all, that I am already dead, and what remains in the place of my will is a kind of ghost of sensation, disintegrated and moveless. My thoughts are torn from me by little fingers that dig deep, deep into my mind, into the regions of me most obscure to myself.

Sometimes these terrible legs that hang inertly to my body grow very heavy—so heavy that they bear me down with their weight and become intolerable to me. Then John has to arrange rags, sacks, all kinds of objects so as to form an elevation to hold them up. I want to forget about them, and I can do so only when I lie in this position with my arms pressed rigidly to my sides. And for hours I lie there perfectly motionless. I do not even dare to take a sip of water or to turn sidewise. I see the little stars in the room dim now—almost extinguished. And John's face far away, receding. I am losing him. Losing the suffering of sympathy he offers, which seems to me, at this moment, the most beautiful thing on earth.

Nannette comes in. She is excited and querulous. After all I am not too ill to fail in a cognizance of her fluttering gestures, her desire, not to help me but to do something which will be recognized as kind, which will relieve her of the obligation to my weakness. In our poverty and misery she, too, is suffering, but she has no awareness of her own misery, no perception of any outward significance. She simply cannot understand how a person born to the luxury, to which, in her youth, she was accustomed, has come to a pass like this. For the solution of concrete problems she has always depended on other people. She thinks that everything which is wrong with us now can be righted by John. In a sense her faith in John is greater than mine, for she believes him capable of the miraculous. "Are you suffering a great deal?" she asks me. "Oh, it wrings my heart to see you like this! Surely there is something John can do to relieve you. If we only had a hot-water bag. Perhaps Estephania can heat a bag of salt. Have you eaten anything today? It is so weakening not to eat." And when John tells her that the best she can do for me is to leave me alone, she gives him a reproachful glance and goes out in utter perplexity, as if something she could not comprehend had frightened her very much.

ESCAPADE

John is so strong that even pain fades under his touch. The little creeping fingers of the other one withdraw themselves and linger only half perceived in my belly and legs.

A LONG centipede striped with coral and black is crawling in and out through the tattered strips of palm branch. He undulates like a snake, and I wonder for a moment if that is what he is. I have always been terrified of these insects, and I wonder why it is that I am no longer afraid of them. I had rather lie here without moving than object to all the centipedes on earth.

I love the rich purplish color of the floor where a sun spot moves on it. I lie here. I am better today. I have had my dinner of our unvarying food, boiled red beans and mandioc mush, with a red pepper to make it tolerable and large crystals of salt like gray-white rock. How warm and comforting food is. How entirely worth while to live to be able to eat. Life seems to me so sweet, so precious, that I wonder that everyone is not kind like John. When there is this awful impersonal Enemy to fight why are not people gentle to each other? Why do they not always stand together protecting themselves against it? I feel that I ought to warn them, to tell them of the danger they are in. It is, almost, that I have a mission to the race. I must make others realize what I alone seem to know, that all of us are subject to the obscure attacks of misfortune, that we have nothing to waste in unnecessary struggles which we ourselves precipitate. But, of course, I only mean that I want people to accept my view of life, my way of looking at marriage and at everything else. I have no wish to force myself on the world, but I want at least a tolerance which will allow me to exist. And at home John and I are actually considered dangerous. Do you not see how pitiful we are? I want to say. But in this also they will misunderstand me, for I love myself entirely, completely, and I will not accept from them any criticism of my acts.

I think sometimes that my pride is as strong as my pain—not quite, perhaps, but very nearly so. If I were the only one made to suffer I should accept everything out of pure defiance. It is through John and Jack that my self-respect can be subjugated. My pride affects me as an exaggeration of myself. Protest expands all of my being. My self-righteousness is much more intense than anything which I can intellectually define or encompass. Because I alone of all the world can understand and pity myself, I am God. I alone of all the world can offer equality to myself.

IT takes very little to make me happy; an hour or two which belong to me, in which my body is quiescent and does not demand anything. John, too, in spite of all his responsibilities and worries, seems cheerful. We walk together up the steep path back of the hut to a spot from which we can see all of the land—land which, though we have done no more than mark it off with little stones like tombstones and register an application, already seems to belong to us. The tops of the trees in the canyon are almost under our feet, the green faintly bronzed here and there by the growth of young foliage on the higher branches. The waterfall, invisible beneath them, makes a noise like wind. A large bird swings upward heavily and falls again into the forest. Late afternoon. Smell of rain, dry and bitter. Still clouds are the color of withered lilacs. Around us bushes of herva ratto—poison plant. Fat wax-green leaves, unmoved, strain and jerk. Hill dark. As rain gathers trees go black with an iron slowness. Dark trees make bright night in a silverness of afternoon where the clouds are like fish. The sky enters its own distance, disappearing sky. There is no sky. Only the motion of emptiness. Trees lie along the slopes, heavy—die along the slopes, night-dead on the hills invisible. The mountains enclose our death, gently, so gently, in a vast embrace which no one can deny, from which there is no escape.

But I do not wish to escape. I want to stay here forever and ever behind the wall that enfolds our peace.

DONA CHIQUINHA sits bolt upright on our only chair, which is quite concealed by the spread-out folds of the flowered material of her skirt. She has asked me some polite questions: how long I have been married, how old I am, how many children I have had. It is easy to see that she is uncomfortably curious. Why should a senhora educada come to such a place? What do we expect to do here? Are we going, perhaps, to build a house and bring some furniture up from the coast? She is a poor woman. She is accustomed to hardship. But a lady from the city—how can she live like this?

Dona Chiquinha asks these last things only indirectly. She understands etiquette and her feeling for what is required of her imposes some restraint. Her broad yellow face is fixed and masque-like as though it were of paste. The only thing which seems to live in this concealment are the small shifting eyes which watch me furtively. From the beginning to the end of her visit she does not so much as lift a hand to alter her rigid attitude. In my attempt to be a hostess to her I am utterly at a loss. I say things, but words spoken in my best Portuguese carry themselves to her ears without any significance.

In the meantime John is discussing crops with Senhor Alfredo. "Oh, yes, this house is only temporary. We are going to build a farinha mill, and, if cane does well here, a sugar engenho. My senhora, of course, is unaccustomed to such surroundings. Her father is very rich." Senhor Alfredo pulls his spare languid mustache and murmurs a wary assent to all John says. Senhor Alfredo wears the large flat hat of a vaqueiro—a hat of leather—and his shirt hangs loosely, unconfined by his thin blue cotton breeches. On his bare broad feet are leather sandals fastened about his great toe with a thong. He rests one hand on his hip and his huge facão, swinging sidewise in its leather sheath, gives him a martial appearance. For the most part he is solemnly impassive. When his curiosity displays itself he is simpler, more naïve than the woman, and I am less afraid of him. His large dark eyes regard me gently with an impersonal bewilderment.

John goes on talking, boasting conscientiously. When I hear all the lies that John is telling I am afraid these people will find us out. In my imagination an abyss opens. On the day on which it is discovered that we are nobodies—that we are as poor as the poorest taborel—we are going to tumble into it. To make myself agreeable to Dona Chiquinha I exert myself more. And she responds by what I psychically feel to be a greater withdrawal. Her remark at every point is, "Ah, the senhora is rich. We are very poor, stupid people. The senhora must take pity on our ignorance." While behind all this deprecating comment it is apparent that no real humility lies, but only malice and suspicion. When Nannette appears Dona Chiquinha asks, "Who is that? A relative?" I have to reply that it is.

Nannette is frightened of our neighbors and tries to go by them hurriedly without stopping to be introduced. But John calls, "Nannette!" And she halts perplexedly, as if stricken with paralysis of the legs. "This, Dona Chiquinha, Senhor Alfredo, is our esteemed relative, Dona Nannetta. Let me give her the great privilege of becoming acquainted with you." Dona Chiquinha gets up and, with a grudging air, holds out a limp fat palm, which Nannette, in her turn, touches with repugnance. Senhor Alfredo coughs, bows, murmurs, "Estimo de conhecel-o," and appears to avoid looking Nannette in the face. As for Nannette, in spite of the fact that she is alarmed, her conviction of innate superiority does not desert her for a minute, and, graciously but condescendingly, she makes a reply in a jargon which no one can understand. Nannette—God knows why—to protect her complexion, perhaps (her complexion which, since her illness, has become completely demolished), always wears the same old panama hat with a ribbon tied under her chin, and I know, in a country where hats for women are never seen, that Dona Chiquinha is amused by it. As I hear later, they call Nannette "the old one"—Nannette, who has always been so careful of her appearance yet always seemed to believe in eternal youth. I am very glad indeed when, with some murmured excuses, she hurries away from us.

The sun is setting. On the upper peak of my most virginal mountain the light falls, as if palpably, in red-lilac flakes. The valley fills with shadows, with the poisonous green of the wild grass that sends its own reflection upward against the oncoming night. The afternoon leaves an attenuated smile of anemic delicacy, the smile of a madonna in a painting by Botticelli, fading from us as if in resignation. Peace. If only there were no Dona Chiquinhas or Senhor Alfredos to disturb us with their suspicions, and to remind us that where people of different temperament or different tradition are gathered together a battle of distrust is always waging. Without actually believing in our wealth, Dona Chiquinha cannot forgive it.

When she rises to tell me goodby she unties an old cloth and pours into the lap of my dress a dozen ash-pink roses plucked off at the blossom, quite stemless, and in the same parcel are some andú, a species of wild bean very good to eat. This touches me, though I realize that a gift at a first visit is a national formality.

John says that he is telling everyone that my father is rich, so that these people will respect me, so that if any harm comes to him I may find assistance in getting Jackie, Nannette, and myself back to the coast.

THROUGH the high grass the crowded backs of sheep going up, up, endlessly. The light touches the massed white wool, and, across the stillness of rocks, the snowy procession resembles a moving cloud. One hundred and thirty sheep. It has taken the very last of our money to purchase them. And while the sheep keep going on like a long dream of hope, Manoel, who is just recovering from snake-bite and is all swelled up until his face suggests a small chocolate pudding, follows behind them, playing shrill music on his bamboo fife. He is ten years old. His clothes are a few rags. But he makes me think of angels—of a little black Saint John, a trifle diseased but quite charming yet. Sheep are close and quiet together. Their personalities are obscure. They have drooped heads, mildly flickering ears, and flat woolly rumps. They go on in steady obedience to secrecy. Occasionally they become agitated and their legs move woodenly in a stiff trot. The separate entities of the flock are like the drops of water in a stream—they flow apart for an instant but immediately reunite, for they have one being, a being which none of them perceives, to which all of them are subjugate. It is for us to guard their timid stolidity, their happiness of patience. If I could tell what those sheep mean— But John and I believe in them. To us they are more actual than anything on earth.

SENHOR CANDIDO is also interested in new arrivals and he has brought the excellentissima senhora a dozen ears of green corn, while to the excellentissimo senhor he has presented a cord of tobacco. For one of the taborel, Senhor Candido is rich, they tell me. In the valley beyond us his whole clan is settled and he presides over it as a kind of dictator. He has recounted to us his feud with Senhor Alfredo. One night Senhor Alfredo's brother came to Milagres to steal, and killed a heifer. Candido's father surprised the marauder in the act.

ESCAPADE

Senhor Alfredo's brother, attempting an escape, shot at Candido's father and struck him through the heart, and Candido himself, witnessing the act, returned the shot so that Senhor Alfredo's brother, too, was slain. Now, Candido never goes west of Milagres, nor does Senhor Alfredo venture in an easterly direction, for on the day they meet there must be an end of one or the other. Candido chuckles in telling this story. His little yellow face is creased with smiles perpetually. But his expression displays less humor than craft. When he is very much amused he covers his upper lip, on which he has some long hairs like a Chinaman's mustache. A few strands of wispy beard dangle from his chin. His arms are so short that, seated on our chair, clasping himself across the stomach, his chubby fingers barely meet to interlace. John's untiring politeness warns me that Candido is a person whose malignant influence is to be reckoned with.

Candido wants to sell us a milch cow. This is a cattle country. Twice a year the beeves are driven to the coast to market. But milch cows are rare, expensive, and hard to find. John says, "We are careful of the milk we give the baby. The doctors have told us that goat's milk is best for him." Oh, how we should like to buy the milch cow! We have no money for the purchase. Candido says, "The senhor is going to purchase a great many sheep? Of course, these will do for a beginning, but later— No doubt a rich man like your excellency, educated, and from the city, will make a great many improvements in this wild place. The senhor is going to show us how they do things 'down there'," and he makes a gesture in the direction of the sea, so far away, that five hundred miles we have traversed. With the gesture goes that invariable throaty laugh that has a peculiarly irritating note. Just then he observes Nannette and her hat and his amusement frankly stifles him. His small eyes glisten. How dare he laugh at Nannette's hat! What consciousness of power allows him to withdraw his deference in a land where even the lowest peon is polite—polite at least in matters which are unimportant to him. I am afraid of Candido's laughter, which seems so natural, so ingenuous.

JOHN is ill. Two years ago—a little more than two years—he underwent an operation for appendicitis, which left him in a weakened condition. He is not really able to do hard work, carry heavy things that put a strain on his side. And I can do nothing to help him. We lie together in the half-darkness. John says very little but his lips are gray and, when he is compelled to move, his eyes have the blind intensity of suffering. I say to myself: If John should die! I want to die also, quickly, at once, so as not to face what may happen to Jackie and Nannette. There are no doctors here, no medicine, but, worst of all, there is no money with which to buy freedom from the necessity to do things for which you are physically unfit. There is no money to buy rest, the right to be ill and to become well again. The currals are only half complete. There is ground to be cleared. Wood to be cut. Candido has sent over two hundred coffee trees to be planted in the hollow on the other side of the stream, and if they do well he is to go shares in the crops, which it will take at least four years to produce. Estephania, though she is ashamed of her distrust, is frightened of our poverty. When we came up to the ranch she looked upon the experience as a lark. She imagined that our discomforts were temporary and that we were going to build a house and buy a quantity of stock. But now she pretends to have had a letter from her mother and is going back to the city. What shall I do without her—she who, in spite of her training as a servant of the rich, is familiar with the ways of the people, with cooking red beans in a pot upon the floor, with roasting green coffee and pounding it in one's own pilão. Then her love for Jackie is a lie. She cares only for her own welfare and comfort.

The truth must be that Estephania has been through all this before. She knows the end that threatens people in our position.

FOR two months now the weather has been perfect. All day the clean sunlight sweeps distantly across us and is like the wind itself. An enormous shadow follows, with the hours, the great curve of the mother mountain, a shadow of rest. I mark every day by the lengthening of that shadow and find myself thinking of the vast depth under the mountain as of the end of everything. Down there in the bottom of the gorge, under the swaying greenness, that is where one goes at the end of everything —when everything above the earth is finished. Pain, make a light for me. Shake the stillness.

YESTERDAY John went to Mucambo. He left in the morning early, barefoot, with a six-mile walk before him. Among the rocks, his figure diminishing, made my heart small with it. I cannot bear to have him go away from me. The sunshine was thin across the sky like a veil of light. Fields of flowers crushed by the glare had two dimensions and were painted flat against the mountains.

In the evening, high up a little figure moving, strange small thing, active, alone in a beautiful stupendous inertia. The world died in the light, yet something survived. I had felt unwell all day and had been lying down, but when I saw John coming I got up and ran to meet him. I ran and ran through the dead light, stumbling up the long path toward the only-thing-alive beyond me. And when I could make out John's face the blankness of fields and rocks converging in him became alive also, too much alive, so that it hurt.

MARIA DA GLORIA, old Januario's sister, has come to help me with the work. We will pay her family out in crops. It is hard for me since Estephania has gone. Maria squats on her haunches in front of our doorway and sings to herself, a strange dissonant tune, monotonously reiterated. Her voice is very shrill and quavers a little. She is making lace on the soiled pillow before her and the click of the small polished bobbins striking against each other is an undertone to her music, music which seems fatuous when I glance at her vague glistening eyes, at her smooth obscure black face. I wonder if somewhere in her soul the melancholy of the music has a place. If she, too, without knowing it, understands that for human beings life is tragic—life is a mistake.

Well, then, now and again something utterly ridiculous occurs which makes us laugh, as if there were no problem of money, no unfriendly world to reckon with.

ESCAPADE

At night, after wading through the long grass in which the cattle of the neighborhood have been grazing, we strip off all our clothes, and, holding the tin lamp so close to our bodies that its heat almost scorches our flesh, we pick the ticks off one another. Hundreds there are, glossy and so minute that one must look carefully or they will escape. They are young ones that suspend themselves from the grass blades like clusters of living fruit and fall all down together whenever anything disturbs their rest. We also bathe ourselves continually in a solution of kerosene and tobacco juice.

At night the thatch rustles. Against the lamplight quick rain-drops flicker brief threads, silver-green, disappearing bright. Like ribbons unwinding, processions of red ants toil up the mud wall steadily. The tin lamp chokes in a diffusion of bronzed smoke. The rats run away from us under the wind. Stiff wind like shredded iron. Boiling sound of wind deep in the world. Flat rush of wind. Full flatness merges with the soft of dark. All soft, dark, deep, rocking and tearing at roots. Through the open doorway I see pulled trees swing apart with a rich pale motion—a motion of shadows, of fire in shadows.

Maria da Gloria makes lace again, lace and more lace. Nannette is treasuring a volume of Anatole France. She tries to read it, but the reflection on the pages is too dim and only jumbles them up. So she finally lays herself down on the cot and goes to sleep. One of her feet in a battered shoe dangles over the edge of the coverlet. I am always trying *not* to see Nannette asleep. She is too terrible—like something lost in itself. Her face is narrow and thin and her eyes are prominent, even through the thin closed lids. Her hair, which I remember as magnificent, is no more than a wisp, always slipping down from its pins. There is gray in the bronze strands which seem to be filmed over with a whitish dust. Everybody laughs at Nannette. Even Maria da Gloria does so in secret. I feel it painfully, as if Nannette were a neglected child who had been given to us to keep.

Not always, of course. When Nannette becomes too querulous and reproaches John because he cannot take us away to America and make everything right, I sometimes hate her. I have hated her as if she were a destructive machine wound up against us—a machine that nobody can stop. Then I think of a long knife in my hand and feel that I must thrust it into her to make her still. Hate after all is only an exaggeration of self-defense. I want to put Nannette out of our lives—to put her out utterly, as one quenches a light. There are days when John refuses to speak to her. Then she comes to me and cries and threatens to kill herself. But I know only too well that she hasn't the courage. To kill one's self requires courage. If John died and we were left alone on the ranch and could get help from no one I should *have* to kill myself. Then the missionaries in Villa Nova would come and get Jackie, perhaps, and send him back to the United States. I imagine Jackie all his life long in these terrible mountains—the only world he will be able to remember. Of course, *we* can't apply to the missionaries for help because our morals are in question and they would disapprove of us.

Little white moon, little white hen, are you another

mother who will lose her baby somewhere over there on the other side of the mountain? Little star, is it because you are sorry for us that, through the rain, you shine so warm and dim, as if you were about to drip into my heart? Little cloud, have you come to hide us with a veil of mercy? Wind in the trees, do not cry like that! I cannot bear to listen to you; for these things are fancies, but it is no fancy that my big little son must go away from me.

THE heavy rains have not yet set in. There is a moon nearly every night. It rushes up from an abyss of obscurity and hurls itself against darkness. Fire breaks upon all the still ridges. The mountains float about the horizon. Frogs bark. Stark white moon. Eternal peace. Blind house. Earth gives up radiance. Across the door-space figures move: John, Nannette. Days, years, centuries. Shadows move. Other shadows. Maybe a leaf stirs, or a tree is swaying. Vague hands reach along the shaken grass. Already the sleeper has turned to a deeper rest. We are fading, fading away in the depths of isolation. We are only memories now. Everyone has forgotten us. Perhaps we are already dead.

WE have sixteen hens. The eggs are for Jack. John made a hen-house very much like the room we live in. I like to go in there at dusk and see the huddled shapes crowded together along the roosts. The pale feathers are clouds that hold the afterglow in the dark enclosure. The clouds stir. A faint dreaming warning. We stuff up all the cracks to keep out vampire bats.

ESCAPADE

Eggs are beautiful to me. White porcelain eggs. They make me feel powerful and rich.

Two hundred years ago pioneers from Portugal came to dig gold from the yellow bed of the river. They died of the fever. There is no trace of them in the sand. Long and low, ridge after ridge, the mountains are tombs, and through the valleys the despondent mists weave in and out. Mists. In the morning—in the madrugada—the startled wet green hillside leaps from the quiet. The sereno is everywhere. The dark trees make sharp sounds like notes of music. The dim sun is a little sick child who caresses the flowers with its withered fingers of light. I think of wings dank with tears, and of silver shoes too worn to dance.

John never says anything now. The beard is long all over his face and he has a gray look. He is beautiful, like something finished that yet lives. If he were less kind to me I should be afraid. I think of his Silence lying breast to breast with a silence that is greater, and I want him to say something to me. On these white days the whole earth is blanched with suffering, and I expect it to disappear altogether. It is as if his path were toward his image and mine toward the image of myself. I want to weep, but if I wept I could be a fountain sobbing—sobbing with happiness.

When it rains the goats huddle close against the walls of the house, but the moment the deluge abates they are up the hillside among the rocks. I go out with a bowl of corn in my arms and whistle to them and they come down to me as straight and swift as water comes down a precipice. When I listen to the clatter they make I imagine they have stars on their feet. With a muffled softness the rain beats on the mud walls. The goats draw near, stamp, nuzzle each other, and I hear the thud of their encountering horns.

John has suspended a broken umbrella over the bed because the fine spray that sifts through the palm-tree roof gets everything wet. In skeins of wool the night envelopes us. Black silence. When the wind tears at the thatch the harsh rattle is like an ache of bones. The little feet of rats running over us are a hurricane of pebbles. I am afraid of night.

Morning. The same shredded mists are drifting against the hut. A few yards beyond the door a sudden tree flings a bright green branch from an invisible trunk. I try to breathe but the cold whiteness of the world is suffocating. I try to breathe through my eyes. There is too much white. John kindles a fire of candeia branches and the thick bitter smoke surrounds us and keeps out the poisonous gnats. We sit there all day with our bare feet on the half-soaked floor, without anything to do. The moment the rain is over the ants will be into the mandioc and John will have to go after them with brands soaked in kerosene. Only yesterday he dug out a city and when he climbed from the hole that was five feet deep his legs were bloody where their mandibles had cut.

I am homesick. Something squeezes up my heart and gives it a fine thin pain. Homesick for what?

In the beginning John talked about the time when we would "get away." We were going home to make money and be comfortable. If we came back here at all it would be an outing, a vacation, a kind of lark. But we speak of such things less and less. When we say anything like that we are ashamed, and we attempt to conceal our secret longings by ignoring them, by changing the subject. Nannette is really the only one who continues to refer to our impossible hope.

Poor Nannette! Her nerves have been so badly shaken by what she has passed through that her hands tremble all the time and at the slightest provocation tears rise to her eyes. She lives in an old calico dress that has been washed almost colorless. Only some brownish stains like rust indicate its former design of flowers. Now that her skin is worse she wears gloves with the fingers out. And all the time she is caring for bits of finery that have survived: a fur neck-piece, a roll of lace, a silk petticoat that is faded and streaked. On good days she spreads these things across the pickets of the wattle fence where the meat is hung to dry. The soles are half off her old shoes and make a flop-flop under her feet so you can hear her coming whenever she walks. She helps a little to care for Jack, but her willingness produces nothing. She has forgotten how to make any motions for herself. If you tell her to put water on to boil you must direct her to the pot, and then again to the fire, and everywhere she goes is the trail of all she has spilled. I feel that she has become a sleepwalker. When she stares at me with her frightened eyes, I want to scream at her, Wake up, Nannette! Wake up!

Jackie's dresses fell apart so I made him a little red coat out of the cloth of a sack. It is very tight in the

arm pits and the buttons are very large, but he is proud
of it. The countrywomen also admire his-red-cotton-
coat-with-its-black-stripes.

John's trousers can scarcely be patched any more
and his skin shows through in the seat. As for myself,
I don't like to think of how I look. The day Maria da
Gloria's small sister came to call on us and was astonished by our looking glass—she had never seen a looking glass before—she went up to it, gazed at herself,
and spat. The mirror, the one precious mirror we
possess, was covered all over with trickles of spittle.
She made grimaces, stuck her tongue out, and spat
again. So I keep away from the mirror for fear I
should be tempted to do the same thing. So long as one
imagines one's self attractive to others one wears a kind
of garment about one's hurt.

AT home I had to admit myself vain, perhaps because I was not particularly pretty. I was curious
to know the opinions of others regarding my appearance,
So I selected a very naïve youth of my acquaintance
and put the question to him. He looked at me candidly,
and told me that I had beautiful eyes and very pretty
teeth. After that, though I considered myself charming,
I was always surprised and elated if anyone agreed with
me. But it is my eyes now that startle me most. My
expression is hard and involuntarily I gaze at myself
from a bitter distance. I have been accustomed to
think of suffering as beautifying and ennobling. Now
I recognize it as distorting. It makes people hideous.
Horrible to be a part of flesh from which there is

no escape. This is the first time since I left Dr. Beach's that I have dared to examine myself critically. The flesh is a night in which one lives without visible sequence, in which everything is mysterious, sinister, and beyond control. I hate this battered thing which is betraying me into a likeness of Nannette. And this is I! What I have become in spite of myself. And I don't know it, though I am longing to know it. I am longing for someone whom I have never seen and shall never see. Does the child long for the mother or the mother long for the child? In the glass the silence quivers. *She* is in the glass, in the room— another silence. When can she break through to herself? Be afraid, you in the glass. The glass is blank, deep— like the eye of God. Are you hating me in the form of beasts and men I despise, you who gave me birth, to whom I give birth?

Well, then, I turn my back on this mystery. I refuse any longer to reiterate a question to which no one replies. And I shut in me the memory of eyes that know more of me than I can ever know of myself. You eyes, you have seen things, but I resent you because you can not give me the vision.

The worse affairs go with us the clearer it becomes to me that true being is behind and beyond words. Awareness is altogether fragmentary and derived. Each man lives his own life submerged in his own darkness, and darkness is much more intimate than light. Our time is created through the imperfection of our sight. People talk of simplicity, but I think I am the only one who really believes in it.

ESCAPADE

Sometimes, for as much as a week, the road that passes through our land remains entirely deserted, and we don't see a human creature from outside. John works at his clearing in the fields. He has to remove stumps and they are very slow to rot and very difficult to take up. He is using whole trunks of trees for the construction of currals that resemble fortifications. All over the mountainsides the people are burning grass so that the new pasturage can come up. Smoke from their distant fires gives a milky appearance to the light. This veil of semiopacity rests heavily in the tops of the trees and along the hollows of the slopes. We sustain a perpetual war against ants that sometimes in a night destroy the whole of a newly planted crop. Yesterday I set out fifty little orange trees and this morning every one of them was stripped of its leaves. The ants at work are wonderful, a fleet of tiny dry-land ships under the rocking sails of the foliage they are carrying off.

The greatest pleasure I have here is in watching the birds which are of wonderful variety and very numerous. The parrakeets with red breasts scatter across the ground like foliage bitten with frost. When the toucans were mating their great sound was like a hunting horn blowing in the distance. There are many, many other birds, but most of them are nameless to me. And in the morning the little tracks of deer are all over the garden patch. Candido has an old flint-lock gun, the only firing-piece for miles around. He comes here to shoot. Muffled echoes from somewhere are always ripping the quiet suddenly. Sometimes he gives us bits of game, an agouti, some armadillo meat, or a piece of paca, a giant rodent. I ought to be grateful to him, but I only detest him for his killing. Men, afraid of each other, huddle apart in straw-thatched huts, and in the forest the cotia, timid and beautiful, listens for their coming, every brown silk hair a-shudder, delicate nostrils dilated in an agony of apprehension. Once we heard the coughing roar of an onça—a jaguar— and we all went out of doors to listen to it. They live in the catingas—in the desert—and only come up here when food is scarce. That roar somehow filled me with an unreasoning elation. Though it told of a danger to our sheep I felt stimulated in the possession of an utterly strange experience.

Jackie and I have seen some enormous snakes—the snakes that have killed our chickens and bitten one of the goats. I enjoy my horror as the whole world falls away from the beautiful shining length of black lacquer and gold, from the symbol of Death which is the name I have given to Nature herself. The toads are as big as dinner plates. Jackie punches one with a stick and its opalescent sides swell out like toy balloons, its mouth gapes, and it hisses ominously.

MANOEL felled a tree in which was an owl nest and when he showed me the small blinded bird I asked him to let me keep it. I cut one of the owl's gray-brown wings and I have allowed him to run loose while we sleep. All night long I hear his hunting moan in the dark. I imagine him free; a gray cloud of feathered quiet drifting, his low cry, and his claws clinging to a young bird—clinging, clinging like an unlifting shadow. From a moral standpoint death, which is most inimical to human relations, should be hideous. But the owl has convinced me of the superficiality of moral judgments. He is the cruelest of creatures and the most innocent. In the morning he sits on my knee and I give him bits of our maggot-laden meat. He is resigned to me utterly. When I call to him in the daylight he always comes feebly toward the sound. And he stares, stares at me with his great helpless eyes, feeling perhaps, because I have given him meat, that I have become a part of his sightless world.

It is different with the hawk. Tilting himself back against the side of his cage, his claws, at the end of his thin stick-like legs, clutch tensely at the air, and when I attempt to feed him his terrible eyes select unerringly my moving finger. More than once he has dragged at it with his beak and torn my flesh. He was wounded when he was captured and it would be useless to free him. Nothing will free him but starvation. He sees us too plainly. His vision has placed us outside him forever. He recognizes our antithesis. He also reminds me of a child. He is another Death.

JOHN had no money with which to build a farinha mill so he followed the custom of the neighborhood and called all of our acquaintances together for a building "bee"—a treat. They came early in the morning and by the time we had taken our coffee they were all at work. In the pit they had dug and were filling with water, the men stood in mud up to their bare knees. And with their hands resting on one another's shoulders they danced through it in a circle, churning the mixture with their feet. The women went back and forth, to and from the brook, with water jars poised on their heads. They were all drunk and that was why they were so industrious. In some wild looking girls with glistening eyes and unloosed hair I scarcely knew the sedate daughters of José Marinho, the voodoo doctor of the district. The men, their shirts unbound, their huge knives clanking against their hips, seemed all alike, wrapped in an enchantment, in the monotonous music of their songs. "Bom dia, senhora! Bom dia! Bom dia nossa senhora que vem para nos fazer rico. Bom dia, excellentissima senhora estrangeira, que nos convidou para dançar. Nos supplicamos todas as santas que ellas mandarem bençôes e felicidade a Vossa Mercê. Viva Senhor João! Viva Joãnzinho! Viva Senhora Dona Evelina! Viva! Viva Dona Nannetta!" With vague gestures they waved their hats to me, half knelt in attitudes of humility and adoration, and their drunken exclamations made great waves of sound across the trees and fields while the mountains flung back a murmur like the harsh voice of a tide. I gazed at them and was unable to respond suitably to their good wishes. They were no longer Manoel, Ruffino, Emilio, Severino, and José. They were mindless. Inscrutable. And their joy was not even joy. By the next day they would have forgotten it.

John had previously prepared the wattled framework of the mill house so that all it needed was to be chinked. The new thatch waved its stiff green fronds in the strong light reflected from the rocky hills. And the visitors, preparing themselves a place to dance, carried huge gluey handfuls of red mud and squeezed it between the gaping sticks. They staggered as they walked, screamed, shouted, and threw themselves into each other's arms. On the grass about them furred shadows laid themselves flat, attenuated and delicate. Trees, fields, mountains, everything familiar to us drew away from the noise. Up a hillside the sunlight ran through the glossy grass stems. A small wind, embroidering the quiet, agitated the death-bright branches of the glowing trees. The sky, milk-blue and infinitely distant, darkened with the oscillation of the little red motes which intruded on our vision whenever we lifted our eyes. Through all the glaring landscape was the silence of stone. When birds flew up their small blanched forms, ascending, were shiningly obliterated. The strong quiet which surrounded everything was stronger than the flutter of wings. And by nightfall, in the new building like an Aladdin's palace created in a day, eighteen drunken men and as many women were dancing the maxixe, dancing magnificently, to the music of a whining accordion and a large bean rattle made of a gourd.

John was a trifle uneasy for, not satisfied with the rum he had provided, the party sent a messenger to Mucambo and brought back more of their own purchase. They made an enormous bonfire in front of the shed and the flames, rushing up against the solitude, threatened the black trees whose leaves looked purplish in the dusky light. The cold air, heavy with dew and with a stale darkness, was poisoned further by the fumes of the kerosene lamps and the bite of the smoke. We heard Candido in the gorge exploding his blunderbus in sheer exuberance. John drew us all inside the house. Drunken people lumbered through the underbrush close to the wall, cursing and calling on all the saints. A

woman's shriek. A snatch of song. A more and more
recurrent stillness. The steady rush of the waterfall in
the deserted gorge bore with it the suggestion of something ominous. I thought of it rushing down to the sea
forever when all these people were asleep—forever and
ever when all these people were asleep.

On Christmas morning I awakened with a kind of
leaden expectancy. What day was it? It was terrifically hot. I had overexerted myself and was feeling
very ill indeed. For breakfast we had, as usual, black
coffee sweetened with raspadura—a crude brown sugar
made into bricks and exchanged for other commodities
at the nearest market. The boiled sweet potatoes with
only salt to make them go down, stick in an unpleasant
mass midway in one's throat. It is months and months
since we have had any butter. Nannette, faithful to
ritual, officiated at the meal. She always does so with
the utmost elegance, her little finger crooked about the
handle of the large tin pot. Miudo was breakfasting
with us. He poured mandioc meal into his coffee mug
and stirred the liquid into a mush. And when he had
buried his face in it he came up with little crumbs of
white clinging to his scrubby mustache and his fat black
face. Miudo eats furtively, now and then wiping his
mouth on the back of his hand—a hand long like a
monkey's, narrow, dark on the top, the pinkish palm
deeply furrowed and grimed with dirt. Nannette made
him uncomfortable. "Senhor Miudo quer more café
com sugar?" Not understanding her thoroughly, he
chuckled politely. "Agradeçido, minha senhora. Estou
muito bem. Agradeço Vossa Mercê. Estou almoçando

bem." When he had finished he set his mug gently upon the ground, smoothed out his trouser legs, and sighed deeply. His smile was childlike but unhappy. As soon as he could make an excuse he got up from the heap of sacks on which he had been resting and went outside. We could hear the quick patter of his bare feet escaping down the path.

I had made Jackie a doll. The body was stuffed with rags and the hair, very stiff and luxuriant, was shredded from the cipó vine with which our thatch is tied to the rafters. Jackie sat flat down in front of the large doll, stared at it bewilderedly, and suddenly began to weep. He was afraid of my work of art—an enormous shape, a pouting red cotton mouth, and astonished blue ging-ham eyes perpetually fixed. He pulled himself to his feet and ran away to a corner to hide. Nannette's gaze clouded with tears. "If I only had something to give him, but I can't buy him so much as a pin!" she said. And because it was painful to be reminded of facts, I answered, "You are as well off as John and I, Nannette." "As well off as you are! At least you chose the thing you wanted and you have each other, while I have no one—nobody on earth! And I am dependent on you and John for everything, for the very air I breathe!" I reflected of course that Nannette had always been de-pendent on somebody and that she always would be. Her education was at fault. Her tears do not make me kind. She suffers from self-pity—the self-pity from which all of us are suffering. Nannette said, "Every bite of bread I eat chokes me." But we don't have bread, Nannette. It is eight or nine months since we were able to get any flour and we have no method of cooking suitable for making bread. If Nannette were less harrowingly pathetic she would be very ludicrous.

Twice on market day we have been able, for a vintem a piece, to buy some little cakes made of tapioca starch, and all of us, I fancy, consider them delicious. When they are set on the table Nannette regards them avidly but with reverence. On the last occasion she was so greedy for them that she refused Jackie his portion, declaring that they were indigestible and might make him sick. John was so disgusted that he left his meal and refused emphatically to touch any of the cakes. Nannette wept indignantly. "John," she informed me, "never misses an opportunity to remind me of the humiliating position in which I have been placed. It is cruel of him to begrudge me the little cakes when for months and months we have had nothing but beans!" So she also refused the cakes. "I haven't a friend or a penny in the world. If we could only get back to the United States I could try to do something—get work. I could be a stenographer or translate French. I don't believe any of you take my translating seriously." I did not permit myself any sympathy—or rather any appearance of it. The truth is that I sympathize with her too much. Her trembling hands, her gaunt face, her terrified eyes, the wisp of grayish hair that straggles about her lean tortured-looking throat.

Fortunately her psychology has its compensations. After leaving me indignantly and hiding herself for an hour or more she came back to the house and, with a relish that could not be disguised, ate four of the cakes.

ESCAPADE

I WANT peace at any price. John and Nannette have quarreled so much that I am no longer interested in fixing responsibilities. Of course I know only too well what actually precipitated this situation. Nannette began to reproach John in an indirect way and finally openly to blame him for my ill-health. To blame John for circumstances which are the consequence of our mutual defiance insults my self-respect even more profoundly than it insults his love for me. But when Nannette begins to complain to me about John, the blind necessity to save myself from further suffering overcomes my sense of justice and my indignation on my own behalf. I have lost all my self-control. I scream at her. "Go away, Nannette! I won't listen to you! When you are like this I hate you both! I don't care whose fault anything is! I don't care who lives or dies. I don't feel sorry for anyone but myself. Both of you are cruel or you wouldn't quarrel. Neither one of you loves me. If you don't get away from me this instant I shall—Oh, I don't know what I shall do!" And intoxicated by my own abandon to passion I look about for something to strike her with. Poor Nannette is afraid of me. She rushes out, weeping. And I throw myself face downward on the cot and hide my head under a pillow. I want to shut away the whole world—everything, everybody, I want to be utterly alone. This is what suffering does to one. It hardens one's heart. It is degrading. Simply hideous.

When Nannette begins her whining talk, John's eyes, so still and kind as he looks at me, turn hard and cold. His pupils contract and are sharp little points of destruction that penetrate to the very depths of Nannette's stupidity and confusion. She is afraid of him and at the same time does everything on earth to agitate and disturb him, especially in regard to me. I don't think she has any clear consciousness of her motives or even of her own words. As a carefully nurtured female her instinct is fixed. When conditions are impossible they can be altered only by stirring to action the man most involved in them. Men have their own engrossments and unless you exhibit your emotions they are apt to ignore troubles under which the helpless other-sex is being crushed. John endured a week of haranguing, but now is silent. If Nannette so much as addresses a word to him he walks out of the hut. I am between two hostilities in which, against all my reasoning, I feel myself ignored. John hates Nannette because he loves me. And Nannette is like a mad woman. She wants to be mad. She is always telling me that she is losing her mind. When I ask her a question her reply is deliberately chaotic. In order to throw everything on us she would like to consider herself insane. The fields, the mountains, and the silence surround her as they do us and imprison her desires. And she is an old woman. She is fifty-three but she is very old. We are, in fact, to remain here forever. The only escape will be through the mind—into a world unmodified by our experience. If she can not go outwardly toward what she wishes she will ignore her surroundings and build her freedom within.

Today when she took Jackie from his bed she dropped him. She wanted us to know that she could no longer be trusted with burdens. On anything but an earthen floor the fall would have hurt his head. As it was he shrieked for an hour. He does not like Nannette any longer. Without understanding her, he is afraid of her. When he sees me in the doorway he runs to me, clings to my skirts, and begs to be taken up. "I wanna go 'way. I don't want Nana. Nana não quer tomar conta de mim. Eu quero ficar comsigo," he says.

Twice Nannette has gone down into the gorge, into the woods with the threat that she was never coming back. And she has stayed away from us a very long time. I have been frightened, though late in the evening, as John had prophesied, she returned. John says, "Leave her alone." When she passes she glances at us with a blank unknowing expression. I may speak to her several times without eliciting any response other than that wild gaze of obliviousness. Her movements are aimless. Her gestures wander. She is dramatically disintegrated, guardedly willless. After Jackie and John are asleep she sometimes calls me to her, flings her arms about my neck, and begs me to forgive her— for what I don't know. She says, "I ought not to give 'way to my emotions. But to think of dying here—— You are younger than I am. You don't realize how horrible it is!" Even John reminds me, "You are younger than I am." He does not speak with reproach, but I begin to feel a sin in my youth. And I think of the biggest mountain with the vast shadow creeping over it.

WE are milling mandioc. The work goes on until late at night. In the big dark shed Candido, naked to the waist and dripping with sweat, is pushing the flaky meal across the flat stone top of the oven. It gives out a warm smell, like toasted flour, and resembles a gilded snow drift as he agitates it, backward and forward, with his long-handled wooden rake. His brother turns the wooden wheel on which the belt of antbear hide whirrs continually with a sound of irritation, of vindictiveness. A sickly child whose large eyes glisten as with fever stares fixedly at the moving saw teeth as she feeds them the peeled root. The trough under her hands is choked with a white mass from which the starch oozes in slow gluey streams. Her thin fingers tremble a little. She is a small danger on guard before her task. Candido laughs, chatters, and finally begins to sing. On the floor a pot of beans warms over a few sticks and the faint glow from the fire gives his nude body the richness of ivory and of gold. The women, squatting in a semi-circle, are scraping the deadly husk from the gnarled root. Their glittering knives scrape pale flesh from the bony white. Their gestures are a brittle rustle. Fatigued, their loosened hair overshadows their faces and they turn and glance at me from under their shawls. Their eyes are still and luminous like the eyes of dumb things in the shadow of a forest. John says, "We are dividing the meal with Candido. Out of this crop we expect to get about eighty sacks." The high droning of songs goes on. Through the open doorway I see the endless night, thick, dark with the moving of leaves, paled here and there with the moving clouds. I am lost in endless songs of which I can comprehend only a few of the words. The songs are as long as the darkness, as long as the night. With all of my being I know them. The songs say that mandioc is our whole future, and that without Candido to whom forty of the sacks belong the crop would be lost. We can not employ labor and it is only through Candido that we can go on living.

BESIDES Bisunga, the donkey, and Boneca, the little white mare, we have another mare, which we bought at a bargain price, who appeared to be in foal. But now we have learned that she has some sort of ailment and that her belly is chronically inflated. Candido also has an old lame mule. To take the mandioc to Lamarão to market all of these animals are required. John and Candido, on foot, accompany the caravan as it goes off up the mountain early in the morning. Ascending the path at the farthest visible distance, the procession looks meager and as if the animals were crawling, climbing upon their bellies over a broken wall of rock. I can recognize John by his coat which is black. For a long time I keep my eye on that tiny black speck. And when it disappears at last the blue and white day before me is like a page on which nothing is written; sunlight, and gold-white sand, fields in which the bony grass bends and shakes, trees in the wind swerving from their very roots —emptiness and silence, sunshine and emptiness. The sky is red-blue through a mist of heat. Some strange cattle browsing by our stream are painted wood, their heads, moving, swinging to one side with the long loose gestures of their necks. Their heavy tasseled tails switch flies, flop inertly, thrash their haunches indolently, flop. Nothing; the consummation of understanding; knowledge obliterated by the thing understood. What one knows one has become and it is impossible to remove this living understanding from one, to look at it and give it a name. Objects—factual or abstract—really

exist only in the past. One's unstated being is all that
is contemporaneous.

Evening. On the virginal mountain there is a glow
like the blooming of heavenly hyacinths in a dark, dark
field. My own warmth goes out of me with the light.
I am as cold as the shadows, I am chill denial, chaos
again, the unnamed thing.

THE tin lamp smokes against the rafters but it gives
no light. I cannot see the fog that is descending over
us, I feel its body against me like the body of a snake.
Consumed by life, our eyes are closed in the undreamt
belly of the night. Every Monday, every market day
there is the same hope which we are afraid to utter to
each other, the hope of mail, any mail, but especially the
hope of the letter with money in it. Somewhere in the
world there is war—a great war. Even the taborel have
heard of it. The war "down there." When they speak so
they jerk their thumbs over their shoulders and indicate
the mountain pass, for they cannot visualize the sea
and the war is in that other world beyond the radius of
their experience. "How many years have the people
down there been fighting?" Miudo asks. "If they are
fighting yet after three years, senhora, how is it there
are any of them left to kill each other?" All the species
of creation exist in enmity and devour one another in
order to survive. Why should people be shocked by
warfare when war is the very law of life. But the
stupidity of it! That men should deliver themselves
directly to conspiring Nature which has dedicated death
to all things, men who are weak even as in this moment
we are weak. If I believed in a God I should despise

him, for my futile defiance is very much superior to easy
strength. Without being able to alter any of my subtler
instincts I have still, in my detachment toward what I
am, a kind of third being which God could not encompass because it is outside inevitabilities, outside intent.
I do not love Life, but I love John and my own awareness for which Nature has no use.

John's gray face, cold with fatigue, his eyes warm,
glad. There is a world after all, a world not dark,
outside me, bright. Fresh meat, too, dripping when
he takes it from the saddle basket, and the bitter odor
of blood. I have a warm satisfied feeling when I look
at it. John and Candido sit down on their empty sacks
and eat hot rose-brown beans. For a treat we have a
jaca as large as a melon—big seeds inside the horny
brown-green case are enveloped in fibrous cream-yellow
flesh. The rum flask in a wicker holder is almost emp-
tied into Candido's tin mug. John and I drink also,
slowly. When rum goes down into your belly it is like
a secret happiness which nobody can touch. Your veins
are alive and they grow over you secretly, filled with
the fluid of life. The fog and the night are pale, meaningless, outside the house. But your belly, with the
feeling of red in it, is the center of significance. It
grows like a fire, stronger and stronger, and all your
desires are burnt in it. The sun is like that, the beginning of all things—a huge empty stomach vacuously
ablaze.

Nannette has been moving about restlessly, glancing
now and again with a hunted expression at John. She
can not endure any more suspense. "I—I don't suppose
there was any mail?" Her eyes are dark, tragic. She

is all open to us. And I am angry with her for sug-
gesting mail. Mail. What a pale strange word. It
pales my whole being, pales the fervor of the rum.
Mail is outside the mountains, outside our life. It is a
silly useless word I want to forget. Of course there is
no mail. We try to talk about other things.

You are not a woman at all. You are a dead thing.
It makes you strong and superior to be dead. Life has
no use for you and so, conversely, you have no use for
life. You lie there and listen to the rain drip and expand
inside yourself in your terrible freedom. When the
gnats besiege you your body is angry. Your face is a
burn. You bury yourself under the frayed blanket and
lie there in your darkness. You resent the people who
love you, who will not let you be dead, who call you
back out of your illness. As for pain—assail you as
it will, it can not overcome your perfect passiveness.
How long have you been here? A year. Years.
Always. You cannot remember anything else. Yesterday two of the sheep died. Every day sheep die.
Everything dies. Years, years. Everything dies. Your
feet walk proudly over the living grass. It cannot
wound you any longer with its agony of green. You
are beautiful, white with sorrow. Your embrace is
eternal. In time the mother becomes the lover of her
son and lays him gently beside her under a green sheet.
But no one will take from you the thing that you are.
You can tell that when you recall the face in the mirror
—pale face, sagging breasts, thin body, starved by its
own ugliness.

ESCAPADE

ONE morning when the dampness permeated the structure of the hut the whole front fell in with the sound of an avalanche. Then indeed it seemed that Nature had penetrated our last retreat. John has reinforced the wall with palm branches. The rain drops rustle in them heavily, and the terrible wind with its profound aspirance pulls up the roots of the earth. There are no longer mountains. The mists have overcome them, and the white darkness of the sereno from all sides surrounds us eternally.

John and I are trying to write. We write on anything —torn scraps of paper, wrapping paper, for paper is hard to get. I wish Nannette could write. It is like saying one's last words.

We have almost no underwear and no nightclothes so we never undress. It is warmer anyway to keep your clothes on. And suppose in the night something mysterious, something terrible happened to you. Suppose the walls fell in again and left you naked and unprotected. It is better to keep dressed. John even wears his coat in bed. I wonder if he too is afraid of being surprised. In the dark I can't sleep. I lie there waiting, on guard. When the last calamity arrives I want to know about it. I want to be awake. With my gaze I must support the light roof on which the sky leans. I must support the roof though I cannot see it—though I hear nothing but the slither of rain and the squealing of invisible rats. We are alive in a grave and the slow walls draw in upon us. If John were only not so good to me. If he would hate me a little so that I could suffer for him now that I have become so useless. He hurts me. His calm gentleness hurts me, his worn hands, his unkept beard, the way the grayish hair grows long on the nape of his neck.

OUR very nearest neighbors are seven miles away from us, and they are squatters, poor ignorant people who do not understand us, who have always regarded us suspiciously. Down in the catingas—in the cattle country, the desert—there are rich cattle owners, but they also are alien. They wear big boots and wide hats, and they do not send their women folk to school. A very, very few of them have been to the city, to the coast. They are not people one could turn to for help —people like us. In Lamarão there is a church, but if the padre makes a yearly visit the parishoners consider themselves fortunate. Among those whom we see frequently José Marinho, the voodoo doctor, has the greatest influence. Once—*once*—a foreigner came here —Senhor Oliveira—John Oliver was his name. We met him in the city. He was a miner. He had been here and staked out land at Milagres. It was then he told us about this place. But he will never come back. There is no one to turn to. He will never come back.

I have written to everyone—to those who have insulted us. To those who have been most unkind. I am too proud to be proud any longer. I recognize in myself an ecstasy of bitterness. I give them all the opportunity to despise me if they will send us a little money. I have written one letter to a woman social worker in the United States and one to a Swedish writer who professes a belief in freedom for women. I have no claim on either of them and perhaps there will be no response. I want my words to live. I want to poison the whole

world with my own suffering. I want to infect people
with the disease of our defeat. If I can disturb them
a little they will buy off their Christian consciences.
They will pay me out of their minds. Christianity has
educated their imaginations and made them susceptible
to the pain of others. I must take advantage of their
weakness. If I am a menace to their complacency they
will cure me to save themselves. But the pagan instinct
of survival persists, and though my words seem to me
sharp and unendurable as the cries of the damned they
may establish for me not sympathy but resistance. I
sent some poetry to a magazine in America and the
woman editor returned it with an admonition to live
more before I began to write. Unfortunately, with the
idea of arousing her interest, I had told my age.

WE must get rid of all we know, go back. Feed ourselves to Nature who is greater than Moloch. Dona
Isabella has walked all the distance from Mucambo in
order to beg of me some of the tin cans which were
bought long ago with milk for Jack. They came sixty
kilometers from the venda at Villa Nova and they are
very precious. Dona Isabella has a dull pale face, tired
eyes, and a belly large with the bearing of many children—or perhaps she is already carrying another.
Without ever having visited her I know the kind of hut
in which she lives. In dull weather like this there is
a damp twilight inside. She has no other belongings
than the pot in which she cooks the beans, and the bed
of sticks bound together on which she and Senhor
Aurelino sleep. Senhor Aurelino has syphilis. He lies
very close to her. The children rest on grass mats which

are half soaked by the rain and wet earth. I asked
her how old she is. "I have twenty-seven years, senhora.
I am an old woman." And she smiles weakly, her
drawn lips parted so that her toothless gums are displayed. Yes, she is an old woman. She has an old— a
very old face. Because she is too tired or too awkward
to sew, she gives me some green and purple calico and
asks me to make her a dress. I gaze helplessly at the
gaudy cloth. I have no idea what is to be done with
it. "But the senhora is educated. She knows how to
sew. I am only a poor woman. I am too poor to learn
things." Her weak vein-corded hands caress the new
material. Its slick texture has to her fingers the flavor
of luxuriance. Dona Isabella has told me her whole
story, how many children she has had, how many have
died. "The senhora is blessed by the saints. What
happiness! To be married four years and have only one
child." With wan incredulity she regards me, smiles
again, and the absence of teeth is even more conspicuous.
And every woman I have spoken to has made the same
remark: "The senhora has only one child! How fortunate she is!"

How is it possible not to pity women, not to respect
the origin, at least, of the instincts which, in a more
advanced civilization, become perverse! Tin cans,
earthen pots—such small things represent a gradual
liberation from the slavery of necessity, from the eternal
obligation to work, work, to create an environment in
which children can be borne, in which there is even a
little time to indulge one's curiousness as to what one
may be, a little time for idleness and rest. Dona Isabella is stupid, she is docile, she is cunning. She clings

to the handsome Aurelino without any resentment of his
contempt. Pride is an opulence beyond her imagination. She may even be glad of Aurelino's illness in so
much as it makes him more helpless and binds him to
her in his dependence. When he is actually too ill to
work she will begin to regret, but that is far ahead. She
has no dream beyond today. I have an infinite respect
for property, for the belongings in the very texture of
which is the blood of those whose strength is expended
to accumulate defense.

Maria Luiza is very pretty, like a little idol. Her
small face has the clear look of ivory, and her eyes, beautiful without intelligence, are sweet and soft. On her
smooth throat shadowed with gold she wears a great
variety of beads. When her chemise, her only garment
beside her skirt, falls from one shoulder I see the swell
of her delicate breast. In spite of Aurelino's malady,
she is in love with him, and he and she have asked John's
permission to build themselves a hut on our place. For
Dona Isabella is very angry. She calls Maria Luiza
"puta" because she has taken her man away and borne a
child to him. Maria Luiza's young baby is very frail
with an abnormally distended stomach. While it is
raining out of doors and the mountains are big and
formless wih mist, Aurelino cannot work at his dwelling, so the three of them sit in our quarters on the floor.
Maria laughs, plays delightfully with the baby, and when
we have our meals she crams a little mandioc into his
toothless mouth. Sometimes I catch in her eyes a furtive
expression of distrust, of fear, and as Aurelino gets up,
swaggers about the room, and jokes with John her gaze

is always secretly following. Aurelino thinks less of
her now that she has given him a child, and she is aware
of this. She has made trouble for him. Before the
baby came everything was all right. She lived with
her people. But they would not have another mouth
to feed and they sent her away. She followed Aurelino
as far as Mucambo. There was a frightful scene when
she and Dona Isabella met. Aurelino is always emphasizing the freedom of his sex. Women are the devil, he
says. For the time being he accepts the situation, but
he is not going to be made a fool of, and some day when
he has a fancy he will take a long journey, far, far
away by himself—as far as the coast perhaps. The
child is well enough. But it is Maria Luiza's child, not
his. When she came running after a married man she
knew what to expect. So Maria Luiza, who is sixteen
years old, never forgets herself in the presence of her
lover and smiles continually. She is very young in her
behavior, coquettish, for youth is her only treasure—all
she holds against Dona Isabella's claims—and she must
make the most of it. She dangles her beads for the baby
to clutch. She has a small nervous laugh, very musical
indeed. And when she thinks Aurelino is observing
her she sings carelessly under her breath. Through
their deep sadness her great eyes always shine. With
instinctive deliberateness she emphasizes her innocence
and charm as against the formulated virtues which she
does not possess. But when we are alone together—she
and I—her words are full of spite. "Dona Isabella is not
married, senhora. She lies when she says that she and
Aurelino are married. It is five years since a priest was
here. When the priest came to Lamarão she was in the

country—in the matto. She lived with Humberto then. One of the children belongs to him. If she wants to fight with me I am ready for her, the dirty old hag." Maria Luiza's soft eyes have a sudden glint and a great understanding of the suffering that has not yet come to her hardens her face. She breathes quickly and I see her little breasts that have already begun to droop somewhat rising and falling under her chemise. The baby clutches at her agitation and exposes the rosy darkness of a nipple and the warm gold of hidden flesh. The baby reaches toward her with its futile hands, but she pushes it away from her crossly. At that moment there is no love for the child in her heart—for the child whose weakness is her weakness, from whom she will never have the courage to escape.

It is eight weeks since my letters were sent, but they have brought no response of any importance. Those who might have been expected to feel a personal appeal in our misery have ignored us entirely. The social worker is evidently a little touched. She has taken the trouble to inquire into our legal status and has discovered that Louise no longer has a definite claim in her pursuit of us. It would be possible for her to secure alimony, but the Mann Act can no longer convict us. I confessed to John that I had written the letters and he says that I should be very grateful for this last reply. To the social worker, besieged daily by the importunities of the very poor, we are only a "case," and it does credit to her imagination that she was affected by what I wrote. I found her reply to my outpourings merely kindly and polite, but what could I expect! When I read her letter I burst into tears and I don't know yet whether the emotion that disturbed me was one of gratitude or bitterness.

How to get money! How to get work! How, in war time, to secure a passport without revealing our true identity! Those problems are no nearer a solution. I look at our ragged clothing and our exhausted faces and remember that we have not a cent of ready money, and that even to reach the nearest consular port means two days on horseback and a long and expensive railway journey. At times I have an austere satisfaction in believing myself severed forever from a world in which sympathy and understanding, in any subtle sense, do not exist. Besides, the thought of the torture of my trip from São Salvador to Lamarão makes me prefer the more negative horror of remaining where I am. If it weren't for Jackie and Nannette it would be easy to accept Cercadinho as the end of life.

To make our falsehoods plausible we must receive some mail. John is always telling these people of my rich father and our influential friends "down there." I have written for a great many seed and dress catalogues and other advertising matter and expect the strange mail carrier at Lamarão to be very much impressed. It will be pleasant to see again a printed word in English. And I can show the pictures to Manoel and Ruffino who are preciously thumbing an out-of-date almanac.

NANNETTE, the fastidious, has lice in her hair, and Jackie had to be shaved quite bald. His curls were in a hopeless condition. When I insulted Miudo and Ruffino about the lice they did not know whether to be ashamed or hurt. They simply could not understand the senhora's rage against so commonplace an occurrence. Has not the senhora lice? Why everyone has lice. They are a part of nature, of existence, like worms in the guts. The dumb brutes have parasites and we have parasites. What else can you expect?

It is the same when our friends spit on the floor and I remonstrate with them. Spit? And why not? Everyone spits. How can you expect us to swallow so much? It isn't nice.

OUR ranch is an utter failure, and for two reasons: we began to work it on inadequate money and could not supply ourselves with implements and stock; and John had overrated his strength. Because in Africa he lived out of doors and went on hunting expeditions which would tax anyone's endurance, he did not take the possibility of ill-health sufficiently into account. His labor is all on shares and when we divide the proceeds of our small crops our own portion is very small, not enough to supply us with things which are the barest necessities. And beyond all that is the problem of the sheep who die and die, and no one can divine the origin of their disease. Sometimes for weeks at a time we have no meat. The last we bought when we disposed of the sick mare and the hides of two of the sheep that were in a better condition than the rest. We eat a little piece and hang the remainder from the rafters, and every day, as long as it lasts, we have a bit. I used to throw away the portions on which the flies had laid, but now I scrape the eggs and maggots away as best I can and we have that, too.

The sheep die every morning, every day. They don't swell up and nothing has got into their wool. As far as can be seen there is nothing the matter with them. Miudo says it is because they came from the hot catingas. It is cold up here. Too cold for plain-bred sheep. Down in the wet curral this morning I saw five stretched rigidly on the ground, their limp tongues protruding, their glazed eyes open. Their legs were bent in the position of running. Their thick yellowed wool was stained and spattered by the mud into which they had fallen. The newborn lambs cling close to the dead ewes and reiterate monotonously their shrill questioning bleat. And the mothers, with their filmed quiet gaze, have a dim look of peace.

The curral is encircled by the charred trunks of heavy trees, and in the rain some of the posts on which there is yet bark are beginning to sprout. The grass blades, thin green through the puddles, are bruised to the earth with the trampling of frightened hoofs. The live sheep go about stupidly cropping the bruised tufts and seem unconscious of the stricken animals lying at their feet. I make out the bald head of a vulture as it rises through the fog. All day long the vultures circle over the sheep-fold, patiently, patiently. Their invisible wings drag heavily through the quiet. I take the smallest of the lambs into my arms and stagger with it back to the house. Its four legs, rigidly extended, are stiffly pendulous. While I carry it, its stupid insistent bleat rises perpetually to a higher note of distress.

John has made a fire in the center of our hut and

we try to feed the young lamb the milk from one of the goats. Its little tongue touches the warm liquid feebly, tentatively, but it will not drink. I soak a rag in the milk and attempt in vain to persuade it to suck. After a while it gives over crying, takes a crouching posture on its tottering resistant knees, and at last sinks down in a heap. We wrap it in some old cloths. In a few hours it is dead. And this is a tragedy which is constantly repeated. Fortunately, some of the strong ewes have adopted the motherless.

JOHN goes out in the white morning and disappears in the fields. Down by the brook he is planting hundreds of banana slips. There is no market for bananas, but at least we will not starve while there are so many of them to eat. Irish potatoes are almost unknown, but he has set out sweet potato slips by the dozens so that next year we will be safe. Too bad that it will take four seasons for the coffee trees to give us a crop. The natives ignore vegetables and it is difficult to secure seeds, but the cabbages we have saved from the ants are growing enormous—great blue roses with the silver of frost on their thick petals, petals corded with hardened veins of white.

We are cultivating wild pineapples and fruit is beginning to rise from the midst of the serrated spears of yellowed leaves out of the rosy bracts. There are monkeys in the trees around the garden, and when I glance up suddenly the foliage reveals a hidden agitation. Sometimes I see little winking eyes, nervous and sad, set in a small grimacing face ruffled with fur.

John lives in wet clothes. His bare feet, bluish with

cold, are stained with the loose soil in which he digs. He looks up at me, smiles, and I love him and wonder who he is. I have brought him some tobacco, another gift from Candido, and he spares a few moments from work to smoke some in a corncob pipe. We take rum when the weather is like this. We have discovered a bee tree and the delicate insects are stingless, so we mix the honey with cachaça and a wonderful liqueur is produced. I am afraid of the rum because it makes you say yes to everything, and when we have said yes finally we shall have become like Manoel and Ruffino and Candido and Miudo, who say yes, yes continually to all of the demands of fate.

YELLOW-GRAY clouds fade with coldness. Trees dragging themselves are wind, are silence dragging, are heaviness of clouds. On mountains light blooms, fades, sinks into the blue dust of the horizon, white-blue-purple-gray dust. Powdery clouds of milk and ink float in rose. Sharp far clouds dilate with the fluid of rose. Clouds float above flat bank of opaque gray. The blue-yellow zenith is filmed whitish with cloud. Slow cloud, bronze-black, pushes at quiet, pushes through glass air. Dust is a curtain, dust of horizon dead gray against hills. Ash-blue atmosphere creeps blankly up the sky. Blue-white wind flutters. Blossoms flutter. Between the rocks trees rise alone on their separate stalks. Grass is alone, millions of dry yellow blades, stiff like dead hair. Light has passed away from them. Higher up, trees along ridge titillate emptiness. White glow makes an end of the world where trees stop on the brink. Sky goes on past the end. Over yonder, farther away from me, trees rush past the wind. Trees are motionless. Dead wind of them trembles along my face. In the valley heavy trees abandoned swing harsh loose branches blackly, swing, lift, swing, lift. Grass blanched in twilight is like a dead youth. Trees are old. They lean forever against space. Dead rocks bulge under them, dead violet rocks. Blanched clouds soar, lather, unroll, make gray surf on a peacock-green dimness. The trees close in and night is apart from the earth.

When the men come up from the market at Lamarão they are all drunk. The night is filled with their cries, shouts, curses. Miudo takes out a lantern and by its glow we can see the eyes of the bareheaded riders, the riders who have lost their hats. The dark eyes of the horses are wild, as they rear in front of us. The blood on their flanks is dark in the dark. Spurs glitter on old boots. The men jerk at the reins and yell joyously as the animals prance. They are gods, able to inflict hurt on living creatures, to make other lives subservient to their life.

Every Monday, when he returns, Aurelino beats Maria Luiza, and I know by the screams in the wood that he has come back. John is away for the evening, so I go down there to their hut by myself. I can just make out the dwelling, the vague walls, the dim thatch, the shadow of a doorway, and Aurelino staggers out. "How dare you strike Maria Luiza? How dare you!" I say. "You remember what Senhor João told you the last time! He will beat you if he hears of it!" Aurelino's eyes glint obscurely. Though I cannot see him plainly I am aware of his still stupid look, of the foolish smile on his lips. He giggles, clutches at the door frame. "O que está dizendo? O que está dizendo?" he repeats. Inside the house Maria Luiza is hiding from me and she keeps perfectly quiet, except that when the baby frets she says, "Psch! Psch!" with a terrified intonation.

Aurelino would like to give me some impudence, but his tongue is thick and he can only stutter and giggle and stutter and giggle without articulating anything definite. I shout at him again. He goes on muttering, but his head sways and his whole body droops limply. A little fear has come to life in him and is stronger even than his stupidity. "Paciença! Paciença! Paciença, minha senhora," he says.

"Maria Luiza?" She does not answer me. (Wings —fine thin gold trembles, shivers, cries, screams. Maria Luiza's gold flesh. Gold-tortured delight, ugly. Fan of gold spreads, burns.) "Maria Luiza, are you all right?" She does not answer me. (The light beats on thin gold eyelids, beats them blind. Light leaps, sways. Gold sobs—heavy metal sobs. Fire spray. Wind shakes, and light runs down feathers. Feathers glisten, heavy with light. Wings fall. Sleep. Light in thread shakes, weaves itself strong. Strong! World sinks. Despair of gold—sinks. Chaos. Light. Wings in cloud obscure the sun.)

NANNETTE is recovering from another illness. As she goes around she clings weakly to the walls. When she sits down to talk to me she tells me things I already know; about the riding horses she had as a girl; about a certain pink satin dress which was handpainted with butterflies and birds; about another dress of ivory satin embroidered with pond lilies in green and white. A toque trimmed with yellow ostrich tips was made to wear with the bronze coil of her hair pushed up through the middle of it. When she was eighteen years old grandfather gave her a real ermine coat. The phaeton with the black span had a rose colored canopy, gray on top. There was a fountain on the lawn. Moss and blue flowers overhung the basin. When strangers came to town they used to stare at the big trees in front of the old house and ask who lived there. Once a millionaire from the East offered grandfather a big price for the place.

RAIN patters on the thatch. A flock of parrots has alighted in the mangaba trees and I hear them screaming through the mist. The discussion of servants, evening dresses, and deteriorated elegance leaves Nannette maudlin with regret, and when John comes in he suffers for her mood. There is a theatrical wildness in her look. She reminds him of the humiliation he inflicts on her, of the horror and impossibility of her position. When he replies plainly in a cold voice she turns to me. Her weak stubby fingers clutch my shoulder and I must hold her in my arms to keep her from falling to the earth. I scream at both of them, as usual, and stamp my foot, while I am conscious of the faint stir of pain.

When Nannette leaves us John tells me, without any repentance in his voice, that if he dared he would take her out at night, tumble her into the gorge, and break her neck. And I believe him. When I think it over

ESCAPADE

I feel that we are going mad, and are as drunk with suffering as any of the mule drivers are drunk with rum.

ANTONIO turns the big wheel of the farinha mill. Sweat drips from his black shoulders. In his dark face his white teeth glisten, and with each revolution of the wheel he shouts ecstatically, like a child excited with playing. But he also is afraid of dying. He has showed me the voodoo charm he wears about his throat.

José Marinho, the witch doctor, is tall and strong. He has little eyes like bugs. When he speaks to John he is very polite. Very, very polite. He laughs at everything John says, laughs quietly, diffidently, with the most delicate appreciation. Miudo keeps at a safe distance, and crosses himself when the old man speaks.

CECILIO GOMES died. Why? The witch doctor was angry with him. He went out in the morning to chop wood. When Dona Isaura followed Cecilio later in the day she found him lying there face downward, cold and stiff but without a wound.

Every morning in the rain, in the sodden grass, dead sheep are stiff. The lambs totter and fall beside their mothers. Why? Miudo tells us to ask the witch doctor, but when we question him for an opinion he smiles very, very politely and doesn't know anything about it.

LITTLE lace maker, little Maria Luiza, little daughter of João the Half-Breed, what are you weaving there on your cushion? What are you weaving with your hundred threads, little brown spider, squatting in the doorway of your hut?

ESCAPADE

"I am weaving lace, senhora. I am weaving a dress so that when the priest comes I shall be ready for him."

Pretty little girl, Maria Luiza, Maria Dolorosa, pretty little weaver, daughter of João the Half-Breed, how many little brown spiders sit in the doorways of their mud huts weaving such webs as this? You and Nature and all the other little brown spiders are weaving together.

The old planter, who has worked until nightfall, shoulders his hoe, and, with his shambling gait, goes off over the hill. Next year his seventh son will be big enough to help him.

The red moon starts up above the mountain, red moon funeral pyre—the funeral pyre of Guarany, the great Indian chief who died so long ago before his people were enslaved. Bats swoop. Whippoorwills circling are shadows in a glass. And the moon grows white, crystal shining in crystal, thin, cold, and as clear as music.

I go to sleep and dream. John and I are in a city looking for a place to live. A lady ushers us into a large front parlor and tells us that sixty dollars is the rental. When I exclaim that the charge is exorbitant she smiles slyly and assures me that none of her neighbors will give it to me for any less. At one end of the room in a glass-fronted bookcase an enormous caterpillar is making his cocoon. "What a lovely cocoon!" I say. "Will that go with the room?" And I clap my hands. The lady smiles, produces a sparrow from her breast, and says, "Eat 'em! Eat 'em!" as she places it in the bookcase. I cry out in horror. She smiles at me again, with an air infinitely mysterious, removes the sparrow, and returns him to his hiding place. John says we will take the room.

Dinner is served and we are escorted to a long bare table on which are some mugs of milk. We sit down and begin to drink. "I am thirsty! Oh, I am so thirsty!" I exclaim continually. The lady keeps on pouring milk into my cup. Suddenly, awfully, I realize that the milk costs two hundred reis and that I must pay for it. I rise abruptly, assume a Delsarte posture, and begin to dance. John and Nannette have left the room. Three strange men are present. They laugh at me. I am indignant. I follow John into the hallway and discover him upon a sofa with his face buried in his hands. He says, "Don't waste time on me. You prefer to dance with other people." But he comes to me and we dance together. Faster, faster. John's arms slip lower and he clings to my hips. His legs are outstretched like windmill paddles. I dance more slowly. When I look down John has disappeared and it is an old shirt and a pair of trousers which remain miraculously attached to me.

I GO to sleep and dream. John and I have gone to a place called The Little Silver Lake. We are walking on foot through a flat country dotted with cacti and low bushes. By a deserted house, the small lake stretches out, and its surface is covered with wild ducks. Ibsen died here, of course, and the wild ducks have a peculiar significance. There is an owl who is trying to eat young sparrows, but he is driven off by my parrakeets.

I GO to sleep and dream. A small-gray-haired woman who resembles Nannette has come to see me, to teach

me French. The lesson progresses indifferently. I interrupt it to rail about the privations of poverty and
the life we lead. We are out of doors, on a sward
under a tree. John is near us, lying on his back on the
grass. I glance down at him, and notice all at once
that there is a small round hole in his neck. The blood
flows from it. When I ejaculate horror he smiles calmly.
He has a penknife in his hand. He tells me he has
"skinned his collar." He excuses himself politely and
walks out of sight. He has no more than gone when
I realize an atmosphere that is peculiarly ominous. I
search everywhere and I cannot find him. I am in a
house. I search among his clothes and I find a note
addressed very carefully to Evelyn and Nannette. I
open it and am surprised by the date which heads it. It
must have been written some months ago. Nannette is
dusting the sewing machine. "John is dead," I say. I
hear my own voice, very loud, terrifyingly distinct. Nannette's eyes fill with tears. Sobbing hysterically, she
turns away from me. As for myself, I do not shed a
tear. I cannot weep. Then I begin to search again,
search, search, for I don't know what. My heart grows
heavier, congeals, and I can scarcely bear its weight.
At last, among some papers, I find a postcard, old and
thumbed and written to John in an unknown hand. On
the card is the picture of a narrow street fronted by
queer-looking houses. Between them runs a car track
almost buried in sand. I read: "This place tries in
vain to ape modernity. All day nothing is to be seen
but sand drifting. Nothing is to be heard but the cries
of the water carriers beating their camels." On the
corner of the card is underlined, Steamship Indian Girl

ESCAPADE

—the doomed ship—a ship in a play, but I remember
it. I understand somehow that the pictured town is
Samarkand, and that John sailed for that port this morning in a vessel which was only permitted to be launched
by the criminal carelessness of the authorities. At the
same time I have a fancy that John is already in Africa,
and something like "from the desert I come, to the desert
I return" keeps going through my mind, repeating itself.
My whole being is as if dissolved in grief.

THIS morning who should ride up to our hut but
Meester Oliver—João Oliveira—the man who first told
us of this place. I remembered him as quite poor, but
now he is well dressed and mounted on a handsome mule
with two others on a lead. He descended heavily. His
spurs glittered and clinked and the sunshine trickled
across the surface of his patent leather boots. His fat
face resembles the face of a stout old woman. His small
blue eyes are vacantly suspicious. His manner was
distrait and, strangest of all, he displayed no surprise at
the condition he found us in. John asked him some
questions. It seems that he was employed by the Company, but that he had trouble and resigned his position.
Miudo has heard gossip to the effect that Senhor Oliveira
is an embezzler and is fleeing from the law. The police
officials never come up here and there are already three
murderers in the district, one of whom has been here
ten years and is quite frank about his crime. When he
has passed twelve years in exile he can go back to his
native village without fear of being prosecuted.

Mr. Oliver says that he is tired of an office, that he
is going to mine, and that he expects to reclaim Milagres.

ESCAPADE

He sat for a long while at our table and drank rum
again and again from the tin cup John filled for him.
I can never forget the hungriness of Mr. Oliver's hand
as it reached out for the rum, while his blank face
pretended to indifference. He took each helping at a
draught, speaking volubly of what he was going to do.
When he was preparing to leave us he mentioned that
his family was coming up. He gave a quick furtive
glance around him at our dilapidated dwelling, walked
unsteadily out to his mule, and pulled himself ponderously into the saddle. As he rode away he did not look
back. I watched his fat shoulders, the dim gloss of
sunlight in the slick coats of his mules, the glitter of his
harness, until he was far up on the path—a mere speck
of moving distance. And I thought of Dona Elvira, his
lean wife with her haggard face—Dona Elvira, the
servant girl he had been forced to marry when he was
studying for the ministry and the missionaries were
attempting his salvation. I recalled her in the city as
she moved about her sala, dusting chairs with the end
of her ragged matinee, nagging and scolding as she
went. When the door into the next room opened, the
pungency of incense from a shrine permeated everything
with its fetid sweetness, and the flowing candle smoke
hung blue and still against the plaster walls. Dona
Elvira has four children. None are entirely normal and
two of them are mute. Her look of hate often swept
past her puny offspring and rested on Senhor Oliveira's
son by another mother—an English-bred boy with bright
blond coloring. Even then I observed that when the
father glanced up vaguely his fat trembling hand

241

strayed incessantly toward the rum bottle on the table before him.

Now that I know we can never leave this place I am resigned to it. It is almost a happiness to imagine one's self forgotten by everybody, liberated by the world's obliviousness. I feel that I shall become everything to myself, as if through me only the trees and rocks exist. When John and I walk down to the log across the brook we can look back to the frayed roof of our dwelling, to the tattered roof of the farinha shed quivering against the wall of the mountain. The stalks of the mandioc are reddish and the bunches of leaves make green stars above the yellow-purple earth. The cabbage patch is a blue shadow in the bleached grass. In the enormous heads cold rain drops have a colorless lustre among the coarse slightly shriveled leaves. Some of the fields are broken by smutted stumps and above one of them, in the twilight, I see the body of an owl, the pointed feathers around the ears in grotesque silhouette. Up the hillside the goats are browsing. They lift their heads and fix us with their sightless attention. Their brush-like tails twitch. When I call them down to feed them they rear themselves against me and scratch ponderously at my breast with their little inert hoofs.

Bisunga has a foal with a lavender-gray coat of the texture of bird's down. Sometimes he follows me, holding the long braid of my hair between his teeth, and if I do not give him attention soon enough, he jerks at it. The monkey Miudo gave to me is named Adám. He stands upright at the end of his chain, and his body, very long and slender in the waist, suggests a lady in a corset. He has lewd gestures of love, and when he chatters to us he moves his scalp forward, wrinkles his small face, and his white teeth are displayed in a menacing grimace of invitation. His little deep-set eyes of a clear shallow brown regard us from the sadness of infinite separation. His lids twitch—thin, pale-colored lids. He cannot sustain concentration for many moments together. He is happy. He regards us sympathetically, but, as it is with dogs, a deep shame has taken possession of his soul and he is chronically apologetic for his own delight.

The armadillo lives in a stone-paved pen. His shelled dust-colored back is hinged and he can fold up like an accordion. To nothing less than a banana will he unroll himself. Then he thrusts forth the quivering snout of a little pig, his sharp ears tremble, and his dim eyes confront the world without receiving any impression from it. The little antbear is thoroughly benevolent, like a domesticated beast. Within the confines allowed to him he ambles about, snuffles, waves his brush, and one has to remember the unpleasant sensation of a caress from his tongue, the clawed danger of his strong front feet. His muzzle is long, narrow, delicate, and he has the quick sly gaze of a fox. But the most unhandsome of my pets is the sloth who follows stupidly wherever he senses the movement of feet. He wants to climb all over us, up our legs, under the clothes of women, or he drapes himself about our shoulders, his tusk-like claws clutch at our necks. His body is as flat as a rug and his awkward legs are set at right angles to it. He runs along with a curious flopping movement. Jackie, in particular, is terrified of these blind and persistent embraces. The sloth has the head of a reptile and can see well only at night. For all that I am fond of him I object to his stink, so pungent and all-pervading that, after I have held him in my arms, my dress, my hands, my hair are saturated with the scent.

Besides the animals, I have a beautiful soffré with a graceful body plumaged in orange and black, black legs like sticks of ebony, a flat head and a wicked-looking black beak that is long and dangerously sharp. In his cage he hops up and down with quick jerks and sings a full woody song. Miudo says he can be taught to whistle a tune. Sometimes he sits on my finger. His quick expressionless eyes are aware of everything. And I have a great stupid red and blue macaw—arara they are called here—who croaks hoarsely at intervals and with the opening of his gorgeous wings illumines the whole world.

I realize the cruel element in this passion for pets. I love them because they are subject to me, because I cannot be hurt by them, and it flatters me to give to them without anticipating a response. Perhaps that is really my attitude among human beings. At any rate I much prefer the society of these creatures to the society of the people I have known in the past.

THE pau d'arco is flowering in yellow clouds. The single mango tree which has survived at this altitude is putting out the stiff red leaves of spring amidst the old winter foliage of green. The rain has passed, or rather the worst of it. An occasional misty day is all we have left to expect. The bright wind is like a storm that shakes the whole glaring world. Its thick hiss grows invisibly between the mountains and when it rises above us I fancy that it has broken the sky with light. The sky is dark, dark blue. The trees are tossed in their own shadows. No rest anywhere. The grass, quivering continually, has a motion which returns to itself like the motion of a sea frustrate between rocks. Pedro believes in the spring, the heavy spring of the tropics that breathes its faint reflection on the unmarked days. Pedro, down by the brookside, is washing for gold, all day long. Among little red flowers, brick-colored, like stains of rust, beyond a boulder his stooped back is visible to me. I see his thin old hands, trembling, sensitive, claw-like, clutching the wooden rim of the batea and rattling the gravel, shaking the gravel back and forth. The angels of gold have begun to sing. José Marinho has spread the story far and wide. At midnight a white cock appears like a vision and over the spot where the conquistadores buried their treasure the fowl crows thrice. Across the gorge below Cabeça de Negro the ghost of the murdered diamond hunter is walking outside the cave in which he was buried alive—the big cave closed miraculously by a huge piece of granite.

JOHN has found a diamond. He looked for two days among the stones at Pedras Pretas, and at last he discovered it. It is small and imperfect, worth only a few milreis if it were cut. But suddenly we have discovered that our dream of aquiescence is only a dream. Each of us, without saying anything to the other, thinks only of diamonds. And we begin to search. Nannette, in her sun hat, stumbles about the fields with a despairing avarice in her eyes. In the path to the curral she hesitates, digs at the gravel with her foot, and stoops to examine a bit of rock. When she brings me her trophy of glittering pebble she asks, in a hushed voice, for my opinion on it. She behaves as though John were an ogre and always waits until he is out of earshot before she says anything. Her long thin face is stupid with fear. It resembles the face of an old horse whose perception has been dulled by many beatings. Her expression is dark, ecstatically intent.

My contempt for her endeavors does not prevent my doing the same thing. Often I go up among the boulders above the house and, lying down on my stomach, examine every little bit of metallic deposit in the surrounding soil. Everything that is small and bright. The lizards creep lightly over my feet. A chameleon in front of me lifts his flat diminutive head, opens his mouth for his prey of insects, and inflates the coralline pouch under his throat until it appears translucent and as if swelling with rosy sunshine. It is quiet among the rocks, quiet save for the tingling of wind in brittle grass, the perpetual oscillation of shadows, the shaking of the dry lilac twigs of the bushes, the pallid motions of blue and white flowers. Up the slope the clouded shapes of evergreen trees revolve against a blue abyss. The sky, the beautiful light, and the earth are all abrupt. They begin here and they end in themselves. A wild plant has a feathery top up against the sun in the frozen distance. The weather is warm but the intensity of space is colder, much colder than the suggestions of a more intimate sense. If only John had not found the diamond. The most terrible disease—the disease of which we thought ourselves cured—the disease of hope has returned to us.

THE sheep are nearly all dead, and this morning there was another death. When I awoke I found that the parrot had fallen from his perch and that he was bleeding profusely from his bowels and mouth. I stroked his stiff roughened feathers and looked into his sunken, half-closed eyes. He had shriveled all up. His breast had flattened, and he was a mere husk of the creature who was alive yesterday. When I took him into my hand he had scarcely any weight. His gnarled pink-gray claws were stiffened in a rigid clutch.

Jackie has been playing on the bare ground before the hut. I had just gone out to him when I looked up suddenly and there, not two feet away, a jaracassú was feeling the wall behind us with his great length. His varnished amber and silver glistened coldly in the sunshine, and his thin tongue, like a forked spear, went in and out. Fortunately John was close by with an axe and that made an end of the snake. But I want very much to catch a harmless reptile and add him to my menagerie.

I haven't yet heard another jaguar. Raimundo Caçador has just come up from the catingas with a quantity of skins. He has a gun little better than Candido's but he knows how to shoot and the cattle men take care of him during the season while he rids them of these pests. Raimundo and John together made an excellent trap and the very first night that it was set they caught a paca in it. It was terrible to look at, its great teeth snarling, its rat head thrown back, its bright eyes dimmed but filled with a still anger even in death. I don't enjoy killing things, but I had rather we ate the wild creatures than the animals we know. The flesh of the goats nauseates me horribly. I haven't yet recovered from the nonsensical prejudice against destroying things, even though I am so determined that we shall live and realize completely that destruction is the very law by which we exist.

IT is night. The flame of the lamp gushes a red jet mingled with smoke. John, with his manuscripts spread on some boards, is writing, making a copy of his book. Without mentioning the fact to him, I observe that the discovery of the diamond has made him more determined and industrious. As for myself, I am eternally in quest of an occupation which will distract me, and I am teaching Antonio and Jovina how to sign their names and to read. Antonio, sadly earnest, clutches his precious stump of pencil in his huge brown fist and pushes it laboriously across a scrap of paper. A-N-T-O-N-I-O B-I-S-P-O. A-N-T-O-N-I-O B-I-S-P-O. He puts it down over and over again. The weak lines, leaning to the edge of the page, trail into space. The pencil marks, in the dim light, are very faint. He looks up at me and smiles consciously and ingratiatingly. His expression is brilliant but softened by the racial melancholy of which he is almost totally unaware. "Agora, senhora, tenho muito orgulho. I am very proud," he says. I feel importantly my own superiority. Antonio, a man, beautiful and perfectly made as a statue of onyx, is absolutely ignorant and looks upon my acquaintance with a pen as nothing short of miraculous. As for Jovina, with her feminine training, she despises these accomplishments. It is only to flirt with Antonio that she agrees to come to the lessons. She exaggerates everything, makes crazy lines with her pencil, and, glancing at me with her great indolent eyes, giggles delightedly, considering her stupidity a joke. "I haven't any head for this. I never heard of a woman who could read and write anyway." If Antonio makes a mistake he is downcast, humiliated. Print represents to him the power of a chaos he has always wanted to reduce.

JOHN heard some marvelous news. Because of the war "down there" a new mining company—an American company—has begun to operate along the coast and is sending men into the interior to locate manganese workings—manganese to be sold for the making of steel armament. One of these "foreigners" who represent the organization has already been to Villa Nova. The news of his activities went on to Lamarão and from there to us. The whole countryside has awakened to a dream of sudden unbelieved wealth. John is neglecting his work, even to the milking of the goats. Here is an opportunity at last, perhaps the only one we shall ever have. If John can find a mine here we can sell our claim to the land for a great deal more than we have paid on it. Imagine, no foreigner has ever been in business here. The only industry is cattle raising. In the mountains the natives are perpetually poverty-stricken. I don't know that I am happier in the thought of escape. It seems easier to continue with old difficulties than to accomplish another readjustment. The passport question is as hopeless as ever, and I can't bear to consider leaving here. I don't feel capable of facing suffering again.

THE miracle has occurred. It happened yesterday when we were all seated in front of the hut in the sunshine, enjoying the heat and our inertia. All at once we heard the clatter of hoofs in the stillness. Then up on the mountain we made out a great crowd of horsemen, dim through the sun-colored dust. We thought they were vaqueiros coming up from the catingas after cattle. They drew nearer and finally passed directly by the gate to the yard, their spurs tinkling and their harness a-rattle. Several were well dressed in conventional outing clothes—soft collared shirts, Stetson hats, riding trousers, and new leather puttees. Some packhorses were burdened with stakes wrapped in red and white tape, and with the tripods that supported instruments for surveying. One man calling to another spoke a word of English which we understood. I glanced at Nannette and was astonished that her expression reflected my own desire. John told me later that he was feeling the same thing, that he was wishing, with all his heart, that we might remain undiscovered, that the strange travelers would not look back.

Fortunately we were satisfied. We were completely ignored. The sound of them grew faint beyond us. Dust rose behind them, and when it settled away we were able to relax again in the familiar quiet. Below the motionless peaks shadowed with blue, on the dullish landscape dotted with trees there were only a few bright specks, moving specks that carried the world with them invisibly like a banner of defiance.

ESCAPADE

Then I began to regard myself, Nannette, John, and my surroundings with the vision of the people who had ridden by almost without observing us, who, seeing our mud and wattle hut, our meager bit of cultivated land, had mistaken us for poor natives who were nearly white. Nannette's clothes are a wreck. She has mended some rents here and there but her skirt hangs every way and the hem is frayed, while below the edge of it her toes peep out of her shoes. Her scraggy arms are sun-blistered. On her thin florid neck the flesh hangs loosely like the skin on the neck of a bird. Her teeth are in a frightful condition, and when she smiles or says anything she shows us their blackened roots. Poor Nannette! She was once so pretty, so chic. And her disturbing eyes with their hectic timidity are all that remain to suggest loveliness. As for John, his garments are patched in every shade of the rainbow. His long hair falls stiffly over his coat and mingles with his wild uncombed beard. His fine face is old and exhausted and he has a nervous concentrated expression of pain— a pain of which he never speaks. I do not see myself, but I know what I am, sallow, dirty, ill-looking, my hair all tangled and allowed to hang down my back. My large thin hands are spotted and rough. Chronic paroxysms of toothache warn me as to what is happening to my mouth.

The passing of the engineers does not stimulate my hope. I prefer not to think of seeing white faces again, and I was stirred unpleasantly by that one word of English. I would like to cling to Portuguese which has no relation to me, in which it is never necessary to infuse a meaning. It is a language behind which I can retreat.

ESCAPADE

JOHN has determined to secure a position with the mining company. He borrowed some clothes from Tenente Alfredo Hylarião in Lamarão and has gone on foot to Villa Nova. When he left here he was barefoot for he had to save the shoes. The blue suit he wore, the work of a provincial tailor, was very tight in the trousers, very small in the waist—almost ridiculous. But at least it suggests an improvement on our true financial condition. I trimmed his beard and cut his hair, but he had no razor so he must wait to reach his destination before he can shave. He is going to represent himself as interested in mining and has thought up a long explanation of our misfortune, a story of a mine he bought which he found it impracticable to work. Luckily the surveyors located nothing in our neighborhood and they aren't likely to return immediately. And they can't speak Portuguese—so we are told—and any stories they may hear of us will be vague and difficult to corroborate.

When John was leaving I walked with him a little distance. It was a hot quiet day. Through the deathly intensity of sunlight the dusty leaves stirred with an unconscious life. The glaring movement of the landscape was like the movement of a sleep. In the stiff burnt grass the small pebbles glittered. The soil radiated the darkness of the heat. When we came to the foot of the mountain I thought of an uplifted hand, the palm turned toward us, warning us back. John's face was pale. He was already beginning to sweat, and little beads of moisture rolled down his temples from under the brim of his hat. I felt as if he were going away from me forever. When he was half-way up among the boulders, he hesitated, looked back, and waved. I think he said something, but his voice broke against the silence and I only caught the gesture of his lips. He was like a memory I was losing. I couldn't watch him any longer. I stared in the opposite direction. When I tried to find him again the dream had come to an end—or was there another dream? Gazing toward the hut I saw Jack running to me, small and far-off. The whole world was small and far-off.

JOHN hasn't come back and I have had no word of him. I am too restless to work. Miudo tells me that Meester Oliver is in Milagres, that he has a negro woman with him, that Dona Elvira objected to her presence, and there was a terrible fight. Meester Oliver, Dona Elvira, and the negress were all quite drunk, mad with cachaça. One of the children was hurt. José Marinho goes about saying that the evil eye is on them, that Milagres belongs to him. The money which Meester Oliver embezzled must have all been used for they are very poor again and have almost nothing to eat.

THE silence of things is more impregnable than any other silence. When I walked out to the gorge today and stared down at the tops of trees, the world was like a pregnant woman asleep. The red sun dropped swiftly in the hollow where the fine plumes of the bamboo crowded the suffused horizon delicately. Across the white path stealing over fields, the cowering moon was silver, voluptuous, and hesitant. Sleep is a thin white hand laid along me in the darkness. I see myself take the form of those hands. White spiders are weaving across dead faces, weaving them into a tapestry, weaving them featureless. The rustle I hear is of night shedding its leaves. My wonder distends the quiet, bursts, and is the quiet. I have never bent anything to my use, but I have been bent. Something beat on my heart—beat with quick fists. And I said, Open. But the thing did not know how to enter me and I did not know how to get out to it. I say to Jackie, I cannot be your mother any longer. I am too small. The earth is too large about me. I will make us a mother, a big God who will be father and mother both. Then we can hide ourselves in the shadow of him. I am not afraid of pain, but of the cessation of pain. I shall ask our new God to tread on us now and then and keep us awake. The bloated lily inflates itself, crushes us with the weight of its petals. I love the warmth that tingles through our mangled fingers squeezed together in the darkness.

Jackie sinks back in his small silence, I into mine. The further we retreat into our separate concaves, the louder the roar of the solitude that encompasses us, an always oppressive roar which each hears alone, which he will hear later from the same sea. With dwarfed inquisitive hands I touch my walls. I draw back on all fours, move my head from side to side timorously. I feel my own nakedness like a cold light surrounding me. My jangling unrelated lustre is an offense to this mystery. A rose burnt with a little white fire, desiring the big fire that would burn clean. Sheltered in opaline softness the fire burnt alone very small and the eaten rose petals fell away one by one. Poor cold helpless flame, aching to be put out. All night it burnt, a fire-lily with a twisted stem, rising from the grave mounds. The moon and the tombstone were steady and white, and the small flickering illumination quite useless, aching to be put out.

JOSÉ MARINHO has spread the story that John has gone away forever, that he has deserted me. Last night two of the goats disappeared. Several of the yellow hens have beri-beri. Their paralyzed legs sink under them and they squat on the floor of the fowl-house and resemble loose heaps of feathers. But their eyes are frightfully alive, hard and quick, and they have hungry pathetically vindictive beaks.

JOHN has come back. José Marinho was visiting us when he arrived and was very much disconcerted, for the witch-doctor had been filling my ears with tales of horrible things that happened to women who were left alone up here, who had no man to defend their rights. John has not yet returned his borrowed clothes and they give an emphasis to his revived confidence. He looked tired but was smiling and excited. José Marinho's little eyes were guarded and alarmed. He began to talk volubly and to express his pleasure that the journey had been a success. He swept the ground with his leather hat, bowed and scraped, and listened with flattering attentiveness to everything that John was willing to relate.

What José Marinho did not hear was that the mining people, ignorant of Portuguese and wanting an American interpreter in their office force, have given John a position at twenty-five dollars a week—twenty-five dol-

lars American gold. He told them that he had an invalid
wife in São Salvador and that he needed a few days
to visit her and talk over the change in his plans. He
is going to take us all to the city and we will remain
there in hiding until we have the clothes to make a
decent appearance. Then we will go on to Villa Nova
and live in one of the houses that the mining company
provides for its employees.

John has thought of everything. He has brought up
some morphine and if the journey is too much for me
I can make myself drunk. Today I am utterly willless.
I'd even like to stay here, to be left in a grave in peace.
Then my loneliness could pierce me forever like the
knife I used to think about with which I wanted to
destroy Nannette. John's energy is terrific. He seems
mad with determination. His face, clean-shaven now,
has an ascetic flush, and his sensitive lips are com-
pressed. Most fortunate of all, he has been able to
borrow some money. He is going to sell the animals
and the crops for whatever he can get. It saddens me
to leave my pets. We will set the antbear and the
armadillo free, and Miudo will take care of Adám
and the birds which we may be able to send for later.

Nannette's attitude is strange. When I told her the
news I expected that some kind of a nervous attack
would expel her astonishment. Apparently she isn't
in the least surprised. Her faith in man is more than
I can conceive. It seems that she knew all the while
that John could liberate us. She did not anticipate a
lifetime in this place. She talks of New York as if we
were already there, dwells on gowns, on places to live,
on the things we will eat. Occasionally, as she speaks,

her brow contracts involuntarily and she stares at me
curiously as if she had forgotten something. She is
most annoyed by the difficulty of going among people
in the rags we wear. She brings me heaps of frayed
ribbon and rotted lace, and her knotted fingers grope
among them, searching for a remnant that can be con-
verted into a dress, into the trimming for a hat. And
on her old panama sunhat she experiments with one
piece of decorative trash after another. I confess I
am depressed by the problem of the old worn-out coat
which I must cut up and make into something else
before I can venture in a train.

On the day of leave-taking it rained. We had very
little baggage for our possessions were of no account—
better to be given away or destroyed. John and I went
on ahead, Nannette, to her distress, being left to follow
with Jackie and Miudo somewhat later. When we were
at the top of the mountain I glanced back, back through
the mist and saw our house, the pink-white roof glistening with moisture, the soft dark walls dripping. Through
the sagging arch without a door I imagined the black
emptiness within. The house looked abandoned and
alive, like something we had betrayed. I could see
the farinha mill too. Wind had lifted some of the
thatch and the cold oven, the empty trough, the still
wheel were exposed. The charred posts of the currals
trickled with moisture. The gorge, with its clouds of
trees, seemed almost under the feet of my mule.
John called to me. Rocks falling beneath us awoke
an echo. We ascended into a deeper stillness. I pushed
against wet branches which swung back stiffly and

brushed my face. We rode between little white stones marked with a K, stones that denoted the claim we were losing, the boundary of our land. The high unbending grass swept damply across my feet and the hem of my skirt. Cercadinho passed away forever and the meadow land of the great plateau was before us. I was calm with the morphine I had taken. My cold white mind went on ahead of me, on through the arrested atmosphere, through the solemn chill. This time there were no cattle in the pasture land, nothing but wild birds. Startled by the mules, they rushed up before us screaming into the mist, sariema with long legs like wands and beautiful fragile crests. Then we began to go down the trail, down, down to Lamarão again, but I had no consciousness of a descent. The catingas stretched under us, below and beyond the fog, below dripping rocks, wet leaves slithering against each other, pale rivers rustling tremendously to an invisible abyss.

IN the early morning the small train of cars makes a great clatter getting itself together. Our coach is almost empty, but an old man with a poncho over his head has entered feebly and taken a seat opposite us. His dim old eyes regard us curiously, with covetous wonderment. Through the dirty windows the town is all pale, with toy houses of stucco, blue and purple, and poorer huts on which the palm thatch lifts harshly to the dawn wind. In a tree by the station platform a horned spiral of night-blooming Cereus has half a dozen enormous dew-bruised blossoms, like giant cream-white moons, fringed, with honey-colored hearts. A small girl wrapped in a shawl is driving a goat across the deserted market place. The mountains are a long way off—a long, long way off. On either side they lie away from us across the catingas, the vast bare plains where the giant candelabra cactus rise gauntly on every hand, their flat branches outstretched like crucified arms, like the arms of all crucified ones of the earth.

The train shudders, starts, jerks, stops, moves on again. Out of the fog that curls up softly from the sleet-gray grass, the familiar horseman appears—the horseman we have seen before—he in the leather coat and wide flat hat, the familiar vaqueiro watching the train go by, watching, watching with a fearful gaze of unconsciousness. Further—and I know that in this dry upland there are not even any cattle, and the mist that lies in pearl and blue above the scraggy undergrowth is the ghost of the sea that one time covered it.

The train begins to descend. A river is pink-brown in the timid light. Stooping figures of washerwomen. One has her skirts rolled to her waist and even her fat buttocks immersed in the stream. A heavy iron door opens, rolls back from one world's end to another, and lets me out.

PART VII

IMPENETRABLE darkness. A moment of silence. Through blackness the sound of laughter, voices, the tinkle of glass. A square of light marks an opening shining through many veils. One by one the veils lift. In an illuminated dining room two men and a woman are seated at table before a meal luxuriously spread. Monsieur Renard, very elegantly correct, all finesse and sophistication, wears a monocle. He is a man of the cosmopolitan world. He has furry pointed ears and, when he displays himself, a bushy tail is uncomfortably depending through a slit in his clothes. Mr. Bulle, surly of mien, is low-browed, ponderously heavy-jawed, and his rapt interest in the glasses at his elbow precludes attention to the lady beside him. Small blunt horns protrude from his temples. His fat hairy hands are ornamented with rings and he has diamond studs in his shirt. Madame Dina ignores him. She is beautiful, sensual, sumptuously dressed. Monsieur Renard drinks sparingly but is arduous in flirtation. Jules, an anemic young waiter, attentively serves the party.

"A beautiful woman, Madame Dina, is the cynic's confession of faith. She contradicts all his doubts. Poof!" Monsieur Renard makes a gesture with the fingers.

"Fie, Monsieur Renard! Do not make the innocent responsible for the guilty." Madam Dina shakes her finger. Her cold eyes are bright.

ESCAPADE

Monsieur Renard is gallant and satiric. "Only the very innocent can be persuaded to accept responsibilities. But we, created to enjoy your beauty, create also for your pleasure and delection. We make sauce for our own banquet."

"Whiskey, waiter. More whiskey." Mr. Bulle, with granite desire, pounds on the table with his fist. Madame Dina, glancing at him, shrugs disgustedly. Monsieur Renard shrugs also but has a delicate tolerance in his contempt. He motions Jules to fill Madame Dina's glass, and lifts his own. "Our friend, Monsieur Le Taureau, has the soul of a sponge. When he dies he will be found stained variously—a life history written between claret and liqueur." He and Madame Dina laugh and drink.

Madame Dina's manner becomes confidential, serious. "Jests aside, my friend, I am taking an incalculable risk to-night."

Monsieur Renard, discreetly, "Allow me, dear lady— I do not doubt my rival's valor, but my devotion insures you against all possible consequences of his displeasure."

Madame Dina is not comforted. "His jealousy is abominable. If he should surprise us now I dare not consider the possible result."

Light lifts. A young man in evening clothes has opened the door with a latch key and is fully revealed to them. His cape is on his arm, his opera hat in his hand, and he is dramatically startled by the group before him. He tosses his hat and cape aside and hisses through his teeth. "Aha! At last! So this was what I had to expect!" Madame Dina screams slightly and rises defensively. "Listen to me, my darling. Allow me to explain this deceptive circumstance." She comes forward, her hands clasped pleadingly. I can hear the swishing of her train. "Away, away! I will listen to nothing. You have deceived me!" She sinks ponderously to her knees. "Have mercy! Allow me one more opportunity to prove my devotedness." Aaron pushes her aside. "My business is with this wretch— not with you." And he confronts Monsieur Renard who strolls insolently into the drawing room, leaving Mr. Bulle asleep, his chin upon his chest, his arms extended among the glasses, his snores valiant.

Monsieur Renard, with his thumb and forefinger, flicks imaginary dust from his sleeve. Then, very deliberately, arranges his rumpled tail. "Come, come, my friend! Have a cigarette with me." He proffers a gold case from his pocket. "It is my benevolent intention to make you listen to reason."

"Faugh!" Aaron quivers with passion and contempt —and refuses the cigarette.

Monsieur Renard accepts the gesture understandingly and takes a cigarette for himself. He bends forward with an air of secrecy. "I know—just the same Consolidated Copper is at par and American Steel is going higher. Reason, my friend. Reason!" He taps himself complacently upon the chest. While Aaron glares at him speechlessly he becomes yet more confident. "I have some other tips which I could give you now. Interurban Traction, for instance——"

"You—you—you—!" Aaron springs forward and attempts to seize his advisor by the throat. "Monsieur

Bulle! Monsieur Bulle! Succor!" cries Monsieur Renard in agitation.

Mr. Bulle staggers to his feet and reveals his jauntily curled tail. He stumbles into the drawing room. "Who dares inshult honor—honor more precious'n blood, honor ish!"

Aaron looses his hold of Monsieur Renard and flings him back. "Enough!" Monsieur Renard recovers himself, adjusts his monocle, and smooths his tail. "Pish, man! You lack poise—poise—the quintessential distillation of civilization."

An uproar in the distance, faint at first, is becoming intrusive. Jules, disappearing for an instant, rushes back on trembling legs into the dining room. "Hélas, Madame, they are upon us! Mon Dieu! Mon Dieu! The brutes attack the establishment of a lady!" Distractedly he clasps his hands.

"Let them come. Better death at the hands of the populace than dishonor later!" Madame Dina lifts her chin proudly and defiantly and welcomes misfortune, her arms outstretched.

"Poor lady," says Jules. "I have barred the doors and windows, but I fear it avails nothing."

"Craven-hearted servant, do you suppose *I* know fear! Anyone can see that you belong to the lower classes."

Jules is humiliated.

The servants rush in: A fat cook; a vinegarish parlor maid; a lady's maid, smart, very pretty, with a delicate face; a butler, pompous and cadaverous; a red-faced heavy-jowled footman; a knowing American chauffeur; a pathetically out-at-heels brow-beaten little kitchen maid. They are in a state of consternation and

seem to have this moment quitted their several occupa-
tions. The cook, one hand to her breast, pants excitedly
and mops her face with her apron. "They're—bat-
batterin'-the-the kitchen!" The chauffeur says, "I was
double crossed. It was impossible for me to get to the
car and put one over on them. We can't escape." All
the servants clamor together: "These ain't our troubles!
We've got troubles of our own. Save us!" Madame
Dina stamps her foot. "Back to where you belong, all
of you. Back to your proper places below stairs."
The servants, murmuring indignant protest, refuse to
move. Monsieur Renard speaks aside, thoughtfully.
"It is the inrush of democracy, but the tide will recede."

The butler, rubbing his chin with a meditative hand,
considers events. "My lady, h'I disapprove as much
as yourself of these 'ere unseemly goin's on. But h'after
all, h'it's the wages of sin. No true gentlefolks would
put the h'interest of h'an old and trusted servitor h'on
the same plane h'as——" Aaron silences him angrily.
There are several crashes of breaking glass.

"Who will protect me?" Madame Dina is hysterical.
A crowd of bill-collectors pour in through the dining
room. Others, ascending the fire escape, enter the
drawing room by the window. They are dressed as
messenger boys or as uniformed employees of large
department stores. Some are placarded like sandwich
men. The boards are inscribed with duns: long overdue
accounts for coats, hats, shoes, jewelry, and wine. Aaron
confronts the mob. "How dare you present yourselves
in this precipitate fashion!" Madame Dina clasps her
hands and gazes heavenward. "Is chivalry a lost art?"

she asks. "Am I to be condemned to ignominious martyrdom?"

Mr. Bulle shakes his head imposingly and, with a sonorous bellow, makes for the crowd. Madame Dina is enthusiastically relieved. "A man at last!" A bill-collector steps forward, removes a red handkerchief from his pocket, and waves it gently in Mr. Bulle's face. Mr. Bulle's advance is halted. He shakes his head once more, regards the handkerchief curiously, until with wounded dignity and great vanity he steps aside. The bill collector carefully folds up the handkerchief and returns it to his vest. From another part of his person he presents what looks like a theater handbill. "Boots and shoes owing since September last."

Aaron, arrogantly: "How much?"

"Five hundred and sixty, not counting interest."

Aaron turns his pockets inside out. He is aghast at their emptiness. The creditors shout: "The tumbril, the tumbril, the guillotine! Off with their heads!"

Madame Dina takes a small mirror from her bosom and gazes heroically at her image. "I will die like a lady." Creditors, all together: "Nine hundred and seventy for hats! Even shop keepers has to live! Kill her, kill her!"

Monsieur Renard steps forward as though about to address an audience. He lifts one hand. "Kindly give me your attention for a moment." The creditors interrupt him. "Choke her! Drown her! Aristocracy!" Monsieur Renard glances at Aaron. "It is my desire to offer a little plea on behalf of the lady." The crowd hisses. Aaron draws away disdainfully. In the dead silence which ensues, Monsieur Renard extracts a gold piece from his wallet and flips the money nonchalantly, humming under his breath. He appears oblivious to the onlooking creditors who are none the less completely electrified by the sight of cash. Creditors, with emotion: "Is it real? We've been fooled before. Bite it." The murmurs continue. "It is perfectly real," says Monsieur Renard, "but anyone who doubts my statement is welcome to make an experiment." The first bill collector eyes the coin suspiciously. "Give it here, will yeh?" With a bow, Monsieur Renard hands him the goldpiece, and he bites it, rings it against the floor, and otherwise assures himself that it is genuine. "Yep, it's the real thing all right." He turns, with a sigh of relief, to his companions. Crowd: "Where do we come in? Where's the rest of it? What is she worth?" Monsieur Renard is very polite. "A perfect lady is without price." He takes money from his pocket and throws it about freely. There is much scooting and scrambling until the booty is secured.

Aaron says, "Circumstances have made me your debtor, Monsieur Renard, but I will not be humiliated by circumstance. This is an obligation of which I will free myself even with the last ounce of my strength. Dina and I will cleanse ourselves of this stain with blood. We will slave—work——" He is unable to proceed.

Madame Dina is scornfully indignant. "*I* work? *I* link my name with that of a failure? Never! I have my pride also—and beside I have no desire to interfere with the process of natural selection. Monsieur Renard, my natural protector, your arm." Monsieur Renard offers her his arm and they proceed together toward the window to which the fire-escape admits. The crowd cheers.

Servants: "Wait! Hold on! Where are our wages? What do I get for workin' in the kitchen? She's owed me four months! Wish I had pulled her hair when I was dressing it!"

Monsieur Renard, airily, "Good people, I leave that to your master. The domestic problem, resting on a personal basis, requires fine psychological adjustments." Gracefully, he assists Madame Dina to mount the fire escape. The bill collectors disperse. The servants clamor at the window. "Stop. Hold on there! We want our money." Mr. Bulle, who is the last to mount the fire escape, turns and bellows, head lowered. The servants shrink back. Monsieur Renard, visible outside, hesitates admiringly. "Virile! Virile! Mr. Bulle has such a fresh unspoiled nature." He and Madame Dina disappear and Mr. Bulle and the remaining bill collectors follow them.

The servants gather about Aaron. "Where's our wages? After all it's 'im as must pay. She's only a weak female. My sick children—— Don't let 'im go until he pays us." Aaron is grand. "Unhand me. Personal liberty is sacred." The servants are insistent. "What's your liberty worth? Pay us, pay us!" Aaron, with proud passion, "I will pay you—yes, I will pay you. You have no conception of the magnitude of my self-respect." Servants, in chorus: "When?" Aaron, angrily, "A gentleman knows no such words as when—"

His manner forces attention. All but the lady's maid regard him with perplexity and antagonism. The lady's maid, in a loud whisper, "He looks grand when he's

267

angry." The chauffeur is disgusted. "Whata we care
for his looks! We want hard cash." Aaron turns to
him contemptuously. "I can't degrade myself by reply-
ing to your vulgarities." The butler speaks thoughtfully. "After h'all, if a person h'accepts 'is word that
'e's a gentleman h'it's somethin' to go on. H'it's a solid
conservative basis for h' argument." The cook inflates
her cheeks scornfully. "I got a sick baby. I asks you
as a mother what good does it do me if he's ten gentle-
men?" The parlor maid elevates her nose. "This 'ere
is w'at comes of takin' service with the *nouveau* rich."
Bessie, the kitchen maid, is timid. "I think——" The
cook gives her a resounding slap. "Nobody couldn't
think on your wages. Shut up!" Jules, in a low tone,
comfortingly: "Don't cry, little one. I will take my
humble little bride away from her persecutors. We will
be married in Gascony in April." Says the cook,
"Humph!" Says the butler, behind his hand, "Ahem."
Says the parlor maid, "You don't mind lowering yourself, Mr. Jules." The chauffeur calls them to order.
"Attention, youse! I'm here to do business."
Aaron presses his hand to his brow. "Quiet, my good
people."

The footman is a jolly fellow. "I suggests we con-
sume the remaining fragments of dinner and drink to the
health of the bride and groom." He goes to the table,
removes a champagne bottle from a bucket, and hands
it to the lady's maid. Lady's maid, drinking from the
bottle: "Poor Bessie has no *chic*, but I wish her well,
anyway." She gives the bottle to Aaron. He drinks
abstractedly and hands it to the parlor maid. They
quarrel among themselves like children and even the

disdainful ones are greedy. Jules snatches the bottle away from the parlor maid and she quivers with indignation. " 'E, 'as no respect for a virtuous character, 'e 'asn't. I 'aven't a doubt but w'at 'e's popish." The cook, in a lachrymose voice: "Champagne goes right to a mother's heart." The servants snatch knives, forks, and pieces of plate from the table and stuff their pockets. A burly policeman enters.

"Perhaps you are not aware that the building contains a system of bells connecting with the apartments." Aaron is withering. The policeman advances. "What's front doors to me! Ain't I the minion of the law? Ain't I got to protect the innocent from the wicked, restore lost property, an' control traffic in the street? Don't I always see that vice is worsted and virtue is triumphant?" Aaron has an air. "I feel myself above your petty morality." The servants are making frantic efforts to conceal the booty they have looted. The policeman, ignoring Aaron: "Look at 'em!" He points accusingly at the footman. "He's got a spoon in his pocket. That 'ooman"—he designates the parlor maid—"is stickin' knives and forks in her bosom. I hope they hurt." Parlor maid, shrilly: "Come near me if you dare! I was born a virgin and I means to die one!" Aaron, calmingly: "This is a case of *noblesse oblige,* officer. The welfare of these needy souls is on my conscience. I present them with the plate." Parlor maid: "Present indeed. 'Tain't paid for." Lady's maid, in a whisper: "And him so generous! Cat!" Butler, self-righteously: " 'Ints 'as been made that the plate hain't paid for, therefore it aren't Mr. Aaron's plate, and if h'it aren't 'is plate and possession is nine points of the law——" The policeman interrupts fiercely. "You ain't the law. I'm the law. The plate's mine." Aaron, mincingly: "That is a technical point. A more primitive justice is involved." The policeman is stubborn. "No matter." The cook begins to cry. "I always had a good character and now he comes with his 'bominable 'sinuations!" The policeman holds out his hand threateningly. "Give it here." She slaps his wrist. "I won't." He scowls ominously. "Then justice must take its course."

The butler steps forward. "I 'appen to be in the possession of valuable h'information. Magnus and Son, 'eads of firm from which silver was bought, departed this life last month." The policeman, from his pocket, produces a scroll-like document. "Magnus and Son, departed life in past month, please come forward and claim silverware." No reply. From another pocket the policeman extracts a tin horn and toots it vehemently. In an attentive attitude, he bends his ear. No reply. Policeman, after a moment's silence: "Rightful owner can't be found. Goods reverts to me."

Aaron, nobly: "This is infamous. The law refuses to acknowledge either your right or mine. I move that we abolish the law." Cheers from all but the policeman. "We will make a higher law of our own." Cheers again.

The policeman taps Aaron on the chest. "Look here, young feller, don't get too fresh with me. The law's settled it." "Can the cop!" say the servants. "Can him, can him! What right's he got!" The policeman swells with pride. "Divine right!" Aaron peevishly pushes the constable aside. "I want it clearly understood that law has been abolished and in place of hard and fast rules we have established the judgment of inspiration." Handclaps. "Hear, hear!" from the servants. The policeman pouts. Butler: "We must consider carefully before we commit ourselves to a revolutionary program. Religion 'as to be kept in decent bounds. Even though a person forsakes the guileful flesh themselves a person 'as to think of 'is duty toward wife and child an' the terrible peril to the social h'order h'ideas h'involve." Aaron is fretful. "No, no. Nothing of the kind. There must be no holding back. All or nothing. Do I think of children, family, friends, or the social order? Look at me!"

A moment's silence. Lady's maid, in a hushed, thrilled voice: "No!" She clasps her hands and gazes with intense conviction into Aaron's face. Lady's maid again, strongly: "No!"

Aaron, with increasing resolution: "The past must be uprooted. All must be swept aside by the flood of divine light which I feel permeating my being." A mellow light has begun to play over him. The details of the drawing room are no longer distinguishable. Servants, after a hush, murmuring among themselves: "What can it be? We never saw the like." All sink to their knees. "A miracle! A miracle!"

Aaron, ecstatically: "I have existed since the beginning of time. I am!"

The lady's maid rises religiously and brings him a purple silk dressing gown, obviously the one-time property of Madame Dina. With an air of devotion she dresses him in it.

Aaron, stretching up his arms: "The light, the light!

How it wells from my soul! Come and drink from the living fountain."

Cook, strangely: "Glory, glory! What is it?"

Darkness. The figure of Aaron is softly illumined above a circle of adoring upturned faces. There is a rumble as of shifting scenes.

Aaron: "Nineveh has fallen! The scenes are being shifted. The kingdom of the future is upon us."

Lady's maid, on her knees, groveling to him: "Save me! Save me! How beautiful he is! I am thine. Thy bride. Thy maid. For thine heart is as strong as thine arm and thine eyes flash lightnings upon me. Sweet, sweet, oh, my soul is naked and ashamed before thee. I cannot hide myself even with my hair." She lets down her hair. "It is sweet to be ashamed. Thine anger caresses me. O Lord of Light, strike thy sweet spirit deep into the flesh of thy handmaiden!"

Bessie, timidly to Jules: "Jules! I am afraid! Let's go away together. I am afraid!"

Jules, in a far-off voice: "Listen! They sing. They call her name. The roses are made of snow and gold. Out of the clouds of incense her little face is like a white-wind-driven flower. O little cold white face in the sky! O thou chaste holy and unattainable! Thou sorrowful and pitying face blooming in heaven! I press my lips to the foam-edged hem of her silver robe and I know the joy of being possessed by her to whom I may never attain. My wretched flesh quivers with ecstatic shame, touched by thy immaculate spirit!"

Bessie, imploringly: "Jules! I am here by your side. Have you already forgotten me?"

Jules is transported. He shakes off her touch.

ESCAPADE

"White woman of heaven! King's daughter! Bessie!"
He is transfixed by his inward vision. Bessie sobs. The
butler is praying loudly, piously. Cook, chauffeur,
policeman, and parlor maid are all praying. The
footman alone is downcast and frightened and says
nothing.

Aaron, with awe: "She comes. The mystery comes.
Truth is about to be revealed." He kneels, his back to
the servants. They murmur and abase themselves.

Grayness lifts. Light shifted from the worshipers
makes a ladder to a distance from which a shrouded
figure is gradually detached. It is a woman, classically
robed. With one hand she holds her drapery across her
face, concealing everything but her heroically commanding stature. She advances.

Aaron, oppressively: "She hides her features that
the eyes of her worshipers be not blinded by their
radiance."

Silence and extreme tension. The marble-like figure
slowly withdraws the veil. The parlor maid screams
sharply. Silence. All watch breathlessly. The face
disclosed is Madame Dina's, pallid and ennobled.

Servants, after a pause: "Goddess! Divine One!"

Aaron: "Have mercy on this, thy priest, thou infinitely wise, showing thy wisdom in beauty."

The glow fades gradually from the limbs of the statue
and leaves the face startled out of the entire obscurity
surrounding it. The face dims, floats, disappears.
Oblique silence descends. Only the sobbing of the parlor maid can be heard. Darkness again.

Aaron, after a devout pause: "Now shall ye behold

273

a miracle. How out of air, earth, and water our faith has created a temple fit for the worship of our divinity!"

In the pallor of dawn, the interior of a cathedral, dim, high, vast. Far back, an altar. Beside the altar a fountain. Through Gothic windows an unearthly radiance beams. Aaron advances toward the altar. From a trunk near the chancel rail—quite an ordinary trunk plastered with Cook's labels and lettered with Madame Dina's name—the lady's maid, rising, takes several garments. The clothing is feminine. She gives Jules a bathrobe and he humbly envelops himself in it. On the parlor maid is bestowed a long, dark cloak and the bonnet of a deaconess. Butler, chauffeur, footman, policeman, and cook are garbed in frivolous negligées. For herself the lady's maid selects a white silk nightdress and, donning it, offers Bessie a similar garment.

Bessie, drawing away: "Oh, Jules, must I wear it?" But Jules, not heeding her, moves toward the altar. She puts on the nightgown and lets down her hair.

Lady's maid, in a high sweet voice: "Dost go unwilling to the bridegroom's feast?"

Aaron, at the altar, turning: "The altar is bare. We who have promised so much have nothing wherewith to deck the altar."

Parlor maid, advancing to the altar: "Out of my little I give all." She takes the pilfered spoons from her bosom. Other servants come forward with the trophies of the feast. Jules, in a passion of devotion, prostrates himself. The lady's maid removes the rings from her fingers and hands them to Aaron. Aaron prays over them. The butler is crowded away from the altar by the women. Butler, protesting: "By right of seniority, as an h'old and trusted servitor, I should be the first to show my devotion to the goddess. As it is, I'm forced to come in at the tail end h'after females that ain't dressed properly." He points with scorn to the lady's maid.

Aaron, shortly: "The discussion is out of order." He begins to pray again.

Policeman: "Your honor, I should like to know ———"

Aaron, alarmed, interrupting: "What's the noise outside? Attend to your business, officer. It's hooting and shouting if I'm not mistaken."

All listen. Policeman, with agitation: "It's worse, your honor. It's mooing and grunting and neighing and barking and screeching!"

Servants, in chorus, falling to their knees: "Our sins have overtaken us!"

Aaron, to policeman, excitably: "Go at once, I tell you, or I'll have you discharged for insubordination." A stone smashes through one of the windows. Servants scream and cower. Moos, grunts, baas, neighs, and the barking of puppies grows louder.

Policeman, his knees shaking: "Your honor—to tell the truth, your honor, I'm afraid to go out there." He gulps miserably. "It's a riot, if I'm not mistaken, your honor."

Aaron, scornfully: "Oh, faithless one!" He strides toward a huge double door which, although barred heavily, sways with the pressure from without. The policeman, continuing to display consternation, anticipates him and opens the upper half of the door which swings in like a window. Immediately a horse, a cow, and a dog thrust their heads in through the space. The grunts, squeals, and cackles become an uproar. The policeman, who wears his club under a kimono, uses his weapon to force back the crowd. Policeman: "It's the squad of pet dogs that's most obnoxious, my lord, and some fancy carriage horses, and a battalion of cows scheduled to be killed next Thursday."

Aaron, screaming above the din: "They're out of order. I can't admit them."

The policeman yells through the upper half of the door. Policeman, to Aaron: "The cows is demanding extreme unction, your grace."

Aaron: "Tell them to go away. It's blasphemous."

The policeman repeats the order. Policeman, to Aaron: "They say they have as much right here as your honor."

Aaron, angrily: "Were they created in the image of God?"

Policeman, hesitating and scratching his head thoughtfully: "I don't know." He turns to the servants. "The topic is now open for discussion." He closes the door and bars it again. The noise of the mob grows fainter and finally dies. Aaron, returning to the altar, knocks on it with a wooden mallet.

Aaron, to the footman: "Little boy in form B, what's God?" The footman sucks his thumb, does not reply. Aaron, severely, "Boy in form B, speak when you're spoken to."

Footman, as a timid child, "I—I don't know, sir." He is suddenly inspired, beaming. "Cake an'—an' plum pudding with brandy sauce."

Aaron strikes the altar again. "Not so! Enough!"

ESCAPADE

The footman is overcome with humiliation. The others hiss. Aaron to the butler: "Big boy in blue kimono, what's God?"

Butler: "God is a person to be treated with great respect, your honor, and I think that certain persons, with especial reference to females——"

Aaron, as before, strikes the altar sharply. "Enough! Next boy, who's God?"

Policeman: "Sure, do ye know yourself, your honor?"

Aaron, briskly: "Beside the point. To be reported for very naughty conduct. Deaconess, what's God?"

Parlor maid: "Terrible are the blows he strikes the wicked! Awful, awful is the flame of his eye! Vengeance on the wicked! Lost are the innocent!" She groans.

Cook, hysterically: "She gets me all excited. I say 'tain't so, your honor. Not that she ain't laid away a tidy bit herself what with taking presents from the gentleman and small pieces o' bric-à-brac from the mistress, bits as nobody noticed was missin'."

Aaron: "You're not called for yet." Cook: "I was only——" He drowns out her words with a blow of his mallet. Aaron, to Jules, who is kneeling with clasped hands and an exalted countenance: "Boy in the bath robe, pay attention!" Jules is oblivious. Aaron, screaming: "Boy in the bath robe!" Jules rises apologetically and wipes the dust from his knees. "Beg pardon, sir. Anything wanted, sir?" Aaron: "God! God! Tell us what God is!" Jules, like well-trained servant: "Very good, sir." He forgets to speak and is immediately lost in his ecstatic vision. Bessie: "Oh, Jules,

ESCAPADE

Jules, can't you hear the master speaking?" Jules, rapt, as though hearing a voice from heaven: "She calls. How can I hear her voice and know that I can never reach her! Oh, sea, how do you wear the rose of your moon? Your billows rise and fall like the breasts of a sleeping woman. Moonlight upon you is like blonde hair spread out." Bessie, sobbing: "Jules!" Chauffeur: "Dry up. Let him alone. He's daffy."

Aaron: "One more woman has failed to express herself." To the lady's maid, "What's God?"

Lady's maid, simply, bending to kiss his robe's hem: "Truly I know not, but I think thou must be God, your honor."

Aaron gazes at her a moment in silence. He seems deeply moved. Hesitating, he leans and kisses her delicately upon the forehead. She closes her eyes, her face upturned in an attitude of worship.

Hidden choirs sing. Aaron grows in dignity. Every suggestion of the ridiculous leaves him. Light streams about his form. A star appears, shining over the altar. The fountain plays in myriad colors. The servants are abashed in the glory.

Aaron, stretching forth his hands in a passion of pity and benediction: "The blessings of thy mercy descend on this, thy handmaiden." More intensely, "I forgive her her sins because she loves me!"

Servants: "Are we not also thine? Do we not also merit forgiveness? Mercy, Lord! Mercy!"

Aaron, as before: "Only this shall cleanse ye, that ye bathe in the fountain."

He advances toward the fountain and thrusts his palms under the bright water. A sprite rises out of the stream. She has an elf-head, eyes half malicious, half caressing, a mocking mouth, and dark wild hair bedecked with leaves. Her arms and breasts are as bare as ivory and as cold. She reaches her embrace beyond the basin and, without seeming able to help himself, Aaron responds to it. Her arms twine about his neck and her full lips pout to his. They kiss. Immediately the star goes out and there is thunder and lightning.

Servants, screaming and running about: "The water sprite! Blasphemy! The church is haunted!"

The sprite sinks into the stream. Aaron turns and tears off his robe. His gesture is protest, blind, intense. Lady's maid, groveling pitifully toward him: "Save me, dear lord! Do not forsake me!" With a shudder, he draws away from her. She lies prostrate in despair.

It grows black. Madame Dina's face appears in the wall over the altar. The lips move.

Jules, with a sharp cry, seeing the face: "Bessie! Virgin!"

Madame Dina, ominously: "From my breast you were fed and yet you have denied me."

More thunder and lightning. The face vanishes. Terrible confusion. The walls of the church totter. Cries, screams. An impression of the last day, or of Pompeii during the eruption. The lightning flashes reveal the walls of the church as they fall. Aaron is erect, defiant. The lady's maid lies at his feet. When the darkness is complete singing can be heard.

VAGUE light shows an open space in the forest. The church is gone with all its débris. The servants have disappeared. Aaron stands alone and around him circle

ESCAPADE

the Seven Daughters of the Wind. They are dressed in blue and green draperies, pale, diaphanous. Their bronzed hair is bound with flowers and fruit. Lightning flashes. Wind blows. Leaves fall. They dance. Their dance is a bacchanal. It grows more and more mad as their singing accompanies it.

> "Amorous and swift we fly,
> Children of the earth and sky.
> Quick our eager feet caress
> Passionate white clouds that press,
> Heavy, patient, blind as fate,
> Each to overpower a mate.
>
> While the stars bind up our hair
> We rest in the swineherd's lair,
> As our languorous arms entwine
> Throats of quivering-bristled swine,
> Lifted snouts in porcine bliss
> Thrilling to our rapturous kiss."

They sing on. Slowly the moon appears, blanched and tremulous, like a stricken face.

> "Modest Moon, so chastely pale,
> Shameless hands throw back your veil.
> Cold and virginal your light,
> Gilding yet our wanton night.
> Fragrant is our fecund breath.
> Life, incestuous, breeds with Death."

The dancers vanish. Aaron is alone. The sun shines. All at once the world has become quiet and prosaic. The ground is covered with autumn leaves. An ape, running on all fours, emerges from the trees. Aaron, as if bewildered, passes his hands across his eyes.

Aaron, to ape: "I'm lost. Be kind enough to direct me——" The ape frisks about, seeming not to have heard. Aaron, patiently, in a conciliatory tone: "Kind and obliging Ape, in this primeval wilderness I don't know what to do with myself."

The ape is still at last. "Where do you want to go?"

Aaron: "I don't know."

Ape, clambering up a tree: "Then why not stay here? Can you hang by your tail?"

Aaron, perplexedly: "Why I—I——" He attempts to ascertain whether or no he has a tail concealed in the rear of his person.

Ape, leaping from bough to bough: "Or this? Or this?" He makes a pinwheel of himself.

Aaron: "I really think—when I was a little more fit——" He takes off his coat and feels his biceps. He makes a leap at the limb of a tree but misses it. The ape watches him from the security of an upper branch.

Ape, scratching his head thoughtfully: "I don't know what we can do about it. You don't belong in our class at all."

Aaron sighs and takes up his coat again. "I'm afraid not." A large white bird walks in. Ape, inspired by the sight of the bird: "Can you fly?"

Aaron tries to see his own shoulders. "There must be pin-feathers at least."

The ape descends from the tree and makes an examination. "Too bad! Not even a suggestion." The bird flies up and alights among the frosted leaves. The ape takes a pair of spectacles from a pocket in his fur and adjusts them. "It's a bewildering situation. Open your mouth." He looks at Aaron's teeth. "Rudimentary

canines. Fangs and tushes both lost. Tail missing."
He shakes his head. He is the very picture of dejection.
Aaron also is humiliated. The ape returns the spectacles to his pocket. "No earthly. What are we to do
about it?"

Aaron, eagerly: "I can do this!"

Ape, skeptically: "What?"

Aaron stares before him fixedly and excitably. "Can't
you see her?"

The ape goes round and round. "Where? What?"

Aaron, pointing a feverish, trembling finger: "There!"

The ape rests his hands upon his hips. "I don't
see it."

The sunshine dims. Against the dusk of trees the
transparent figure of a woman like a magic lantern
shade.

The ape is unmoved. "No use. I can't see it."

"There! Don't you see that?" The woman is followed by a ghostly ape. The true ape pokes his finger
into the apparition. "I can see that, of course, but
what's the use?"

Aaron, with disgust: "Use! Try it yourself!"

"My time is better employed." The ape jumps into
a tree and disappears. The bird flies away in the opposite direction.

Aaron passes his hands once more across his eyes.
When he speaks he is like a sleepwalker. "In the be-
ginning she was created from a rib. I will imagine that
she exists." He reclines by a rock and falls asleep.
Except for his evening clothes, he recalls a painting of
Jacob's dream. Several moments pass.

In the night that has fallen a well of light opens. The

lady's maid appears. She is elevated in a niche like a holy statue. She yet wears a nightgown and her hair is loose. On her head is a crown of thorns. She is deathly pale and her forehead is streaked with blood. There are bloody nail prints on her hands and her bare feet. She holds a baby in her arms. The servants, in their costly negligées, kneel at her feet, adoring her. She lifts one hand in benediction, palm up, showing the wound. Far-off cries. Oriental street music always drawing nearer, cymbals clashing, blatant trivial obscenity. An ecstatic smile of unearthly peace, thrilling in its compassion, illumines the maid's face. The baby laughs and crows.

Aaron, in his sleep, lifting his arm as if to ward off a blow: "No, no! Not that!"

The vision fades.

Madame Dina's face again. It becomes distinguishable only to vanish.

Where the face has been a rough mass of unhewn marble looms in the well of light. A form takes shape out of the marble. It is dead white, the statue of a girl, virginal and delicate. A thin veil covers her. She stirs, moves. Her flesh takes tint.

With a cry, Aaron awakes and springs to his feet. The young girl is clothed in light. She steps forward. Behind her the radiant chasm closes itself. Aaron seeks the veiled figure, while he shields his gaze from her brightness. His gestures are of unutterable longing. The girl flits among trees. She seems barely to touch the earth. Aaron, painfully thrilled: "Galatea!"

Here and there the white shadow flits. Again and again Aaron would clasp her. She is gone. At last he

succeeds, overtakes her, draws her to him. She throws
back her shrouding. The figure has a man's head,
Aaron's face so like that one head can only be differ-
entiated from the other by the body that accompanies it.
The two identical heads stare at one another in tragic
silence. Aaron releases the despairing shade and it
vanishes in the forest. He throws himself by the rock.

Madame Dina, in a ball gown, wearing a cloak with a
hood, comes briskly from among the trees. Her face is
averted. Aaron rises to his knees. Aaron, wretchedly:
"Dina! Madame Dina!" She hesitates and, without
speaking, turns slowly to him. The features of a woman
are no longer hers. Under the satin hood shows a bare
skull, eyeless sockets and fleshless cheeks. She goes on.

Aaron leaps to his feet and shakes his fist. "Fiends!
Devils! Torturers! I defy you! Come out in the
open!" No answer. Aaron, more wildly: "Where are
you? Come out and fight me! I'm not afraid of you,
you cowards!" Laughter from nowhere. Aaron glances
desperately about him. Nobody. The branches rustle.
With a groan, he buries his face in his hands.

In the trees and rocks, doors open. Dozens of figures
emerge. Figures of men who, in the vague light, show
themselves Aaron's doubles, the features his, the appearance duplicate even to the smallest detail of dress. They
surround him stealthily.

At first he is not aware of them. He looks up. Their
eyes—his own eyes—mock him in the silence. Aaron
tears at his hair. The ghost men sink into the trees and
rocks. Everything is as before. Again the laughter of
the invisible.

The sun is rising. A beautiful glow like an alpine

morning. Birds twitter. Dew glitters on the sere grass, the old leaves. The world is ecstatic with life, with happiness. The little kitchen maid, Bessie, in her nightgown, walks in. She carries a bedroom candle. In the dawn the flame is pale. The hair that falls about her shoulders is gray. Her small face is old and wan. Two men in their shirt sleeves, ordinary property men of the theater, but with large white angel wings protruding from their shoulders, appear with a white iron crib, a crib such as children sleep in, magnified, however, to the dimensions of a man. When the crib is in order they fly away.

Bessie, smiling maternally as she places the candlestick upon a convenient boulder: "Time to go to bed, dear." She takes Aaron's hand, leads him to the crib, and lowers the side so that he can climb into it. He lies down and she tucks the covers about him. As she stands looking down on him, the sun dies. Twilight. Moonrise. The moon is a death's head. The crib, Bessie's guarding figure, a tableau wraithlike and motionless under the death's-head moon. Bessie sings:

> "Innocent the tigers creep
> From the dens where cat cubs sleep.
> Innocent the young lambs bleat,
> Tugging at the old ewe's teat.
> Innocent the serpent coils,
> A little fawn caught in her toils.
>
> On the clouds my baby stands,
> Garnered stars are in his hands.
> From his heavenly judgment seat,
> Saint and sinner at his feet,
> He tosses flowery missals wide,
> Pelts the lion's sinewy hide.

ESCAPADE

Innocent the tigers creep
To lap the blood of little sheep.
Innocent the serpent's start,
Her fangs poised for the weak bird's heart.
Glorified my baby stands,
Soothes their wounds with snow-soft hands."

The moon is dim. Instead of the mellow glow, a vague indeterminate radiance. The song and the light pass away together. Silence and darkness, as it was in the beginning.

END